Good Reasons to Run

Good Reasons to Run

Women and Political Candidacy

Edited by

Shauna L. Shames, Rachel I. Bernhard,

Mirya R. Holman, and Dawn Langan Teele

TEMPLE UNIVERSITY PRESS

Philadelphia • *Rome* • *Tokyo*

TEMPLE UNIVERSITY PRESS
Philadelphia, Pennsylvania 19122
tupress.temple.edu

Library of Congress Cataloging-in-Publication Data

Names: Shames, Shauna Lani, editor. | Bernhard, Rachel I., editor. |
Holman, Mirya, editor. | Teele, Dawn Langan, 1983- editor.
Title: Good reasons to run : women and political candidacy / edited by
Shauna L. Shames, Rachel I. Bernhard, Mirya R. Holman, and Dawn Langan
Teele.
Description: Philadelphia ; Rome ; Tokyo : Temple University Press, [2020]
| Includes bibliographical references and index. | Summary: "Examines
the current landscape of opportunities for women in electoral office to
determine what kinds of messages, support, and training are most
effective in getting women candidates to run"— Provided by publisher.
Identifiers: LCCN 2019039558 (print) | LCCN 2019039559 (ebook) | ISBN
9781439919552 (cloth) | ISBN 9781439919569 (paperback) | ISBN
9781439919576 (pdf)
Subjects: LCSH: Women political candidates—United States. | Political
campaigns—United States. | Campaign funds—United States. |
Classification: LCC HQ1236.5.U6 G6665 2020 (print) | LCC HQ1236.5.U6 G6665
2020 (ebook) | DDC 320.082/0973—dc23
LC record available at https://lccn.loc.gov/2019039558
LC ebook record available at https://lccn.loc.gov/2019039559

♾ The paper used in this publication meets the requirements of the American National
Standard for Information Sciences—Permanence of Paper for Printed Library Materials,
ANSI Z39.48-1992

Printed in the United States of America

9 8 7 6 5 4 3 2 1

Our country—indeed, our world—must get smarter and make women 50% of its leaders and legislators. If we did, I guarantee we would see changes for the better in policy priorities and communities—not just for the sake of women, but for men as well. At the rate we're going, however, it could take several centuries to achieve gender parity. Considering the massive issues we face, that is not an option. I suggest we hurry history, bringing women to all decision-making tables before it's too late.

—**MARIE C. WILSON**, president emerita and honorary founding mother of the Ms. Foundation for Women, founder and president emerita of the White House Project, and creator of Take Our Daughters to Work Day

The LUPE Fund's organizational growth is happening at a time of flux and change in our country. More than ever, education and civic engagement for young women is critical in building strong leaders that can advance quality of life issues for New Jersey diverse communities. With more than a decade of experience, LUPE is ready to move to the next chapter of its work and reach more young women to help them realize their potential as local and state leaders.

—**SARA PEÑA**, president, LUPE Fund Inc.

When women run for office, they face stereotypes; sexism; statements about their hair, their clothes, their voices. Women are held to higher standards and face higher barriers on the path to public office. It is the reality that female politicians face, and yet we see that when women candidates have the tools to succeed, they are able to overcome obstacles and thrive. Voters are hungering for change, and see women as different from the status quo. At the Barbara Lee Family Foundation, we know that when women focus their energy and resources, gender parity is possible.

—**BARBARA LEE**, president and founder of the Barbara Lee Family Foundation

Contents

Part III: Why Not Run?

Part IV: How Nonprofits Help Women Run for Office

Part V: The Special Role of Money

Good Reasons to Run

Introduction

Sometimes events in the real-world leap ahead of our research-based understandings of them, and scholars have to race to catch up. Such is the case with women and politics in the first two decades of the twenty-first century. Around the world, and especially in the United States, new approaches, programs, and trends cry out for greater exploration. We have seen rapid growth in nongovernmental and nonpartisan programs specifically designed to recruit and train women as political candidates. And, particularly since the 2016 U.S. presidential election, the huge cohort of women that stepped forward to run for office has changed the landscape of candidates and representation. The early decades of this century have also produced changes in the types of women who run, with female candidates and elected officials in the Democratic Party far outnumbering Republican women. Indeed, the 2018 election featured the most women (including the most women of color) of any election to date, and the 2020 Democratic primary alone featured more female candidates for the presidency than all parties together fielded in any prior U.S. presidential contest.[1] And although in the past women of color have faced heightened discrimination based on both race and gender, the post-2016 landscape has also seen a record number of women of color run—and succeed. The essays in this volume are meant to serve as a primer on the current landscape of opportunities and constraints faced by women who are considering electoral campaigns.

Although most of the essays herein focus on U.S. politics, placing the experience of one country into conversation with others is an essential part of this project. The electoral system of the United States—where we typically elect only one candidate out of each district, and where the person with the

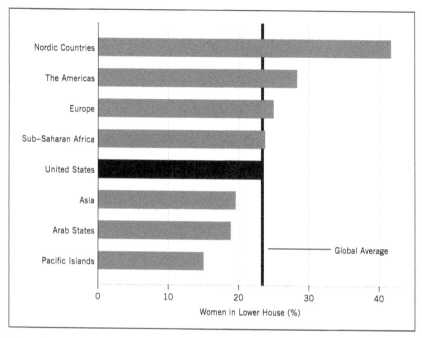

Figure I.1. Women in lower houses around the world (percent), 2019. The global average is 24.5 percent. (Source: Editors' calculations based on Inter-Parliamentary Union data 2018, and 2019 data for the United States; European average excludes Nordic countries and Americas average excludes the United States. Figure created by the editors.)

most votes takes the seat—is relatively candidate-centric compared to other systems.[2] Unlike in other countries, where parties play a much larger role in recruiting and funding political candidates, in the United States we rely on individuals to step forward somewhat independently to pursue electoral office. Within this environment, the personal and financial costs of running for office are high. Given the vitriol in recent elections and the high level of hyperpartisanship, negative advertising, and animosity in even lower-level elections, it is fair to ask: Why would anyone run for office? Indeed, as many have found, the costs—in actual pay cuts, in other career opportunities lost, and in time away from family and friends—may be too much to ask for many people.[3] Research suggests that these costs may weigh more heavily on some groups, especially those already marginalized in politics and economics, such as the working class, women, and people of color.[4]

What do these costs mean for women's representation in the United States? The United States lags behind most other countries; in 2019, women held 24 percent of seats in the U.S. House of Representatives, placing the United States as 104th out of 190 countries worldwide (see Figure I.1).[5] Although a woman has never been president of the United States, globally, women head 7.2 per-

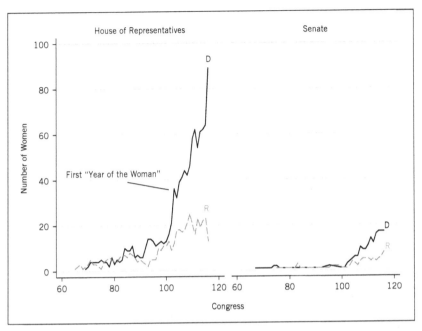

Figure I.2. Women in U.S. Congress, 1907–2019. The figure lists, on the left-hand side, the total number of women that have served in the House of Representatives since the first woman was elected to serve with the Republican caucus in the 65th Congress in 1917. There are 535 members of the House in total. The right-hand side lists the total number of women that have served in the Senate, which has 100 members, since the first woman was elected to the Democratic caucus in the 67th Congress in 1921. (Source: Graphic by the editors, based on data from Center for American Women in Politics 2018.)

cent of states and women lead the government in another 5.7 percent of states.[6] In the Americas alone, eight women have served in the most powerful political office.[7]

Despite the dismal track record in comparison to other countries, women's representation in the United States has increased dramatically over the past half century. Figure I.2 presents the number of women that have served in Congress between 1907 and 2019, in both the Democratic (top line) and Republican (bottom line) Parties. As Figure I.2 shows, the Democratic Party has elected many more women to Congress, with particular success since the 1990s. As of 2019, 101 women serve in the 435 member House (88 D, 13 R), and 25 women serve in the Senate (17 D, 8 R). (This shows the growth in the number of women serving in the House from that of 2018, when 64 Democratic and 23 Republican women served.) There has also been a marked improvement in the representation of women of color. At the national level, Black women now hold 22 seats (21 in the House and 1 in the Senate). In the House, there are now 13 Latina representatives, 8 Asian American/Pacific Islander women, 2 Native American women, and 1 female representative from Middle Eastern descent. And although there are still twice as many Black male state legislators as Black female state legislators, there has been a growth of more than 50 percent in Black women's representation—from 170 women in 1995 to 275 (272 D, 3 R) in 2019. These figures suggest that, as the U.S. Congress and state legislatures have increased women's representation, they have also diversified on other fronts.[8]

Why Don't More Women Run?

As with anything in politics, scholars have engaged in a vigorous debate about whether, and to what extent, women are less likely to be supported as political candidates. While women may sometimes be equally likely to win elections as men (as advocates like to say, "When women run, women win"), other research shows that voters harbor biases (both explicit and implicit) that make women's campaigns more challenging. In many studies, stereotypes and gender schemas have been found to color voters' perceptions of the competence, ideology, and policy priorities of women as candidates.[9] Still other studies counter that overt bias has all but faded, and, since similarly situated men and women win at equal rates when they run as candidates, the underrepresentation of women can best be explained by women's relative lack of political ambition to run.[10] Reconciling these disparate findings has made for a lively debate among scholars in recent years.[11]

Even if voters are equally likely to support men and women, other scholars see persisting inequalities: Jenkins, for example, finds that, although men and women raise the same amount of money when they run for Congress, women generally have to make twice the number of phone calls to raise this same amount.[12] And women themselves clearly anticipate that they will face an unfair fight as candidates, including bias on the part of voters, funders, news and social media, and party leaders.[13]

The most perplexing aspect of women's continued underrepresentation is the fact that most research shows that the women who make it to the top are highly successful in their posts: they are good at bringing money and projects back to their districts, they receive high ratings for the service they do in their own constituencies, they are more likely to get their proposed bills passed, and they are even more likely to get reelected than men.[14] All of these findings have left feminists, advocates for democratic representation, and researchers with the conclusion that more women *can* run for political office, and, in fact, they *should*.

Even setting aside practical concerns, potential candidates often express displeasure with aspects of campaigning and governing. Some prefer careers that provide more opportunities to work collectively and help others.[15] And

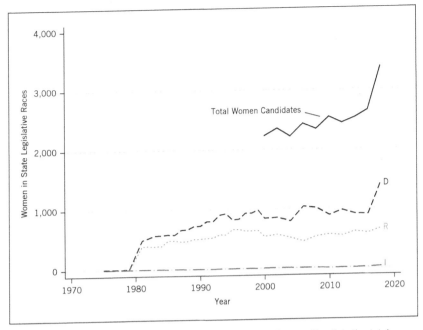

Figure I.3. Women in U.S. state legislatures, 1975–2019. The top line lists the total number of women who were candidates for state legislative offices (from 2000 to 2018), while the marked lower lines list the number of women winners from the Democratic, Republican, and Independent nonheritage parties. In 2019, there were a total of 7,383 in state legislatures. (Source: Graphic by the editors, based on data from Center for American Women in Politics 2018.)

many otherwise eligible people may willingly avoid the process of running for office itself, including selling oneself to voters, soliciting donations, facing a hostile media, and making tough compromises.[16] The problem may be more acute for female candidates, as women seem to be averse simply to putting themselves up for election, even in the low-stakes environment of laboratory experiments.[17] Some recent research suggests that, although male and female candidates face the same type of costs-versus-benefits structure of decision-making in deciding whether to run, women typically see more costs and fewer rewards to running and feel the costs more keenly.[18]

And yet, there are those women who do run for office. In the 2016 election cycle alone, 2,648 women ran in state legislative races as major party nominees (see Figure I.3), 183 women ran for Congress as their party's nominees, and 1 woman ran for the highest office in the land as the Democratic Party's nominee. The numbers of female candidates in the 2018 election exceeded this by 150 percent, with more women running for Congress than ever before. So, what would prompt someone to subject herself to the rigors of a political campaign and the potential antipathy of the general public?

Political Ambition

A lot of the recent debate about why women are underrepresented has centered on the role of women's *political ambition* in limiting gender parity in U.S. politics. Intuitively, the focus on ambition makes sense; no other term affixes itself as firmly to our image of politicians. But on deeper inspection, ambition as an explanation for candidate emergence appears to be more useful as a description than as an explanation. Here, in this collection, we engage broadly with the idea of ambition, with a focus on why some individuals or groups might want to run for political office in an environment where so many forces point to the irrationality of political candidacy.

Despite the widespread use of the term and relative simplicity of the definition, there have been surprisingly few theoretical explanations for how or why some individuals possess political ambition while others express no interest in public office.[19] Beginning with Schlesinger's study of political careers in 1966, researchers have defined political ambition in terms of commitment to running (expressive ambition) or desire to move to higher office once elected (progressive ambition).[20] More recently, a set of studies on "nascent" ambition look further upstream, tracking the early antecedents of individuals' desires to run.[21] But "ambition" itself is not well defined in these works; we suspect, instead, that ambition is an outcome in search of a theory. Indeed, the phrase *political ambition* suggests a sycophantic, vote-maximizing individual, plotting her way to the top of the political system like the Frank—or Claire—Underwood character in Netflix's *House of Cards*. Such a caricature hardly describes every individual (or even most individuals) who might be interested in holding elected office. Further, the term *political ambition* suggests an ambitious personality, but most studies have found that thinking of ambition as related to one's seeking of status, desiring of salary, or having an ingrained personality trait does not predict actual people's level of political ambition.[22]

In many ways, research on political ambition supports the idea that ambition is largely affected and shaped by external factors; the early works focused on how things like incumbency, open seats, and district composition affected the "political opportunity structures" facing potential candidates, and more recent research has expanded this understanding to also include the role of recruiters and party "gatekeepers."[23] *Recruitment* refers to the process by which political parties, interest groups, and peers persuade individuals to run for office. Political parties exist, in part, to recruit individuals with broadly similar ideologies and worldviews to run for office.[24] Not surprisingly, recruitment matters for the decision to run for office; in short, simply asking people to run for office will lead to more of those people running for office.[25] But recruitment does not happen in a vacuum. Often, the people recruited by party operatives are already known by the party and already have the type of "nascent political ambition" that led them to be visible to recruiters in the first place.[26]

Although we suspect that some people really are "born to run," new research suggests that ambition is not innate but fluctuates based on contextual, structural, institutional, and psychological factors.[27] Women, in particular, on the whole appear to be more strategic about how, when, and where they run and are likely to make more "relationally-embedded"[28] decisions about candidacy. In other words, women are more likely to think about the consequences their candidacies will have for those around them.

This volume attempts to take seriously the idea that women's candidacies, and their political ambition more generally, are contingent, malleable, and relationally embedded. What this means is that when something major happens in the social or political environment, we may expect women's interest in running for office to undergo profound changes. Here we ask not who has ambition, as much previous work has done, but how to activate and encourage ambition among a larger population of potential female candidates. Such ambition is not innate; it can be created anew from new experiences and understandings, coached, and supported or quashed. How and for whom these processes work is the starting point for many of the studies in this book.

Book Overview

Electoral democracy requires that voters have meaningful choices about who serves in office. To provide voters with real choices, we need willing candidates. In this book we strive to combine rigorous scholarship with a focus on the "real world" of women as potential candidates, both in the United States and more broadly. This unusual compilation is the result of an innovative conference, held in November 2017 at the University of Pennsylvania, that brought together academics and advocates working in the field of women and politics. We believe that this sort of collaboration is essential: scholars may overlook important problems on the ground for lack of shoe-leather experience, while practitioners may be unaware that solid, peer-reviewed research has already attempted to answer many important questions in their field.

Part of the disconnect between practitioners and scholarship revolves around language; academics in particular are often used to speaking to each other and to focusing far more on data and methods than most advocates may want or need. This volume, therefore, presents original research but in an accessible format; to the extent that our authors' comments draw on statistical techniques, an online appendix includes additional scholarly information[29] but the main body of each chapter attempts to tell a clear story about some aspect of women's political ambition, recruitment into political parties, training to run for office, or fundraising campaigns. The central question our authors address is how to get more women to run for public office.

The essays in Part I, "Who Runs?" assess who does and who does not seem interested in running (Bernhard et al.), with particular explorations into key demographic subgroups, including elite women (O'Connor and Yanus), Republican women (Och), and Black women (Scott, Dickinson, and Dowe). Part II asks "Why Run?" as in, what are the "good reasons" that would generate women's candidacies? Some potential answers arising from these chapters include the idea of making good public policy (Thomas and Wineinger), understanding electoral politics as civic service (Deen and Shelton), and thinking of elected office as a way to promote one's activism (Mo and Anderson-Nilsson).

Part III, "Why Not Run?" flips the question, asking how larger contextual factors might make even those women who would otherwise make great candidates choose not to run. The answers offered through the original data and reasoning in this section include the idea of geographically strategic candidates (Ondercin), the role of party leaders in recruiting and promoting women as candidates (Gimenez Aldridge et al.; Brown and Dowe), and the negative messages that can come from a prominent female candidate's defeat (Bonneau and Kanthak).

Parts IV and V turn to the new and emerging strategies that nonprofit training and funding organizations are using, both here and more globally, to help more women run for and win office. Part IV, "How Nonprofits Help Women Run for Office," focuses more on what these organizations are, what they do, and why, with chapters devoted to a broad overview of the organizational landscape (Kreitzer and Osborn), specific organizations and their effects (Sanbonmatsu and Dittmar; Schneider and Sweet-Cushman), and examining campaign training for women on a global scale (Piscopo).

Part V, "The Special Role of Money," examines the special role of money and fundraising in campaigns, looking at how this affects women as candidates in particular (Swers and Thomsen), the role and impact of training and funding in a comparative case study (Johnson), and an innovative look at contributions to a diverse set of candidates within the United States (Kettler).

The essays in this book thus seek to move beyond description toward answering "how" and "why" questions, with the goal of increasing women's candidacies for public office. In a time of declining public trust in government, not to mention increasing political polarization, gridlock, and animosity among public officials, we firmly believe that a key part of the solution will be giving more power to women.

NOTES

1. CAWP, "Current Numbers | CAWP" (New Brunswick, NJ: Center for American Women and Politics, Eagleton Institute of Politics, Rutgers University, 2018), accessed November 20, 2019, available at http://www.cawp.rutgers.edu/current-numbers.

2. Proportional representation systems typically elect more than one candidate out of a district. In those systems, parties and not individuals tend to be more important in candidate entry.

3. Richard L. Fox and Jennifer L. Lawless, "Reconciling Family Roles with Political Ambition: The New Normal for Women in Twenty-First Century US Politics," *Journal of Politics* 76, no. 2 (2014): 398–414; Shauna L. Shames, *Out of the Running: Why Millennials Reject Political Careers and Why It Matters* (New York: New York University Press, 2017); Jerome H. Black and Lynda Erickson, "Women Candidates and Voter Bias: Do Women Politicians Need to Be Better?" *Electoral Studies* 22, no. 1 (2003): 81–100.

4. Nicholas Carnes, *White-Collar Government: The Hidden Role of Class in Economic Policy Making* (Chicago: University of Chicago Press, 2013); Sarah A. Fulton, Cherie D. Maestas, L. Sandy Maisel, and Walter J. Stone, "The Sense of a Woman: Gender, Ambition, and the Decision to Run for Congress," *Political Research Quarterly* 59, no. 2 (2006): 235–248; Nadia E. Brown, *Sisters in the Statehouse: Black Women and Legislative Decision Making* (New York: Oxford University Press, 2014); Nadia E. Brown and Sarah A. Gershon, eds., *Distinct Identities: Minority Women in U.S. Politics* (New York: Routledge, 2016); Christina E. Bejarano, *The Latina Advantage: Gender, Race, and Political Success* (Austin: University of Texas Press, 2013); Pamela Stone, "Ghettoized and Marginalized: The Coverage of Racial and Ethnic Groups in Introductory Sociology Texts," *Teaching Sociology* 24 (October 1996): 356–363.

5. Accessed November 20, 2019, more information available at https://www.ipu.org /resources/publications/infographics/2017-03/women-in-politics-2017.

6. The head of state is the chief executive position (like president) while the head of the government is often a prime minister. Some countries like France have both a president and a prime minister.

7. Farida Jalalzai, "Women Rule: Shattering the Executive Glass Ceiling," *Politics and Gender* 4, no. 2 (2008): 205–231.

8. For a discussion of how this might happen and the methods of measurement, see Tiffany D. Barnes and Mirya R. Holman, "Taking Diverse Backgrounds into Account in Studies of Political Ambition and Representation," *Politics, Groups, and Identities* (November 8, 2018): 1–13; Tiffany D. Barnes and Mirya R. Holman, "Gender Quotas, Women's Representation, and Legislative Diversity," *Journal of Politics,* forthcoming.

9. Kira Sanbonmatsu, "Gender Stereotypes and Vote Choice," *American Journal of Political Science* 46, no. 1 (2002): 20–34; Deborah Alexander and Kristi Andersen, "Gender as a Factor in the Attribution of Leadership Traits," *Political Research Quarterly* 46, no. 3 (1993): 527–545; Kim Kahn, "Does Gender Make a Difference? An Experimental Examination of Sex Stereotypes and Press Patterns in Statewide Campaigns," *American Journal of Political Science* 38, no. 1 (1994): 162–195; Mirya R. Holman, Jennifer L. Merolla, and Elizabeth J. Zechmeister, "Terrorist Threat, Male Stereotypes, and Candidate Evaluations," *Political Research Quarterly* 69, no. 1 (2016): 134–147; Leonie Huddy and Nayda Terkildsen, "The Consequences of Gender Stereotypes for Women Candidates at Different Levels and Types of Office," *Political Research Quarterly* 46, no. 3 (1993): 503–525; Jeffrey W. Koch, "Do Citizens Apply Gender Stereotypes to Infer Candidates' Ideological Orientations?" *Journal of Politics* 62, no. 2 (2000): 414–429; Kathleen Dolan, "Voting for Women in the 'Year of the Woman,'" *American Journal of Political Science* 42, no. 1 (January 1998): 272–293.

10. Jennifer L. Lawless and Richard L. Fox, *It Still Takes a Candidate: Why Women Don't Run for Office* (Cambridge: Cambridge University Press, 2010); Edmond Costantini, "Political Women and Political Ambition: Closing the Gender Gap," *American Journal of Political Science* 34, no. 3 (1990): 741–770.

11. Kathryn Pearson and Eric McGhee, "What It Takes to Win: Questioning 'Gender Neutral' Outcomes in U.S. House Elections," *Politics and Gender* 9, no. 4 (December 2013): 439–462; Jennifer L. Lawless and Kathryn Pearson, "The Primary Reason for Women's

Underrepresentation? Reevaluating the Conventional Wisdom," *Journal of Politics* 70, no. 1 (2008): 67–82; Mirya R. Holman, Jennifer L. Merolla, and Elizabeth J. Zechmeister, "Terrorist Threat, Male Stereotypes, and Candidate Evaluations," *Political Research Quarterly* 69, no. 1 (2016): 134–147; Erin C. Cassese and Tiffany D. Barnes, "Reconciling Sexism and Women's Support for Republican Candidates," *Political Behavior* (May 18, 2018): 1–24; Erin C. Cassese and Mirya R. Holman, "Party and Gender Stereotypes in Campaign Attacks," *Political Behavior* 40 (2018): 785–807; Cecilia Hyunjung Mo, "The Consequences of Explicit and Implicit Gender Attitudes and Candidate Quality in the Calculations of Voters," *Political Behavior* 37, no. 2 (May 16, 2014): 357–395.

12. For a review of the debate about bias against female politicians, see Dawn Langan Teele, Joshua Kalla, and Frances Rosenbluth, "The Ties That Double Bind: Social Roles and Women's Underrepresentation in Politics," *American Political Science Review* 112, no. 3 (August 2018): 525–541. Shannon Jenkins, "A Woman's Work Is Never Done? Fund-Raising Perception and Effort among Female State Legislative Candidates," *Political Research Quarterly* 60, no. 2 (June 1, 2007): 230–239.

13. Shames, *Out of the Running*.

14. Jeffrey Lazarus and Amy Steigerwalt, *Gendered Vulnerability* (Ann Arbor: University of Michigan Press, 2018); Mary Layton Atkinson and Jason H. Windett, "Gender Stereotypes and the Policy Priorities of Women in Congress," *Political Behavior* 41, no. 3 (2019): 769–789; Sarah Anzia and Christopher R. Berry, "The Jackie (and Jill) Robinson Effect: Why Do Congresswomen Outperform Congressman?" *American Journal of Political Science* 55, no. 3 (2011): 478–493; Tiffany D. Barnes, *Gendering Legislative Behavior: Institutional Constraints and Collaboration in Argentina* (New York: Cambridge University Press, 2016).

15. Monica C. Schneider, Mirya R. Holman, Amanda B. Diekman, and Thomas McAndrew, "Power, Conflict, and Community: How Gendered Views of Political Power Influence Women's Political Ambition," *Political Psychology* 37, no. 4 (2016): 515–531; Amanda B. Diekman, Elizabeth R. Brown, Amanda M. Johnston, and Emily K. Clark, "Seeking Congruity between Goals and Roles: A New Look at Why Women Opt Out of Science, Technology, Engineering, and Mathematics Careers," *Psychological Science* 21, no. 8 (2010): 1051–1057.

16. Shames, *Out of the Running*; Lawless and Fox, *It Still Takes a Candidate*.

17. Kristin Kanthak and Jonathan Woon, "Women Don't Run? Election Aversion and Candidate Entry," *American Journal of Political Science* 59, no. 3 (November 1, 2014): 595–612.

18. Melody Crowder-Meyer and Benjamin E. Lauderdale, "A Partisan Gap in the Supply of Female Potential Candidates in the United States," *Research and Politics* 1, no. 1 (April 1, 2014); Shames, *Out of the Running*.

19. Thanks to Patrick Meehan for some of the research, thinking, and writing on political ambition used in this section.

20. Joseph A. Schlesinger, *Ambition and Politics: Political Careers in the United States* (New York: Rand McNally, 1966); David W. Rohde, "Risk-Bearing and Progressive Ambition: The Case of Members of the United States House of Representatives," *American Journal of Political Science* 23, no. 1 (February 1979): 1–26; Gordon S. Black, "A Theory of Political Ambition: Career Choices and the Role of Structural Incentives," *The American Political Science Review* 66, no. 1 (March 1972): 144–159; Linda Fowler and Robert McClure, *Political Ambition: Who Decides to Run for Congress* (New Haven, CT: Yale University Press, 1990).

21. Jennifer L. Lawless and Richard Logan Fox, *It Takes a Candidate: Why Women Don't Run for Office* (Cambridge: Cambridge University Press, 2005); Melody Crowder-

42. Male Republican party leader, as quoted in Och, "The Grand Old Party of 2016," 11.

43. Political Parity, 2015.

44. Kathryn Pearson and Eric McGhee, "What It Takes to Win: Questioning Gender Neutral Outcomes in U.S. House Elections," *Gender and Politics* 9, no. 4 (2013): 439–462.

45. Wineinger, "Gendering Republican Party Culture."

46. As quoted in Och, "The Grand Old Party of 2016," 11.

47. Male Republican national party leader, as quoted in Political Parity, 2015, 15.

48. Och, "The Grand Old Party of 2016."

49. Personal communication.

50. Marie Solis, "Women Candidates Aren't All Running against Trump—Republicans Say They Are Answering a Different Call," *Newsweek*, January 16, 2018, accessed February 8, 2018, available at http://www.newsweek.com/record-number-women-are-running-office-2018-where-are-all-republican-women-771055.

51. Och, "The Grand Old Party of 2016."

52. Och, "The Grand Old Party of 2016," 14.

53. Abbie Erler, "Moving Up or Getting Out: The Career Patterns of Republican Women State Legislators," in *The Right Women. Republican Party Activists, Candidates, and Legislators*, ed. Malliga Och and Shauna Shames (Denver, CO: Praeger, 2018), 176–196.

54. Och, "The Grand Old Party of 2016," 19.

55. Danielle Thomsen, "Republican Women, Then and Now: Ideological Changes in Congressional Candidates from 1980–2012," in *The Right Women: Republican Party Activists, Candidates, and Legislators*, ed. Malliga Och and Shauna Shames (Denver, CO: Praeger, 2018), 74–92.

56. Political Parity, 2015.

57. Shames, "Higher Hurdles for Republican Women."

58. Shames, "Higher Hurdles for Republican Women."

59. Political Parity, 2015.

60. As quoted in Political Parity, 2015, 30.

61. Political Parity, 2015; Shames, "Higher Hurdles for Republican Women."

62. Political Parity, 2015.

63. Republican congresswomen, as quoted in Och, "The Grand Old Party of 2016," 13.

64. Simone Pathé, "Stefanik Launches PAC to Boost Female Candidates, Now with GOP Leadership Support," Roll Call, January 18, 2019, accessed February 14, 2019, available at https://www.rollcall.com/news/campaigns/stefanik-launches-pac-leadership-support.

65. Open Secrets, "E-PAC Summary," Center for Responsible Politics, February 1, 2019, accessed February 14, 2019, available at https://www.opensecrets.org/pacs/lookup2.php?strID=C00570945.

66. Republican Women for Progress, Mission, accessed February 19, 2018, available at https://gopwomenforprogress.org/.

67. Personal communication with Lisa Zeriax, communication director, NFRW.

4

Who Is Stacey Abrams?

An Examination of Gender and Race Dynamics in State-Level Candidacy

Jamil Scott, Kesicia Dickinson, and Pearl K. Dowe

Conversations about women vying for public office tend to be couched in the experiences of White women.[1] To truly understand the experiences of women who seek political office, and those who have won political positions, we have to look beyond White women. This is especially important as we think about the gains for women of color in the 2018 midterm election cycle.[2] An intersectional approach allows us to think about how race and gender produce distinct political experiences for women from different groups. For instance, Black women are often associated with more masculine traits[3] as well as other pervasive and negative images.[4] While these stereotypes about Black women may not directly relate to their role in politics, these images may play a role in how the public perceives and responds to the candidacy of Black women; although, the stereotypes associated with Black politicians can be distinct.[5]

Black women officeholders have propelled the representation of both Black leaders in politics and women's representation more generally.[6] Over time, the proportion of Black leaders that are women has grown, particularly in state legislatures. In Figure 4.1, we show Black women's representation in state legislatures, along with that of the representation of women of color more broadly. By 2018, Black women accounted for about 14.7 percent of all women legislators;[7] in addition, all women of color, representing a large and growing group of women in politics more generally, made up 24 percent of women state legislators.[8] This proves women of color can and do win political office; however, attaining office is not without challenges.[9] Women of color are less likely to be recruited by political parties.[10] At the state level, women of color respond to multiple constituencies—representing the interests both of women and of their racial group.[11]

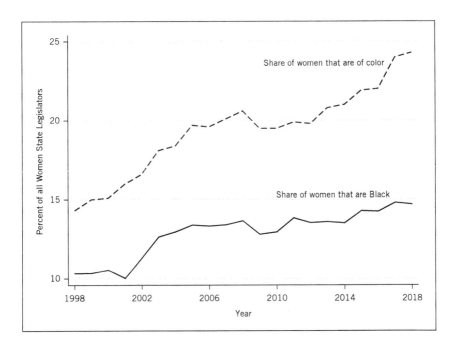

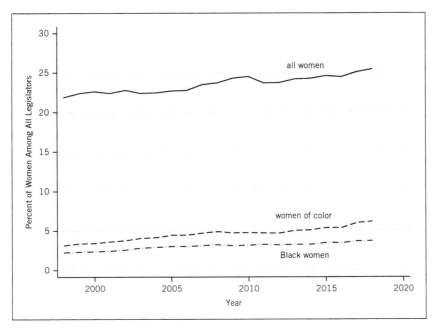

Figure 4.1. Representation of women of color in state legislatures. The figure lists the share of women state representatives that are of color or Black.

There is an open question as to whether Black women's intersecting identities disadvantage or advantage their electoral ambition. While there is some
evidence that the combination of race and gender places women of color at a
disadvantage in the electoral arena,[12] there is also evidence that the combination of race and gender allows women of color to have a broader appeal and
leads to electoral success.[13] Even still, there is reason to believe that women
of color have nuanced electoral experiences and their intersectional identity
can help or hurt their electoral chances depending on the context.[14]

The extant literature argues political parties are less likely to recruit women
of color, but it is limited in helping us understand what we know about how
voters' perceptions of Black women candidates influence the selection process.
Whereas the question of how women of color fare in the electoral process tends
to be examined after elections, in this chapter we examine how voters perceived
Stacey Abrams, a Black woman who ran as the 2018 Democratic nominee for
the gubernatorial seat in Georgia. Due to the historic nature of the Abrams's
campaign and the support from high profile Democratic party leadership outside of the state, this case study is critical to understanding how the intersection
of race and gender influence the candidacy process and particularly how the
candidate both is perceived by voters and seeks to represent herself.

We engage in a case study of Stacey Abram's candidacy using a mixed
methods approach. Our primary data on self-presentation and voter evaluation come from Abrams's presence on Twitter (@staceyabrams). She maintains an active Twitter account and has also received attention on Twitter
because of her political candidacy. We specifically use two sets of Twitter
data: tweets in which Stacey Abrams is mentioned and tweets from her official Twitter account. Specifically, we want to know: (1) how tweeters discuss
the candidacy of a woman of color in a statewide election contest, (2) how a
woman of color represents herself as a candidate in a statewide election contest, and (3) how participation in a candidate training program influences
her candidacy. Our initial hypotheses are twofold. First, we suspect that conversations about her candidacy will include considerations of her intersectional identity. Second, we believe she will use a deracialized approach to
appeal to non-Black voters while using subtle and intentional strategies in
her campaign rhetoric and materials to maintain the support of Black voters.

There are some advantages to our approach. We are able to test theories
of deracialized candidacy in relation to a Black woman's emergence as a major
contender for the nomination in a statewide race. We also take a novel approach to examining if the stereotypes and perceptions of women candidates
in the literature extend to women of color. Furthermore, we consider the crit-
icisms of quantitative research in regard to the intersectionality research paradigm.[15] Quantitative research often treats intersectionality as a multiplicative
term. Though this is methodologically sound, it violates the strict assumption in the intersectionality approach that identity can be reduced to fixed

categories. Using qualitative analysis and a text-as-data approach, we are able to hold true to the intersectionality assumption because we consider the Twitter utterances as a measure of sentiment toward Abrams as well as a way to measure the ways in which Abrams represents herself.

Who Is Stacey Abrams?

Stacey Abrams is a native of Gulfport, Mississippi. She earned an undergraduate degree from Spelman College, a historically Black college for women, and advanced degrees from the University of Texas at Austin and Yale Law School. Abrams has an impressive history of leadership and service. She was the first woman to lead a party in the Georgia General Assembly and the first woman and person of color to lead the House of Representatives as House minority leader. She also founded the New Georgia Project—an organization that registered over 200,000 voters of color in a two-year time span. Given her accomplishments and her evident passion for public service, she has received support from political forces across the nation like Congresswoman Barbara Lee and Senator Cory Booker. If Abrams had won, she would be the first woman to serve as a governor of Georgia, the first Black governor of Georgia, and the first Black woman elected as a governor in the country.

Stacey Abrams's candidacy contains an important narrative, not only because she could have been one of the first or the few gubernatorial officeholders who look like her but also because she had taken a crucial step to do so via program initiatives. Abrams's path to office can be traced through her participation in political training programs. Before being elected to the state house, Abrams participated in Leadership Georgia, Leadership Atlanta, and the Regional Leadership Institute. During her journey to the Georgia General Assembly, she was endorsed by Georgia's Win List. After announcing her gubernatorial candidacy, she was endorsed by EMILY's List and again by Georgia's Win List. While endorsements by notable organizations garner votes from the organizations' followers, such endorsements also carry financial, strategic, and political support from these organizations. Also, Stacey Abrams is a candidate who we know has completed several candidate training programs,[16] and she continually relies on these organizations to move her political campaigns forward.

The national attention Abrams has received speaks to the political success and broader acceptance of a new cohort of Black elected officials—a group known for their deracialized approach to politics.[17] This group of leaders is careful to convey a nonthreatening, amiable image. Their campaign platform centers around general issues like education and health care. They also avoid addressing issues explicitly alluding to race to appeal to a larger portion of the electorate, more importantly, non-Black voters.[18] Though they refrain from pushing a race-specific agenda, they are still committed to representing and advocating for voters of color. Former president Barack Obama and former governor Deval Patrick are commonly mentioned when discussing Black leaders who called attention to this method through their success.

Methods and Data

Our analysis focuses on tweets collected from May 2017 to January 2018. We mark the start of our data in May because this is the month in which there was some indication that Abrams was going to run. Former governor of Michigan, Jennifer Granholm, even congratulated Abrams on her decision to run in May: "Thrilled that @staceyabrams is going to run for gov in Georgia! She's brilliant." However, we acknowledge that Stacey Abrams officially announced her candidacy in June. Overall, our data sample includes 2,181 tweets from Abrams's Twitter account and 19,724 tweets about Abrams.

The qualitative analysis involves examining how Abrams fits into Andra Gillespie's typologies of the current generation of Black candidates and officeholders.[19] Gillespie characterizes the current generation of Black leadership on three dimensions: crossover appeal, perceived trajectory, and ties to the Black establishment. *Crossover appeal* captures a politician's ability to capture support from Black and non-Black constituencies. The *perceived trajectory* dimension encompasses not only whether a Black leader has progressive political ambition but also if the opportunity structure exists for upward mobility and the ability of the leader to generate media attention. Finally, the *ties to the Black establishment* assesses whether a leader is included in the network of "traditional centers of Black political power," such as being connected with or supported by civil rights leaders.[20] Gillespie's dimensions of Black leadership capture both image management on the part of Black leaders and how these Black leaders fit into the political landscape in which they rise to power. Here, we examine how Abrams engages in image management and expression via her Twitter account.

The quantitative analysis involves a text-as-data approach in which we analyze tweets about Stacey Abrams. We do this to capture how she is perceived by Twitter users (both within and outside of Georgia). In analyzing the tweets, we use latent Dirichlet allocation (LDA). LDA is modeling technique that gets at the topics that are the best probabilistic representation of the Twitter discussion about Abrams.[21] We also use a dictionary-based approach (i.e., electronically coding for the presence of certain words) to descriptively examine how race and gender play into conversations about Abrams.[22]

We first take a subset of the sample (10 percent of each set of tweets) to determine the initial patterns in the data and the best fitting topic model before running analysis on the remaining data. Because the modeling technique we use is a parametric model and relies on user input to set the number of possible topics for which words can be sampled, we chose 10 topics to both capture topics in the tweets and be parsimonious.

Results

In the analysis of tweets from Stacey Abrams's Twitter account, we consider Gillespie's typologies but also note the ways in which Abrams is divergent. As previously mentioned, Gillespie's typology is focused on three dimensions: crossover appeal, perceived trajectory, and ties to the Black establishment. Abrams exhibits high crossover appeal, meaning that she has been able to garner support from both Black and non-Black potential voters. Not only does she make statements like "every Georgian deserves the chance to succeed," but she also openly rejects the idea that she would only serve Black interests. For instance, in one tweet she says, "I am running not just for Atlanta." In another, she states, "I want this campaign to build a coalition from Appling to Atlanta." The mention of Atlanta, a majority Black city, and its juxtaposition to Appling, a majority White city, is meaningful here. This is a nod to non-Black voters that projects her ability to represent the interests of all Georgians. In conjunction with her rhetoric, Abrams's crossover appeal is evident in her popularity both within and outside of Georgia with the media attention she has received and her endorsements. In her tweets, she notes endorsements by trade organizations, EMILY's List, the AFL-CIO of Georgia, and others. In addition, Abrams is one of the few women of color who have been able to build a national profile from a more local position.

In terms of Abrams connection to the Black political establishment, there are important distinctions that should be considered here. In accordance with Gillespie's typology, politicians that have high crossover appeal tend to lack a strong connection to the Black political establishment and struggle with connecting to Black leaders of earlier cohorts. While the tweets suggest that Abrams cares a great deal about voting and voting rights, she is not counted among the members of traditional organizations like the NAACP nor is she part of a Black political activist family. However, Abrams indicates that she has been endorsed by individuals who are considered authentic leaders like John Lewis and Rev. Dr. Joseph Lowery, both civil rights leaders. In addition, Abrams is explicit about attending a historically Black undergraduate institution, and, throughout her tweets, she is often explicit about race and its impact on the political experience. In one tweet, Abrams is noted as saying, "My people are the Black people who people told to pick cotton but not to vote." These explicit invocations of the impact of race serve to align her more closely with older Black leaders, like Lewis, who fought for equal rights for people of color in the South.

While Abrams's run for governor is certainly indicative of political ambition for higher office, having previously served in the Georgia state house,
the extent of her political trajectory is yet to be determined as her upward
mobility may be limited. Although Abrams ran in an open seat election, her
intersectional identity as a Black woman and her liberal stances may have in-
hibited her political ambition in a largely Republican state. However, it must
be noted that across the country voters are responding to the negative national political climate and turning red states, like Georgia, blue. This may
bode well for Abrams's future political prospects. Abrams is vocal about her
support for transgender rights, reproductive rights and the #MeToo movement. She is also vocal about gender issues, more generally, with concern for
issues facing women of color. One such example of this is Abrams's tweet,
"Equal pay for women is an economic security issue for all families. Georgia's next governor must commit to closing the wage gap #EqualPayCant-
Wait." Similarly, she tweeted, "The gender wage hurts women of color the
most." As a candidate, Abrams not only paid credence to issues for all Georgians, the prescribed behavior for the current generation of Black politicians,
but also specifically addressed issues for women.

Turning to how Abrams is perceived by tweeters (both within and outside
of Georgia), we look to the quantitative analysis. Given that Stacey Abrams is a
woman of color, it would be natural to expect that her gender and race would
play into conversations about her online. To examine this, we use an electronic count of how many times words associated with race, gender, or both are
included in tweets. The results of this analysis are shown in Figure 4.2.

The graph in Figure 4.2 is labeled for the mention of a characteristic (race,
gender, or both) on the x-axis and the number of tweets that explicitly mention these characteristics on the y-axis. The graph indicates that more Twitter users mentioned Abrams's gender than her race. Twitter users discussed
Abrams's intersectional identity (her gender and her race) the least. Moreover, it must be noted here that there are 19,724 total tweets about Abrams
and, in seeking to examine explicit mentions of race and gender, we have cap-
tured less than half that number. This shows that the vast majority of the
tweets that mention Stacey Abrams do not explicitly mention either race or
gender. This is not to say that both race and gender dynamics are not at play
in the discussion about her but that the discussion is likely more nuanced.
We will further explore this in the analysis of the LDA model.

In Figure 4.3, we show the predicted number of tweets associated with
the 10 topics from the LDA model. From the graph, it is clear that Topic 4 is
associated with the most tweets followed by Topic 1 and Topic 2. Thus, most
of the discussion surrounding Stacey Abrams during the period of data collection is related to Topic 4. For clarity, we focus on the three most prominent topics. In Table 4.1, we show the terms from the fitted model that are

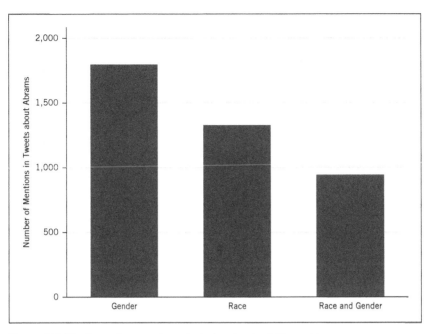

Figure 4.2. Mentions of race and gender in tweets about Stacey Abrams.

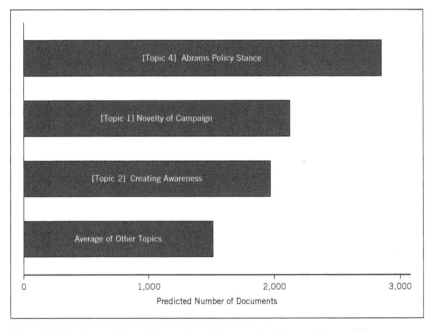

Figure 4.3. Topic model predicted coding of tweets about Stacey Abrams. The average of the other topics is the average over seven other modeled topics.

TABLE 4.1. TERMS ASSOCIATED WITH THE MOST FREQUENTLY
PREDICTED TOPICS FEATURED IN TWEETS ABOUT STACEY ABRAMS

Topic 1 Novelty of Abrams's Campaign	Topic 2 Creating Awareness of the Campaign	Topic 4 Abrams's Policy Stances
"governor"	"stacey"	"candidate"
"black"	"abrams"	"history"
"abrams"	"governor"	"gubernatorial"
"first"	"georgia"	"right"
"stacey"	"news"	"stone"
"woman"	"race"	"mountain"
"win"	"story"	"confederate"
"female"	"endorses"	"leader"
"wants"	"john"	"democrat"
"change"	"lewis"	"government"

associated with Topics 1, 2, and 4. Again, these three topics were most frequently predicted in the test data.

The topic model produces the most likely terms associated with each topic.
These terms inform the theme or topic that can be deduced from the probabilistic model fitting. The terms in Topic 1, Topic 2, and Topic 4 all reference
Stacey Abrams's campaign, but in distinct ways. The terms in Topic 1 refer
to the novelty of Stacey Abrams's candidacy. As previously noted, Stacey Abrams's
run for governor had the potential to make history as she could have been the
first Black woman to serve as governor of Georgia and, more notably, she could
have been the first Black woman governor in the United States. It is no sur-
prise that tweeters are noting this moment and discussing its potential impact. Stacey Abrams's candidacy could have also meant a big change for Georgia
as she could have been the first Democratic governor elected in Georgia in 15
years.

The terms in Topic 2 refer to creating awareness about Abrams's campaign and who is supporting her. Stacey Abrams received John Lewis's endorsement during the time of our data collection, and this was reflected in
the tweets. Not only does Lewis have political capital as a congressman but
also as a civil rights leader. This is an implicit racial reference as this crucial
endorsement for Abrams speaks to her connection to the Black political establishment and may reflect on the support she receives from the Black community in the primary. Abrams's primary opponent, Stacey Evans, not only
has a similar name but also similar credentials. The endorsement from John
Lewis likely makes Abrams stand out in comparison to her opponent.

Finally, the terms in Topic 4 refer more to the political stances that Abrams has espoused as a candidate, in particular, her stance that the confederate monument at Stone Mountain be removed. This is a bold stance to take and generated a lot of conversation both with and about Abrams. There was even an article that questioned whether this stance would hurt her electoral chances for the gubernatorial seat. Although this topic is strongly tied to race and race relations in Georgia, there was no explicit use of race-related words. However, Abrams's stance garnered strong support both for and against it. While sentiment in some of the tweets made it clear that she would not receive the support of some voters in the primary and that they did not believe she could win, she did receive strong support from others who were with her in the belief that the monument should be removed. The fact that Abrams is willing to take a position on such a polarizing issue, particularly in a state like Georgia, speaks to the type of campaign she is running.

Conclusion

Gillespie[23] lays out a political typology that allows us to think about how Stacey Abrams fits among other current Black politicians. Among her contemporaries are politicians like former president Barack Obama and Cory Booker. Although Abrams exhibits some of the characteristics that have made both Booker and Obama widely popular, she does diverge from them in important ways. As a woman who was supported by EMILY's List, Abrams had both resources and national attention that her Black male counterparts would not be able to access. Furthermore, Abrams's attention to issues surrounding gender and race not only speak to her dual identities but also separate her from her Black male contemporaries who do not necessarily bring these issues up on the campaign trail. Despite Abrams's choice to talk about issues surrounding race and gender, tweeters couched discussion about her candidacy in terms of the benefits her election would bring, her stances on political issues, and the historic relevance of her candidacy.

By ending our data collection in January, we were not able to follow Abrams's election bid through the Democratic primary and subsequently to the general election. Thus, our analysis here is instructive but incomplete. However, we do expect that the attention she received on Twitter during the general election will be different and reflect a stronger voice of nonmembers of her base now paying attention to her election bid. We do note that our analysis is distinct in that we are able to capture the utterances of a candidate during the campaign phase. Our analysis speaks to how a woman of color presents her policy stances and politics to voters in a state-level election. As a candidate, Abrams must both engage Black voters and appeal to a broader voter base in a largely Republican state. Her self-presentation in and of itself is interesting because there are few women of color running for state-level positions. Her policy stances and political discussion could certainly be enlightening for women of color who follow her in the electoral process.

NOTES

1. N. Alexander-Floyd, "Why Political Scientists Don't Study Black Women but Historians and Sociologists Do: On Intersectionality and the Remapping of the Study of Black Political Women," *National Political Science Review* 10, no. 2 (2014): 135–159; Jane Junn and Nadia Brown, "What Revolution? Incorporating Intersectionality in Women and Politics," in *Political Women and American Democracy*, ed. Christina Wolbrecht, Karen Beckwith, and Lisa Baldez (New York: Cambridge University Press, 2008); J. L. Prestage and M. Githens, *A Portrait of Marginality: The Political Behavior of the American Woman* (New York: D. McKay Company, 1977).

2. W. Smooth, "Standing for Women? Which Women? The Substantive Representation of Women's Interests and the Research Imperative of Intersectionality," *Politics and Gender* 7, no. 3 (2011): 436–441.

3. M. C. King, "Oppression and Power: The Unique Status of the Black Woman in the American Political System," *Social Science Quarterly* (1975): 116–128.

4. J. S. Jordan-Zachary, *Black Women, Cultural Images and Social Policy* (Routledge, 2009).

5. M. C. Schneider and A. L. Bos, "An Exploration of the Content of Stereotypes of Black Politicians," *Political Psychology* 32, no. 2 (2011): 205–233.

6. W. Smooth, "Intersectionality in Electoral Politics: A Mess Worth Making," *Politics and Gender* 2, no. 3 (2006): 400–414.

7. Facts on Women of Color in Office, accessed July 1, 2019, available at http://www.cawp.rutgers.edu/fact-sheets-women-color#blackStateLeg.

8. Women in State Legislatures 2018, accessed July 1, 2019, available at https://cawp.rutgers.edu/women-state-legislature-2018.

9. W. Smooth, "African American Women and Electoral Politics: Translating Voting Power into Office-holding," in *Gender and Elections: Shaping the Future of American Politics*, ed. S. J. Carroll and R. L. Fox (New York: Cambridge University Press, 2014), 167–189.

10. K. Sanbonmatsu, S. J. Carroll, and D. Walsh, "Poised to Run: Women's Pathways to the State Legislatures (New Brunswick, NJ: Center for American Women and Politics, Eagleton Institute of Politics, Rutgers University, 2009).

11. K. A. Bratton, K. L. Haynie, and B. Reingold, "Agenda Setting and African American Women in State Legislatures," *Journal of Women, Politics, and Policy* 28, nos. 3–4 (2007): 71–96; Luis Ricardo Fraga, Linda Lopez, Valeria Martinez-Ebers, and Ricardo Ramirez, "Gender and Ethnicity: Patterns of Electoral Success and Legislative Advocacy among Latina and Latino Officials in Four States," in *Intersectionality and Politics: Recent Research on Gender, Race, and Political Representation in the United States*, ed. Carol Hardy-Fanta (New York: Haworth Press, Inc., 2006).

12. Prestage and Githens, *A Portrait of Marginality*.

13. R. Darcy, C. D. Hadley, and J. F. Kirksey, "Election Systems and the Representation of Black Women in American State Legislatures," *Women and Politics* 13, no. 2 (1993): 73–89; Smooth, "Intersectionality in Electoral Politics"; T. S. Philpot and H. Walton, "One of Our Own: Black Female Candidates and the Voters Who Support Them," *American Journal of Political Science* 51, no. 1 (2007): 49–62; C. E. Bejarano, *The Latino Gender Gap in US Politics*, vol. 14 (Routledge, 2013).

14. N. E. Brown, *Sisters in the Statehouse: Black Women and Legislative Decision Making* (Oxford University Press, 2014).

15. L. Bowleg, "When Black + Lesbian + Woman ≠ Black Lesbian Woman: The Methodological Challenges of Qualitative and Quantitative Intersectionality Research," *Sex Roles* 59, nos. 5–6 (2008): 312–325; A. M. Hancock, "When Multiplication Doesn't Equal Quick Addition: Examining Intersectionality as a Research Paradigm, *Perspectives on Politics* 5, no. 1 (2007): 63–79.

16. Training programs have been considered instrumental in advancing women's political ambition by undertaking recruitment, training, and developing resources for women candidates.

17. A. Gillespie, ed. *Whose Black Politics? Cases in Post-racial Black Leadership* (Routledge, 2010).

18. J. McCormick and C. E. Jones, "The Conceptualization of Deracialization: Thinking through the Dilemma," *Dilemmas of Black Politics: Issues of Leadership and Strategy* 66 (1993): 84.

19. Gillespie, *Whose Black Politics?*

20. Gillespie, *Whose Black Politics?*

21. We use LDA on preprocessed text. We preprocess the text using the quanteda package. We treat each tweet as an individual document here. LDA attempts to get at the underlying topics contained in a document or set of documents (in this case a set of tweets) by generating a set of words based on probabilistic topic representation. LDA is a topic model that takes a Bayesian data analysis approach, making use of collapsed Gibbs sampling to iteratively go through each document, randomly assign words to one of k topics, and generate the probability that a word appears in a topic and that a topic appears in a document.

22. The dictionary for the analysis consisted of the following words to capture gender, race, and the intersection of the two: "woman," "women," "female," "girl," "lady," "ladies," "black," "African American," "Black American," "black woman," "black women," "black girl," "African American female," "Black female," and "Black lady." The words associated with our dictionary were derived from the coding of the training data (the initial 10 percent of the data that we used to train the LDA model).

23. Gillespie, *Whose Black Politics?*

PART II

Why Run?

Why should women run for office? The chapters in this part take up two key themes. The first is that women's representation as candidates and in political office is important not only for descriptive reasons but also for the ideas and issues that women bring to the table.[1] The second is that women's interest in holding office can be galvanized by participating in local or voluntary organizations.[2]

Decades of research into gender and politics has revealed that the motivations that propel women and men to seek public office are different. Whereas men tend to think of themselves as carving out a career in politics, women's political ambition tends to emerge out of a desire to fix a problem in the world.[3] These gendered motivations have implications for the arguments that we can and should use to convince more women to become involved in politics.[4] Becoming involved in local issues can set in motion the imaginative process that is crucial for furthering a policy agenda and can help women to establish the networks that will put them in the public eye. The authors in this part propose that even small steps toward community involvement can have a large impact on women's political careers down the line.

In the past, certain institutional features of American politics, such as high rates of incumbency (of predominantly men), the candidate-centric electoral process, and the fact that elections are so expensive, have all been analyzed as key barriers to women's candidacies. Yet as Thomas and Wineinger suggest in Chapter 5, "Ambition for Office: Women and Policy Making," the largest barrier to women's candidacies may be the fear that they won't be able to make a difference. Thomas and Wineinger argue that rebranding political ambition as a desire to make public policy widens the appeal of politics, especially to women. This is because people who desire specific changes are likely to be motivated to engage in the basic tasks of identifying political social problems, working to put these issues on the agenda, and then striving to create alliances for meaningful change. They draw on interviews with scores of female leaders around the United States to describe the efficacy of women as policy makers, highlighting how alliances that women form across party lines have been crucial to women's policy successes.

In Chapter 6, "From Civic Mindedness to Electoral Politics: Citizen Advisory Committees and the Decision to Run for School Board" Deen and Shelton trace the way that prior experiences as volunteers in community organizations can pave the way for continued civic involvement. In particular, they examine the path to running for the local school board and argue that there may be a multiplier effect, where engagement in organizations like the PTA breeds more engagement down the line. School boards were some of the first realms in which women were allowed to serve in office in the United States and have tended to have the highest levels of gender parity among any elected office.[5] As other scholars have shown, women who make it to higher political echelons, including state- and national-level positions, are much more likely to have served on a school board than men who make it into the same positions.[6] Deen and Shelton conducted interviews with all members of the school board in a midsize town in the southwestern United States and analyzed school board elections in several other towns. They argue that local-level officeholding may push people to consider other realms of politics because it gives them the civic skills to pursue further positions. Although the women they interviewed often became involved in PTAs for nonpolitical reasons related to motherhood, the tasks that are involved—wrangling donations, herding volunteers, and mobilizing on important issues—breed the types of skills necessary for policy making more generally.

Picking up on similar themes, in Chapter 7, Mo and Anderson-Nilsson describe how early career activism can lead to an interest in holding office. In "Youth National Service and Women's Political Ambition: The Case of Teach For America," Mo and Anderson-Nilsson study applicants to Teach for America, a large youth service organization that puts young college students into public schools. In this retrospective study, the entire pool of applications from 2007–2015 was invited to answer a survey where, among other things, they were asked a battery of questions about political participation (such as whether they had ever or would ever sign a petition, join a protest, or participate in a political campaign) as well as whether they would consider running for office. They compare responses for a group of applicants that were nearly offered slots in the program with those who just passed the threshold for admittance and found that Teach for America participants were more likely to show an interest both in running for office and in running political campaigns than applicants who did not participate in the program. Most important, the effects were huge for women of color: participation in the program caused their political interest to skyrocket. These findings suggest that the kind of civic capital that scholars have long deemed important for cementing political interest and participation may also be critical for bolstering women's political ambition. The chapters in this part provide novel approaches to understanding what actually works to convince a more diverse set of candidates to run for office. Several of these papers use cutting-edge techniques to understand which institutions and experiences matter for political ambition, and for whom. In doing so, these chapters contribute to our understanding of gender and political ambition and also to what we know about the diversity among women, revealing that the same message may not matter equally for all women.

NOTES

1. Tiffany D. Barnes, *Gendering Legislative Behavior: Institutional Constraints and Collaboration in Argentina* (New York: Cambridge University Press, 2016); Zachary Greene and Diana Z. O'Brien, "Diverse Parties, Diverse Agendas? Female Politicians and the Parliamentary Party's Role in Platform Formation," *European Journal of Political Research* 55 (2016): 435–453; Mirya R. Holman, "Sex and the City: Female Leaders and Spending on Social Welfare Programs in U.S. Municipalities," *Journal of Urban Affairs* 36, no. 4 (2014): 701–715; Tracy Osborn, *How Women Represent Women: Political Parties, Gender and Representation in the State Legislatures* (New York: Oxford University Press, 2012); Melanie M. Hughes, "Intersectionality, Quotas, and Minority Women's Political Representation Worldwide," *American Political Science Review* 105, no. 3 (2011): 604–620; Michele Swers, "Are Congresswomen More Likely to Vote for Women's Issue Bills Than Their Male Colleagues?" *Legislative Studies Quarterly* 23, no. 4 (1998): 435–448; Nadia E. Brown, *Sisters in the Statehouse Black Women and Legislative Decision Making* (New York: Oxford University Press, 2014); Anna Mahoney, *Women Take Their Place in State Legislatures the Creation of Women's Caucuses* (Philadelphia: Temple University Press, 2018).

2. Mirya R. Holman, *Women in Politics in the American City* (Philadelphia: Temple University Press, 2015); Melody Crowder-Meyer, Shana Kushner Gadarian, and Jessica Trounstine, "Electoral Institutions, Gender Stereotypes, and Women's Local Representation," *Politics, Groups, and Identities* 3, no. 2 (2015): 318–334; Jo Freeman, *A Room at a Time: How Women Entered Party Politics* (Rowman and Littlefield, 2002); Jane Mansbridge, "Rethinking Representation," *American Political Science Review* 97, no. 4 (2003): 515–528.

3. Monica C. Schneider, Mirya R. Holman, Amanda B. Diekman, and Thomas McAndrew, "Power, Conflict, and Community: How Gendered Views of Political Power Influence Women's Political Ambition," *Political Psychology* 37, no. 4 (2016): 515–531; Mirya R. Holman, "Women in Local Government: What We Know and Where We Go from Here," *State and Local Government Review* 49, no. 4 (September 25, 2017): 285–296; Osborn, *How Women Represent Women*; Melody Crowder-Meyer, "Baker, Bus Driver, Babysitter, Candidate? Revealing the Gendered Development of Political Ambition among Ordinary Americans," *Political Behavior*, September 11, 2018.

4. Mirya R. Holman and Monica C. Schneider, "Gender, Race, and Political Ambition: How Stereotype Threat and Perceptions of Discrimination Influence Interest in Political Office," *Politics, Groups, and Identities* Online First (2016); Elisabeth Gidengil, Ja-

nine Giles, and Melanee Thomas, "The Gender Gap in Self-Perceived Understanding of Politics in Canada and the United States," *Politics and Gender* 4, no. 4 (December 2008): 535–561.

5. Dawn Langan Teele, *Forging the Franchise: The Political Origins of the Women's Vote* (Princeton, NJ: Princeton University Press, 2018) (especially chapter 4); Melissa Marie Deckman, "School Board Candidates and Gender: Ideology, Party, and Policy Concerns," *Journal of Women, Politics, and Policy* 28, no. 1 (2007): 87–117; Jennie Sweet-Cushman, "Where Does the Pipeline Get Leaky? The Progressive Ambition of School Board Members and Personal and Political Network Recruitment," *Politics, Groups, and Identities* (2018): 1–24.

6. Susan J. Carroll and Kira Sanbonmatsu, *More Women Can Run: Gender and Pathways to the State Legislatures* (New York: Oxford University Press, 2013).

5

Ambition for Office

Women and Policy-making

SUE THOMAS AND CATHERINE WINEINGER

This moment in our nation's history requires that,
as women, we step up.
—WENDY CARRILLO, California Assemblymember[1]

The election of Donald J. Trump to the presidency has reinvigorated and recast our understanding of and commitment to electing more women into office. From the start, a large and diverse contingent of women has risen to resist the president's agenda. Aided by women's organizations dedicated to increasing the number of female candidates at all levels of office, record numbers of women signed up for campaign training programs, launched campaigns, and won elections in the 2018 cycle.[2]

What can we do to ensure that this momentum continues beyond the specific political moment and that the number and diversity of women running for local, state, and national offices increases? One answer comes from the public policy motivations of politically interested and active women. More than men, women tend to get politically involved because of specific policy concerns—and those concerns address a distinctive array of issues. It follows then that offering prospective candidates evidence that holding office can lead to high-priority policy success may translate the impulse to make a difference into active, viable campaigns.

Thus, in this chapter, we synthesize long-standing and extensive political science evidence that: women officeholders have long been motivated to run by policy concerns, these concerns are often more diverse than those of men, and women successfully pursue those policies to enactment. Ultimately, understanding that the path to office has been trod by women much like them may make the difference between having an interest in running for office and committing to throwing their hats into the ring.

Women and Political Ambition

In the United States, women vote in greater numbers than men. Since the 2016 election, more women than men say they are paying increased attention to politics. When women run for elected offices on school boards, city councils, state legislatures, the U.S. Congress, and other offices, all else equal, they win as often as men. Yet, depending on the office, currently, only one-fifth to slightly more than a quarter of elected bodies are women. What is the reason for this discrepancy? Scholarship over the past 40 years has focused extensively on this question. Among the findings are that women candidates face different and sometimes disproportionate obstacles than men and that those hurdles can dampen ambition. We classify these obstacles into two broad categories: political variables and sociological variables.

Political variables include: high incumbency rates that leave few opportunities for new members; differential levels of party support for female and male candidates; fundraising opportunity gaps (see Swers and Thomsen in Chapter 16, in this volume); differences in candidate support by Republican and Democratic women's organizations; heightened media portrayals of women; stereotypical, gender-based public perceptions; positive and negative biases toward female candidates; and levels of voter support of women who run for legislative and executive offices. Further, many of these obstacles are intensified for women of color (see Brown and Dowe in Chapter 10, and Scott, Dickinson, and Dowe in Chapter 4, in this volume, for additional illumination of this point). The nonprofit research group, the Center for Responsive Politics, reports on campaign contributions to women of color: "Female candidates of color received an average of around $330,000, compared to around $450,000 for men of color, and almost $700,000 for White candidates of both genders."[3] Higher Heights, a nonprofit political organization supporting African American candidates and officeholders, reports that African American women are more likely to be discouraged from running for office than other women and less likely to be recruited to run.

Sociological variables include the responsibilities women have for care of the home, children, and elders and inequities in educational and experiential backgrounds that impel people toward political careers. Additionally, political socialization of women tends to result in lower levels than men of political knowledge, efficacy, and activity. Each of these factors rests on a foundation of generalized gender inequalities in society that still operate powerfully.

To be sure, many of these political and sociological hurdles have been reduced over time. Yet, none have been eradicated. The result, as much contemporary research has demonstrated, is that women tend to see higher and more costs relative to benefits of running for office. From college onward, women are less likely than men to want to run. This is true even among millennials in prestigious schools of public policy and law, which are, according to traditional models of political ambition, the professions from which candidates are most likely to emerge. Moreover, the cost-benefit analysis differs among groups of women. As Och demonstrates in Chapter 3, and, as borne out in the 2018 electoral cycle in which just one new Republican woman was elected to the U.S. Congress, compared to Democrats, Republican women are affected by lack of party support. And, women of color often face more potent challenges across the board than White women.

Clearly, the costs of running for elected office have been well documented, well publicized, and internalized among those interested in politics. The benefits of doing so have not enjoyed the same breadth and depth of scrutiny. It is up to us then to provide an evidence-based counterpoint to conclusions that the costs of running are prohibitive—especially for women. To do so, we couple political science literature with voices of women officeholders. The result is a persuasive case that women in office make a big difference in people's lives. If the efforts of organizations that recruit, train, and fund women candidates are augmented with this message, running for office may be a more compelling prospect. Indeed, in "What It Will Take for Women to Win," Amanda Ripley asserts: "The third and most ambitious strategy [to encourage women to run] is for party recruiters to approach women—and men—with an entirely different sales pitch: one that reframes politics altogether. It turns out that the gender gap [in political ambition] disappears once women start thinking of politics as it should be. When women see political office as a way to fix problems and improve their communities, they become just as eager to run as men."[4]

Women's Ambition: Furthering Good Public Policy

"I decided all the men I'd been working for hadn't gotten it done," she said. "So, I needed to run myself."

—SENATOR JEAN SHAHEEN, Democrat of New Hampshire on why she first became a candidate for public office (Bash, "How New Hampshire's First Female Senator Moved Off the Sidelines")

Often, women run for office[5] to help people remedy problems that stem from inadequate public policy. Many times, something that has touched women deeply prods them to become involved.[6] Moreover, among women, this reason for running has become even more pronounced over time.[7] In contrast, although there are many men who run for office with deep concern for good public policy, men are more likely to run to achieve a certain office. As Erin Loos Cutraro, cofounder of the nonpartisan group She Should Run, puts it, "When women run for office, they run to get things done, not to get power. . . . Men run for office to get power."[8]

"As women and women of color we are speaking up and standing up on issues that matter most for people who are marginalized or do not see themselves represented in the halls of government." She goes on to say, "I ran because people wanted someone who could stand up for public education, LGBTQIA rights, speak out against the school-prison pipeline, someone raising the wage for people who work paycheck to paycheck. That was my platform: bringing people along who feel like they don't have a voice."

—**Member, U.S. House of Representatives, Attica Scott (D-KY)**[*]

"It wasn't until I was raising my child on my own and I started a job training program that set me up on this path. My son had serious medical conditions, and I was on welfare and Medicaid. . . . Raising my son, I joined the local PTO and was elected president. I wanted to become a better advocate. I was volunteering more, too, working on campaigns and getting active in the community. I think the more you know, the better you do. I started to hear input and started to have experiences; and all of a sudden I was awakened to some of the challenges my community was having."

—**Member, House of Delegates, Hala Ayala (D-VA)**[†]

"I didn't think I was ever going to run for office. . . . But I was disappointed in the 2012 elections. I think we need new candidates who are able to talk about a positive vision to getting our economy moving again. Specifically, in upstate New York, where young people are leaving in historic numbers for lack of jobs."

—**Member, U.S. House of Representatives, Elise Stefanik (R-NY)**[‡]

[*] Nicole Lewis, "The Presidential Glass Ceiling Is Still Intact, but New Report Shows Black Women Made Gains in 2016," *Washington Post*, July 31, 2017, accessed September 19, 2017, available at https://www.washingtonpost.com/news/the-fix/wp/2017/07/31/the-presidential-glass-ceiling-still-intact-but-new-report-shows-black-women-made-gains-in-2016/?utm_term=.e6a9f1523ab5.

[†] Mattie Kahn, "How Hala Ayala Is Running for the Virginia House of Delegates after Charlottesville," *Elle*, August 23, 2017, accessed October 1, 2017, available at http://www.elle.com/culture/career-politics/news/a47128/maggie-hassan-interview-americans-with-disabilities/.

[‡] "Elise Stefanik Biography," *Biography*, July 6, 2016, accessed November 21, 2019, available at https://stefanik.house.gov/about/full-biography.

Women's policy motivations bear fruit once they get to office: extensive research demonstrates that women's contributions across the policy-making process—from their distinctive and diverse policy priorities to their successes— are central to encouraging more women to run for office.

Here is detailed evidence of that success for three critical stages of the policy-making process: problem identification, agenda setting, and legislating.[9]

Problem Identification

Members of the public or politicians are displeased with an existing policy or
lack of policy for a problem. The problem is named and explained. A large and
growing volume of research shows that women policy-makers bring new
issues/problems to governing. It is not that male officeholders are uninterested
or inactive on a range of issues. Or that women limit themselves to particular issue areas. Still, everyone's experience informs her policy perspective and
affects her priorities. Because women have different life experiences from men
that range from reproduction to sexual harassment and domestic violence, it
is not surprising that women officeholders prioritize issues differently.[10]

Following are two perspectives on the difference women officeholders make
in identifying policy problems that had, heretofore, not been prioritized. U.S.
senator Mazie Hirono, Democrat of Hawaii, says: "There are seven women
now on the Senate Armed Services Committee—more than ever in the history of that committee. It's a very macho committee. I believe that all of us
women on the committee have experienced sexual harassment at some point
in our lives, whether in college or wherever. And it's when the women sat on that
committee that the issue of sexual assault in the military very much came to
the forefront. It was really the women, in my view, who drove that issue, and
got some changes made."[11]

U.S. representative Kristi Noem, Republican of South Dakota, cites her
experience as mother when she is asked about her motivation to work on
anti–human trafficking legislation: "I'm a mother of three—I've got two
daughters . . . I never would have dreamed that when I sent them out the door
to go to school, or to the mall, or to a store, that they were in jeopardy of
being trafficked. . . . The more that I learn about this issue, the more it keeps
me up at night." Noem's Human Trafficking Prevention, Intervention, and
Recovery Act became law in 2015.[12]

Legislative efforts on women's behalf also show how women's perspectives expand and diversify legislative agendas by identifying problems that
have been overlooked. At issue, it may be attention to insurance coverage for
pregnant women, or high rates of maternal mortality experienced by Black
women, or mandating leave for new parents, or expanding social support
programs such as the Supplemental Nutrition Assistance Program (SNAP),
or ensuring that women are included in clinical trials of new drugs, or enacting equal pay for equal work mandates, or expanding legal protections for
LGBT people, or strengthening sexual harassment prohibitions, or reducing
violence against women. All these issues and others are more likely to be
accorded governmental attention when women are at the policy-making
table. A specific example is the Women's Health Equity Act, a bipartisan,
multiyear, multi-item bill in Congress with mandates that: women and mi-

norities be used as subjects in clinical research, research be conducted on breast cancer, and improved methods be sought for contraception, infertility treatment, osteoporosis, adolescent pregnancy prevention, and more. In short, making strides toward significant progress in the clinical understanding of women's health through the life cycle is the result of the determined and consistent efforts of women officeholders.[13]

Agenda Setting

New policy options are formulated and space on the issues agenda is secured. Research on women legislators shows that they are as active in bill introductions and cosponsorships, introduce and cosponsor more bills on a wide array of women's issues than men, and have more diverse policy agendas.[14] That does not mean that all women think the same way about women's issues or that the same types of solutions are sought for identified problems. Nor does it mean that all women are equally active or successful on women's issues (factors such as party, committee assignments, seniority, leadership status, racial/ethnic diversity, and more are discussed below). But, it does mean that women bring issues to the legislative process that were not being addressed or not being addressed as extensively or comprehensively prior to their involvement.[15]

> "More women in office means more women and child-friendly legislation and—particularly as hostile politicians attempt to roll back our rights at the federal level—it is critically important that we stand together and advocate for women in our cities and states."
>
> **—Helen Rosenthal, New York City Democratic Councilwoman and Co-Chair of the Women's Caucus***
>
> * Jillian Jorgensen, "New York City Lags behind in Number of Women Holding Office," *New York Daily News*, August 24, 2017, accessed October 1, 2017, available at http://www.nydailynews.com/news/politics/new-york-lags-behind-numbers-women-holding-office-article-1.3436937.

It is important to emphasize that the category "women's issues" is not exclusively those considered to be feminist issues. Rather, women's issues are governmental initiatives that focus on inequality between the sexes and those that expand women's autonomy—regardless of ideological perspective. One definition centers on the following: (1) issues that address women's special needs, such as health concerns; (2) issues with which women have traditionally been associated, such as education and children; (3) measures that seek equality for women. The ideological foundation of policy approaches, both conservative and liberal, are included.[16]

An example of how women contribute distinctively to the policy-making process comes from a bipartisan team of women in the U.S. Congress and a governor who together are concerned about the number of women incarcerated for low-level criminal offenses. Senator Kamala Harris of California and Representative Sheila Jackson Lee of Texas, both Democrats, joined with Representative Mia Love of Utah and Governor Mary Fallin of Oklahoma, both Republicans, to hold a conference on the subject. Hearing evidence of the effect of incarcerations on women and families, the team concluded that rehabilitation and mental health services would be more effective than harsh sentences. Senator Harris and her colleagues introduced legislation to "improve conditions for incarcerated women, including banning solitary confinement and shackling of pregnant women, provide better visitation policies for parents and children, and make available a range of counseling and treatment services."[17]

The flip side to agenda setting is what can be called agenda limiting—or strategic efforts to prevent legislation that could damage women's interests from becoming law.[18] In 2017, Republican women of the U.S. Senate were widely credited for repeatedly blocking the repeal of the Affordable Care Act. In what a journalist called the "revenge of the GOP women," Senators Susan Collins of Maine, Shelley Moore Capito of West Virginia, and Lisa Murkowski of Alaska announced that they would not vote for a repeal bill before the chamber. Their announcement led to its defeat. Some analysts speculated that the original committee appointed by the Senate Republican leadership to draft the repeal legislation epitomized the problem because the committee excluded diverse voices and perspectives: the committee had 13 male senators and not a single female one.[19] Another example comes from the state level: in Utah, in 2006, two lesbian officeholders, Representatives Jackie Biskupski and Christine Johnson successfully prevented anti–gay-lesbian measures from being enacted. The first was a bill that would have banned domestic partner benefits, and the second was an anti-LGBT section of a bill that regulated student clubs in public schools.[20]

Legislating

From among alternative solutions to a named policy problem, policies (legislative bills) are formulated. To be successful, these bills must be adopted by legislative bodies, such as the U.S. Congress, state legislatures, or city councils/county boards of supervisors, and either signed by executives or permitted to become law without signature. If women with distinctive priorities distilled their priorities into problem identification and bill introduction, but stopped there, little beyond the symbolic would be achieved. Fortunately, extensive study of legislative effectiveness shows that women officeholders are as or more successful as men. They usher their bills through the process to enactment and do so on a wide range of policies, including women's issues.

An analysis of legislative effectiveness in the Pennsylvania statehouse exemplifies what is found more generally among women legislators and executives in municipalities, statehouses, and the U.S. Congress.[21] Using multiple measures of effectiveness, the study's authors concluded that female legislators in the General Assembly were more likely than men to pursue diverse agendas, more committed to women's issues, more effective at attracting cosponsors to their bills, and more effective at passing legislation, including women's issues. This was true regardless of party affiliation.[22]

What is true about legislation broadly is also true across a range of issues. For instance, the League of Conservation Voters compares the records of members of Congress on environmental protection legislation, such as on pollution, climate change, food and energy insecurity, chemical safety, and biodiversity loss. Their most recent study examines votes from 2006–2015. The findings show that women legislators in both the House and the Senate voted for environmental protections more often than men. The conclusion: "If we want to make progress on protecting the environment and public health, we should help elect more women to public office, and support them during their tenure."[23] This conclusion illustrates the point, emphasized above, that women tend to prioritize issues differently than men. As a result, policy decisions on a range of issues may be different from those emerging from all-male political institutions.

It may be on women's issues, though, that the strongest difference between female and male officeholders is evident. On these issues, female legislators on the local, state, and federal levels are more successful at introducing and securing passage of bills pertaining to women, children, and family. And, at all stages of the process from introduction through committee hearings, floor debate, and roll call votes, women are instrumental in supporting legislation and defending bills from crippling amendments.[24]

"You know, you just assume that everybody else has the same [familial] arrangement and until somebody stands up and says, 'No, that is not the reality for many in this country. That's not my reality,' they don't ever consider that perspective. It just never even crosses their mind. So, I feel like my role as a woman on the committee is very important because I don't just speak for myself. I speak for many similarly-situated women. . . . [Were I] not there, that perspective is totally absent from the debate."
—Member, U.S. House of Representatives, Linda Sanchez (D-CA)*

* Kelly Dittmar, Kira Sanbonmatsu, Susan J. Carroll, Debbie Walsh, and Catherine Wineinger, *Representation Matters: Women in the U.S. Congress* (New Brunswick, NJ: Center for American Women and Politics, Eagleton Institute of Politics, Rutgers, State University of New Jersey, 2017), 23.

Behind the statistics are stories of women's legislative effectiveness. On the local level, in 2016, Los Angeles County supervisors Sheila Kuehl and Hilda Solis, both Democrats, introduced a five-year Initiative on Women and Girls to direct the county to refocus its resources to increase women's opportunities.[25] At the state level, in 2016, Massachusetts senator Pat Jehlen, representative Ellen Story, and senator Karen Spilka, all Democrats, successfully steered a pay equity measure through the legislative process.[26] And, on the national level, Representative Kristi Noem, Republican of South Dakota, authored the Women, Peace and Security Act that mandates that State and Defense Department leaders develop a "comprehensive strategy that increases and strengthens women's participation in peace negotiations and conflict prevention."[27]

Context Matters

As Dittmar cautions us, "In weighing whether or not to run, women need to perceive the electoral terrain as navigable, political success as possible, and officeholding as worthwhile."[28] Without acknowledgment of the obstacles that women face in the best and worst of times coupled with evidence that they can be surmounted, efforts to encourage women to run for office may not be as effective as they could be. First, overcoming obstacles starts with identifying and defining challenges, understanding their dynamics, and strategizing to meet the challenges they pose. The discussion below of institutional, temporal, and proportionality obstacles can help dispel the idea that policy success happens only when political contexts are optimal for enacting women's policy preferences. Rather, for those willing to persevere, success is possible—even in challenging times.

Institutional Factors

For legislators, a representative's committee assignments, seniority, leadership roles, and chamber—and its partisan balance—all facilitate or constrain how much individual or collective efforts (such as caucuses) can succeed.[29] For instance, if a state or federal legislator is a first-term member in a chamber governed by the opposite party and holds committee assignments unaligned with her policy priorities, she will enjoy less legislative success.

Even if a legislator is fortunate enough to hold a committee chair or leadership ladder position and be a member of a governing party, there may be barriers to passing priority legislation. In 2019, the Republicans are the majority in the U.S. Senate. But, because Republican Party culture has not been heavily supportive of many women's issues, all else equal, Republican women senators who want to pursue women's issues may not have a great deal of success.[30] Similarly, for executives, being a first-term mayor or governor in a state or municipality with a council or legislature governed by the opposite party will make major policy success more challenging.

Still, there are paths forward for those who are determined to enact good public policy. Among the ways women accomplish their goals despite obstacles are their pragmatism and their collaborative styles. Studies of women in office at all levels of government make clear that they are more likely than men to work across the aisle, attract broad support for policy efforts, and use a consensus style of leadership. This is likely one of the reasons women legislators have often been more successful than men in enacting their priority policies.[31]

"Women tend to be less partisan, more collaborative, listen better, find common ground." "Every time I've had a bill that's important to me, I've had strong Republican women helping me pass it."
—Member, U.S. Senate, Kirsten Gillibrand (D-NY)*

"There is good research that shows women tend to have different leadership styles, . . . We tend to be more inclusive, we're less autocratic in our decision-making. We like consensus, we like to get people around the table, and so I think that has made a difference."
—Member, U.S. Senate, Jeanne Shaheen (D-NH)†

* Claire Cain Miller, "Women Actually Do Govern Differently," *New York Times*, November 10, 2016, accessed November 3, 2017, available at https://www.nytimes.com/2016/11/10/upshot/women-actually-do-govern-differently.html?mcubz=1.
† Linda Feldmann, "How Women Lead Differently," *Christian Science Monitor*, October 8, 2016, accessed October 4, 2017, available at http://www.csmonitor.com/USA/Politics/2016/1008/How-women-lead-differently?cmpid=editorpicks&google_editors_picks=true.

Presence and Proportionality

Well, hell, we're an institution that runs by numbers. You have to have the votes and there are not enough of us here.
—U.S. Representative Rosa DeLauro, Democrat of Connecticut
(Dittmar et al., "Representation Matters," 49)

As discussed throughout this book, women are only a small share of those who hold elected office in the nation—and, even factoring in the heartening results of the 2018 midterms on the federal and state levels, the proportions are not rising quickly nor uniformly.[32] It is also abundantly clear that not only do we need many more women to run for office if parity is to be achieved; we need a diverse array of women from both parties to run so that the full spectrum of policy innovation is considered.[33] For example, women of color are often more supportive of women's issues than are White women. African American women, in particular, are more likely to introduce legislation on women's issues than men.[34] Illustrating this point, U.S. Representative Joyce Beatty, Democrat of Ohio, says: "Because I am female and African American, I know that I have a laser eye on gravitating to women's issues, issues for minorities [so] that I can make sure that they are included more."[35]

Research has also demonstrated that Latina officeholders are more likely than their male counterparts to highly rate family and children's policy.[36] California State Democratic assemblymember Lorena Gonzalez Fletcher is a case in point. She has introduced bills to protect working women who become pregnant, including prohibiting employers from discriminating against women's reproductive health choices, ensuring equity in workers' compensation payments for pregnant women, and mandating pregnancy leave for school employees. Says Gonzalez Fletcher: "There are employers who cross the line by invading the privacy and personal lives of the women who work for them, and far too often women are punished financially for becoming pregnant and having children."[37]

Another way in which proportionality matters is how well women are represented within their party. At the congressional and state legislative levels, there are far fewer Republican women than Democrats and fewer Republican women party leaders. This has been true for some time.[38] An imbalance in institutional support and resources is a significant contributor to this trend. Says Erin Loos Cutraro, CEO of She Should Run: "Feeling that you're not going at it alone makes a big difference . . . and it can feel really isolating for Republican women. They don't have the same networks, just in sheer numbers . . . or the same level of institutional support. If you're a Democratic pro-choice woman, and you have EMILY's List there to support you, that can be incredibly powerful. Republican women don't have anything that plays at the same level."[39] Indeed, U.S. representative Elise Stefanik (R-NY) created Elevate PAC (E-PAC) after the 2018 midterm elections to address the paucity of Republican women in the House. After that cycle, Republican women representatives went from 23 to 13.[40] In comparison, 89 Democratic women sit in the House of Representatives in 2019, which is a rise from 64 in 2018.

Even though they face significant challenges, Republican women continue to work to accomplish legislative goals that are important to them. For example, the 24 Republican congresswomen in the 112th U.S. House of Representatives created the Republican Women's Policy Committee "to build coalitions among Republican women, to mentor newer women members, and to promote women's perspectives within their party."[41] More recently, New York also enacted the Reproductive Health Act to codify the abortion protections provided to women by the 1973 *Roe v. Wade* Supreme Court decision.[42] And, in the U.S. Congress, new female members are prioritizing issues such as sexual harassment and sexual violence. Representative Ayanna Pressley (D-MA), who is a survivor of sexual violence, has said that she plans to prioritize this issue in her work in Congress.[43]

Political Eras

Temporally, the political context matters very much to legislative and executive success. Political eras differ from each other, sometimes dramatically, and the issues that dominate each era can differ just as dramatically.

In our political culture, issue ownership is often gendered. Republicans are perceived as "owning" issues that are often associated with masculinity, such as defense and economics. In contrast, Democrats are perceived as owning issues associated with femininity, such as health, education, social policy, and women's issues.[44] Therefore, in times of crisis, such as the attacks of September 11, 2001, Republicans and "male" issues tend to dominate. On the other hand, when Anita Hill testified against the nomination of Clarence Thomas to the U.S. Supreme Court because he had sexually harassed her, Democrats and women's issues came to the fore. In the subsequent election, women's issues were accentuated and women candidates were elected to the U.S. Congress in record numbers. Subsequently, leaders took pains to ensure that women were represented on committees that had previously lacked their presence. And women's legislative priorities were more successful in Congress.[45]

Political eras are also dominated by political actors who command the media spotlight by virtue of position or by engagement with high-profile issues or events. Their issue preferences and leadership styles may be more or less in harmony with women's priorities. In the age of Trump, the president's issue stances and governing style of disruption, distraction, inconsistency, and unpredictability makes moving agendas more difficult (see Bonneau and Kanthak in Chapter 11, in this volume). Still, purposeful legislators are finding ways to meet the challenge. For example, in many states, representatives have created alternate paths for their issue priorities such as preserving and expanding women's reproductive rights. In New York, a new regulation requires insurance plans to cover all contraceptive methods; other states have done the same.[46]

Conclusion

The aim of this chapter has been to spotlight the benefits to women of running for elected office—and to sustain the momentum from the 2018 electoral cycle. One big benefit of running is the opportunity to improve public policies in ways that matter most to women. To make our case, we have linked political science research focused on women's ambition for holding office—highlighting the finding that policy is and has long been a prime motivator for candidacies—to the literature that affirms that women officeholders are successful policy-makers, particularly when it comes to women's issues. This chapter has also sought to provide a clear-eyed analysis of research on obstacles to women's success and the ways those obstacles can be surmounted. This is especially important in the present political era in which resistance is strong to the policy goals of many women candidates and officeholders.

The best way to summarize this chapter might be to expand an old saying among those who study women candidates: "When women run, women win." Here we coin a new saying: "When women legislate and govern, women make big policy differences." That knowledge can help encourage women to be the change they seek. And it can help Emerge America, Ready to Run (see Sanbonmatsu and Dittmar in Chapter 13 and Schneider and Sweet-Cushman in Chapter 14, in this volume), She Should Run, EMILY's List, ROSA PAC, Higher Heights, LPAC, Running Start, Get in Formation, Project GROW, VIEW PAC, Winning for Women, Off the Sidelines, the California Leadership Collaborative, Young Women's Political Leadership Program (see Mo and Anderson-Nilsson in Chapter 7), and many more organizations support women on their political journeys.

NOTES

1. "Q&A with Candidate Wendy Carrillo: 'This Moment in Our Nation's History Requires That, As Women, We Step Up.'" September 28, 2017, Off the Sidelines, accessed October 4, 2017, available at https://medium.com/@getots/q-a-with-candidate-wendy -carrillo-this-moment-in-our-nations-history-requires-that-as-women-we-226223d68e60.

2. Suzanne Dovi, "Preferable Descriptive Representatives: Will Just Any Women, Black, or Latino Do?" *American Political Science Review* 96 (2002): 729–743; Suzanne Dovi, "Theorizing Women's Representation in the United States," *Politics and Gender* 3, no. 3 (2007): 297–320; Jane Mansbridge, "'Should Blacks Represent Blacks and Women Represent Women?' A Contingent 'Yes,'" *Journal of Politics* 61 (1999): 628–657; Anne Phillips, *The Politics of Presence* (New York: Oxford University Press, 1995); Mary Hawkesworth, "Congressional Enactments of Race-Gender: Toward a Theory of Race-Gendered and Institutions," *American Political Science Review* 97 (2003): 529–550; Michele L. Swers, *The Difference Women Make: The Policy Impact of Women in Congress* (Chicago: University of Chicago Press, 2002); Michele L. Swers, *Women in the Club: Gender and Policymaking in the Senate* (Chicago: University of Chicago Press, 2013).

3. Judith Warner, "Opening the Gates: Clearing the Way for More Women to Hold Political Office," May 19, 2017, Center for American Progress, accessed September 10, 2017, available at https://www.americanprogress.org/issues/women/reports/2017/05/19/427206 /opening-the-gates/.

4. Kim Zetter, "Why Isn't the GOP Electing More Women? Republican Strategists Weigh In," June 9, 2017, Politico, accessed September 10, 2017, available at https://www .politico.com/story/2017/06/09/women-rule-podcast-republican-women-239356.

5. Dana Bash, "How New Hampshire's First Female Senator Moved Off the Sidelines," August 9, 2017, CNN, accessed September 1, 2017, available at http://www.cnn.com/2017 /06/19/politics/jeanne-shaheen-badass-women-of-washington/index.html.

6. Sue Thomas, Rebekah Herrick, and Matthew Braunstei, "Legislative Careers: The Personal and the Political," in *Women Transforming Congress*, ed. Cindy Simon Rosenthal and Richard F. Fenno Jr. (Norman: University of Oklahoma Press, 2002).

7. S. Carroll and K. Sanbonmatsu, *More Women Can Run: Gender and Pathways to the State Legislature* (Oxford: Oxford University Press, 2013).

8. Christina Cauterucci, "How Do You Inspire Women to Run for Office? Elect Trump," January 16, 2017, Slate, accessed October 17, 2017, available at http://www.slate.com/articles/news_and_politics/cover_story/2017/01/when_women_run_they_win_and_trump_s_election_is_inspiring_a_surge_of_new.html.

9. J. W. Kingdon, *Agendas, Alternatives and Public Policies* (Boston: Little, Brown, 1984); C. E. Lindblom, "The Science of 'Muddling Through,'" *Public Administration Review* 19 (1959): 79–88.

10. Dittmar et al. "Representation Matters: Women in the U.S. Congress" (New Brunswick: Center for American Women and Politics, Eagleton Institute of Politics, Rutgers, State University of New Jersey, 2017); Barbara Mikulski, Kay Bailey Hutchinson, Dianne Feinstein, Barbara Boxer, Patty Murray, Olympia Snowe, Susan Collins, Mary Landrieu, Blanche L. Lincoln, and Catherine Whitney, *Nine and Counting: The Women of the Senate* (New York: HarperCollins, 2001); Susan Molinari and Elinor Burkett, *Representative Mom: Balancing Budgets, Bill, and Baby in the U.S. Congress* (New York: Doubleday, 1998); Linda Sanchez and Loretta Sanchez, *Dream in Color: How the Sanchez Sisters Are Making History in Congress* (New York: Grand Central, 2008); Swers, *Difference Women Make*; Swers, *Women in the Club*.

11. "The Senator: Mazie Hirono, First Asian-American Woman to Be Elected to the U.S. Senate," accessed October 12, 2017, available at http://time.com/collection/firsts/4898538/mazie-hirono-firsts.

12. Congresswoman Kristi Noem, "Noem Offers Remarks on Human Trafficking at Congressional Hearing," Press Releases, February 26, 2014, accessed October 1, 2017, available at http://noem.house.gov/index.cfm/press-releases?ContentRecord_id=1638D E88-454D-4E12-9155-1AA9A16E126D.

13. Debra L. Dodson, "Representing Women's Interests in the U.S. House of Representatives," in *Women and Elective Office: Past, Present, and Future*, ed. Sue Thomas and Clyde Wilcox (New York: Oxford University Press, 1998); Peg A. Lamphier and Roseanne Welch, eds., *Women in American History: A Social, Political, and Cultural Encyclopedia* (Santa Barbara, CA: ABC-Clio, 2017), 258.

14. Mary Atkinson and Jason Windett, "Electoral Security and the Strategic Legislative Behavior of Women in Congress," Working Paper, 2015, 1–30; Sue Thomas, *How Women Legislate* (New York: Oxford University Press, 1994); Michelle A. Barnello and Kathleen A. Bratton, "Bridging the Gender Gap in Bill Sponsorship," *Legislative Studies Quarterly* 32, no. 3 (2007): 449–474; Kathleen A. Bratton and Stella M. Rouse, "Networks in the Legislative Arena: How Group Dynamics Affect Co-Sponsorship," *Legislative Studies Quarterly* 36, no. 3 (2011): 423–460; Michele L. Swers, "Connecting Descriptive and Substantive Representation: An Analysis of Sex Differences in Co-Sponsorship Activity," *Legislative Studies Quarterly* 30, no. 3 (2005): 407–433; Jennifer Hayes Clark and Veronica Caro, "Multimember Districts and the Substantive Representation of Women: An Analysis of Legislative Cosponsorship Networks," *Politics and Gender* 9 (2013): 1–30; Sarah F. Anzia and Christopher R. Berry, "The Jackie (and Jill) Robinson Effect: Why Do Congresswomen Outperform Congressmen?" *American Journal of Political Science* 55, no. 3 (2011): 478–493; C. Volden, A. E. Wiseman, and D. E. Wittmer, "Women's Issues and Their Fates in the US Congress," *Political Science Research and Methods* (2016): 1–18.

15. Debra L. Dodson and Susan J. Carroll, *Reshaping the Agenda: Women in State Legislatures* (New Brunswick, NJ: Center for the American Woman and Politics, 1991); Susan J. Carroll, "The Personal Is Political: The Intersection of Private Lives and Public

Roles among Women and Men in Elective and Appointive Office," *Women and Politics* 9 (1989): 51–67; Susan J. Carroll, "Representing Women: Congresswomen's Perceptions of Their Representational Roles," in *Women Transforming Congress*, ed. Cindy Simon Rosenthal (Norman: University of Oklahoma Press, 2002); Susan J. Carroll, "The Politics of Difference: Women Public Officials as Agents of Change," *Stanford Law and Policy Review* 5 (Spring 1994): 11–20; Thomas, *How Women Legislate*; Kathleen Dolan and Lynne E. Ford, "Change and Continuity among Women State Legislators: Evidence from Three Decades" *Political Research Quarterly* 50, no. 1 (1997): 137–151; Swers, *Difference Women Make*; Barnello and Bratton, "Bridging the Gender Gap"; Dodson, "Representing Women's Interests in the U.S. House of Representatives."

16. Swers, *Difference Women Make*; Swers, *Women in the Club*.

17. Vanessa Williams, "Officials from Both Parties Say Too Many Women Are Incarcerated for Low-Level Crimes," July 18, 2017, *Washington Post*, accessed September 10, 2017, available at https://www.washingtonpost.com/news/post-nation/wp/2017/07/18 /officials-from-both-parties-say-too-many-women-are-incarcerated-for-low-level-crimes /?utm_term=.9d92b40ca31c&wpisrc=nl_daily202&wpmm=1.

18. Suzanne Dovi, "The Institutional Non-Presence of Women," article presented at conference on Gender, Institutions and Change: Feminist Institutionalism after 10 years. University of Manchester, April 3–4, 2017.

19. Robert Pear, "13 Men, and No Women, Are Writing New G.O.P. Health Bill in Senate," *New York Times*, May 8, 2017, accessed August, 12, 2017, available at https://www .nytimes.com/2017/05/08/us/politics/women-health-care-senate.html.

20. Donald P. Haider-Markel and Chelsie Lynn Moore Bright, "Lesbian Candidates and Officeholders," in *Women and Elective Office*, 3rd ed., ed. Sue Thomas and Clyde Wilcox (New York: Oxford University Press, 2014).

21. *Few, but Mighty: Women and Bill Sponsorship in the Pennsylvania General Assembly*, Pennsylvania Center for Women and Politics, May 2017, Chatham University Women's Institute, accessed September 10, 2017, available at www.pcwp.org.

22. *Few, but Mighty.*

23. "A Decade of Women's Environmental Voting Records in Congress, 2006–2015," 2016, *Rachel's Network*, accessed September 8, 2017, available at https://rachelsnetwork .org/wp/wp-content/uploads/2014/09/WhenWomenLead.pdf.

24. Nadia Brown, *Sisters in the Statehouse: Black Women and Legislative Decision Making* (New York: Oxford University Press, 2014); Dodson and Carroll, *Reshaping the Agenda*; Sue Thomas, "Voting Patterns in the California Assembly: The Role of Gender," *Women and Politics* 9 (1990): 43–56; Thomas, *How Women Legislate*; Sue Thomas, "The Personal Is Political: Antecedents of Gendered Choices of Elected Representatives," *Sex Roles: A Journal of Research* (2002): 343–353; Dolan and Ford, "Change and Continuity"; Dolan and Ford, 1998; Swers, *Difference Women Make*; Dodson, "Representing Women's Interests in the U.S. House of Representatives"; Debra L. Dodson, "Acting for Women: Is What Legislators Say, What They Do?" in *The Impact of Women in Public Office*, ed. Susan J. Carroll (Bloomington: University of Indiana Press, 2001); Arturo Vega and Juanita M. Firestone, "The Effects of Gender on Congressional Behavior and Substantive Representation of Women," *Legislative Studies Quarterly* 20 (1995): 213–222; C. Volden, A. E. Wiseman, and D. E. Wittmer, "When Are Women More Effective Lawmakers Than Men?" *American Journal of Political Science* 57, no. 2 (2013): 326–341; Brian Frederick, "Are Female House Members Still More Liberal in a Polarized Era? The Conditional Nature of the Relationship between Descriptive and Substantive Representation," *Congress and the Presidency* 36 (2009): 181–202; Brian Frederick, "Gender and Patterns of Roll Call Vot-

ing in the U.S. Senate," *Congress and the Presidency* 37, no. 2, 2010), 103–124; Barnello and Bratton, "Bridging the Gender Gap"; Bratton and Rouse, "Networks in the Legislative Arena"; Clark and Caro, "Multimember Districts and the Substantive Representation of Women"; Swers, *Difference Women Make*; Swers, "Connecting Descriptive and Substantive Representation"; Anzia and Berry, "The Jackie (and Jill) Robinson Effect"; Stefano Gagliarducci and Daniele Paserman, "Gender Differences in Cooperative Environments? Evidence from the U.S. Congress," NBER Working Paper No. w22488, 2016.

25. Jennifer M. Piscopo and Nancy L. Cohen, "What's Good for Women and Girls Is Good for L.A. County," *Los Angeles Times*, December 12, 2016, accessed September 4, 2017, available at http://www.latimes.com/opinion/op-ed/la-oe-piscopo-cohen-county -womens-initiative-20161212-story.html.

26. Shirley Leung, "Pat Jehlen and Ellen Story: The Champions of Equal Pay for Women," *Boston Globe*, December 14, 2016, accessed September 10, 2017, available at https://www.bostonglobe.com/magazine/2016/12/14/pat-jehlen-and-ellen-story-the -champions-equal-pay-for-women/JsI1q8U2VGbVQ0BDc7QA4I/story.html.

27. Congresswoman Kristi Noem, "House Passes Noem's Women, Peace, and Security Act, Sends Bill to President Trump," Press Releases, September 25, 2017, accessed October 4, 2017, available at http://noem.house.gov/index.cfm/press-releases?ContentRecord_id =95AC0A89-5EC1-4425-83CF-A8E85AB67726.

28. Kelly Dittmar, "Encouragement Is Not Enough: Addressing Social and Structural Barriers to Female Recruitment," *Politics and Gender* 11, no. 4 (2015): 759–765.

29. Matt Grossman and David A. Hopkins, *Asymmetric Politics: Ideological Republicans and Group Interest Democrats* (New York: Oxford University Press, 2016); Jo Freeman, "The Political Culture of the Democratic and Republican Parties," *Political Science Quarterly* 101, no. 3 (1986): 327–356; Volden, Wiseman, and Wittmer, "When Are Women More Effective"; Volden, Wiseman, and Wittmer, "Women's Issues and Their Fates"; Jocelyn Jones Evans, *Women, Partisanship, and the Congress* (New York: Palgrave Macmillan, 2005); Colleen Shogan, "Speaking Out: An Analysis of Democratic and Republican Woman-Invoked Rhetoric in the 105th Congress," *Women and Congress: Running, Winning, Ruling* (Philadelphia: Haworth, 2001); Laurel Elder and Steven Greene, "The Politics of Parenthood: Parenthood Effects on Issue Attitudes and Candidate Evaluation in 2008," *American Politics Research* 40, no. 3 (2012): 419–449; Heather L. Ondercin and Susan Welch, "Women Candidates for Congress," in *Women and Elective Office: Past, Present, and Future*, ed. Susan Thomas and Clyde Wilcox (New York: Oxford University Press, 2005), 60–80; Kira Sanbonmatsu, *Gender Equality, Political Parties, and the Politics of Women's Place* (Ann Arbor: University of Michigan Press, 2002); Kira Sanbonmatsu, "Do Parties Know That 'Women Win?' Party Leader Beliefs about Women's Electoral Chances," *Politics and Gender* 2, no. 4 (2006): 431–450; Rebekah Herrick, Jeanette Mendez, Sue Thomas, and Amanda Wilkerson, "Gender and Perceptions of Candidate Competency," *Journal of Women, Politics and Policy* 33 (2012): 126–150; Barbara Palmer and Dennis Simon, "Political Ambition and Women in the U.S. House of Representatives, 1916–2000," *Political Research Quarterly* 56 (2003): 127–138; Haider-Markel and Bright, "Lesbian Candidates and Officeholders"; Danielle M. Thomsen, "Why So Few (Republican) Women? Explaining the Partisan Imbalance of Women in the U.S. Congress," *Legislative Studies Quarterly* (2015): 295–323; Susan J. Carroll, "Committee Assignments: Discrimination or Choice?" in *Legislative Women: Getting Elected, Getting Ahead*, ed. Beth Reingold (Boulder, CO: Lynne Rienner, 2008); Cindy Simon Rosenthal, *When Women Lead: Integrative Leadership in State Legislatures* (New York: Oxford University Press, 1998); Swers, *Difference Women Make*.

30. Evans, *Women, Partisanship, and the Congress*; Catherine Wineinger, "Gendering Republican Party Culture," in *The Right Women: Republican Party Activists, Candidates, and Legislators*, ed. Och, Malliga, and Shauna Shames (Santa Barbara, CA: Praeger/ABC-Clio, 2018); Volden, Wiseman, and Wittmer, "When Are Women More Effective"; Volden, Wiseman, and Wittmer, "Women's Issues and Their Fates."

31. Mirya R. Holman and Anna Mahoney, "Stop, Collaborate, and Listen: Women's Collaboration in U.S. State Legislatures," *Legislative Studies Quarterly*, 43, no. 2 (2018): 179–206; Alana Jeydel and Andrew Taylor, "Are Women Legislators Less Effective? Evidence from the U.S. House in the 103rd–105th Congress," *Political Research Quarterly* 56, no. 1 (2003): 19–27; Sue Tolleson Rinehart, "Do Women Leaders Make a Difference? Substance, Style and Perceptions," in *Gender and Policymaking: Studies of Women in Office*, ed. D. L. Dodson (New Brunswick, NJ: Center for the American Woman and Politics, Rutgers University, 1991); Thomas, *How Women Legislate*; Volden, Wiseman, and Wittmer, "When Are Women More Effective."

32. Dittmar et al., "Representation Matters," 49.

33. Carol Hardy-Fanta, Pie-te Lien, Dianne Pinderhughes, and Christine Marie Sierra, *Contested Transformation: Race, Gender, and Political Leadership in 21st Century America* (New York: Cambridge University Press, 2016); Wendy Smooth, "Intersectionality in Electoral Politics: A Mess Worth Making," *Politics and Gender* 2, no. 3 (2006): 400–414; Cathy J. Cohen, "A Portrait of Continuing Marginality: The Study of Women of Color in American Politics," in *Women and American Politics: New Questions, New Directions*, ed. Susan J. Carroll (New York: Oxford University Press, 2002); Christine Sierra and Adaliza Sosa-Riddell, "Chicanas as Political Actors: Rare Literature, Complex Practice," *National Political Science Review* 4 (1994): 297–317; Byron Orey, D'Andra Orey, Wendy Smooth, Kimberly S. Adams, and Kisha Harris-Clark, "Race and Gender Matter: Refining Models of Legislative Policy Making in State Legislatures," in *Intersectionality and Politics: Recent Research on Gender, Race, and Political Representation in the United States*, ed. Carol Hardy-Fanta (New York: Haworth, 2006); Brown, *Sisters in the Statehouse*; Nadia Brown and Kira Hudson Banks, "Black Women's Agenda Setting in the Maryland State Legislature," *Journal of African American Studies* 18, no. 2 (2014): 164–180; Lisa Garcia Bedolla, Katherine Tate, and Janelle Wong, "Indelible Effects: The Impact of Women of Color in the U.S. Congress," in *Women and Elective Office: Past, Present, and Future*, eds. Sue Thomas and Clyde Wilcox (New York: Oxford University Press, 2005): 152–175; Evelyn M. Simien, "Race, Gender, and Linked Fate," *Journal of Black Studies*, 35, no. 5 (2005): 529–550.

34. Kimberly S. Adams, "Different Faces, Different Priorities: Agenda-Setting Behavior in the Mississippi, Maryland, and Georgia State Legislatures," *Nebula* 4 (2007): 58–95; Kathleen A. Bratton, Kerry L. Haynie, and Beth Reingold, "Agenda Setting and African American Women in State Legislatures," in *Intersectionality and Politics: Recent Research on Gender, Race, and Political Representation in the United States*, ed. Carol Hardy-Fanta (New York: Haworth, 2006); Orey et al., "Race and Gender Matter"; Beth Reingold and Adrienne R. Smith, "Welfare Policymaking and Intersections of Race, Ethnicity, and Gender in US State Legislatures," *American Journal of Political Science* 56, no. 1 (2012): 131–147.

35. Dittmar et al., "Representation Matters," 21.

36. Luis Ricardo Fraga, Linda Lopez, Valerie Martinez-Ebers, and Ricardo Ramirez, "Gender and Ethnicity: Patterns of Electoral Success and Legislative Advocacy among Latina and Latino State Officials in Four States," *Journal of Women, Politics, and Policy* 28 nos. 3–4 (2006):121–146.

37. "Assemblywoman Lorena Gonzalez Fletcher Proposes Pregnancy Protections for Gender Fairness at Work," Press Release, February 14, 2017, accessed September 2, 2017, available at https://a80.asmdc.org/press-release/assemblywoman-lorena-gonzalez -fletcher-proposes-pregnancy-protections-gender-0.

38. Sanbonmatsu, *Gender Equality*; Sanbonmatsu, "Do Parties Know That 'Women Win?'"; Palmer and Simon, "Political Ambition and Women"; Grossman and Hopkins, *Asymmetric Politics*; Freeman, "Political Culture"; Volden, Wiseman, and Witmer, "When Are Women More Effective"; Volden, Wiseman, and Witmer, "Women's Issues and Their Fates"; Evans, *Women, Partisanship, and the Congress*; Shogan, "Speaking Out"; Elder and Greene, "Politics of Parenthood"; Ondercin and Welch, "Women Candidates for Congress"; Rebekah Herrick and Jeanette Morehouse Mendez, "Women and Campaigns," in *Women and Elective Office: Past, Present, and Future*, ed. Sue Thomas and Clyde Wilcox (Oxford, NY: Oxford University Press, 2014), 97–110; Haider-Markel and Bright, "Lesbian Candidates and Officeholders"; Danielle M. Thomsen, "Partisan Polarization and the Representation of Women in the US Congress," in *APSA 2012 Annual Meeting Paper* (2012).

39. Jocelyn Noveck, "For GOP Women in Politics, a Needle That's Not Moving," September 30, 2017, ABC News, accessed October 4, 2017, available at http://abcnews.go.com /Politics/wireStory/gop-women-politics-needle-moving-50194519.

40. Simone Pathé, "Stefanik Launches PAC to Boost Female Candidates, Now with GOP Leadership Support," January 18, 2019, Roll Call, accessed February 2, 2019, available at https://www.rollcall.com/news/campaigns/stefanik-launches-pac-leadership-support.

41. Wineinger, "Gendering Republican Party Culture."

42. Andrew M. Cuomo, "Trump's Assault on Abortion Rights Must Be Rejected," *New York Times*, February 6, 2019, accessed February 6, 2019, available at https://www .nytimes.com/2019/02/06/opinion/cuomo-roe-abortion-trump.html.

43. "Ayanna Pressley Releases Plan to Address Violence and Trauma in Our Communities," July 12, 2018, *Sampan*, accessed January 2, 2019, available at https://sampan. org/2018/07/ayanna-pressley-releases-plan-to-address-violence-and-trauma-in-our-comm unities/.

44. John R. Petrocik, "Issue Ownership in Presidential Elections, with a 1980 Case Study," *American Journal of Political Science* 40, no. 3 (1996): 825–850; John R. Petrocik, William L. Benoit, and Glenn J. Hansen, "Issue Ownership and Presidential Campaigning, 1952–2000," *Political Science Quarterly* 118, no. 4 (2003): 599–626; Leonie Huddy and Nadya Terklidsen, "Gender Stereotypes and the Perception of Male and Female Candidates," *American Journal of Political Science* 37 (February 1993): 119–147; Kathleen Dolan, "The Impact of Gender Stereotyped Evaluations on Support for Women Candidates," *Political Behavior* 32 (2010): 69–88.

45. Elizabeth Adell Cook, Sue Thomas, and Clyde Wilcox, *The Year of the Woman: Myths and Realities* (Boulder, CO: Westview, 1994).

46. Elizabeth Nash, Rachel Benson Gold, Lizamarie Mohammed, Olivia Cappello, and Zohra Ansari-Thomas, *Laws Affecting Reproductive Health and Rights: State Policy Trends at Midyear, 2017,* Guttmacher Institute, July 13, 2017, accessed February 13, 2018, available at https://www.guttmacher.org/article/2017/07/laws-affecting-reproductive-health -and-rights-state-policy-trends-midyear-2017.

6

From Civic Mindedness to Electoral Politics

Citizen Advisory Committees and the Decision to Run for School Board

REBECCA E. DEEN AND
BETH ANNE SHELTON

W hy does someone run for elected political office? Perhaps he has always had an interest in politics and thinks he would make a good candidate or would be good at the job at hand. Perhaps she was raised in a home with high levels of political activity. Maybe she grew up block walking for candidates with her mom or attending political rallies with her dad. It might be the case that he never really considered seeking an elected position, but, after years of serving in civic organizations and on community boards, people began to approach him to run. Maybe a particular issue or event lit the spark or was the final push to convince her that she could be an effective problem solver and public servant.

What motivates an individual to run for elected office may involve one or more of the scenarios just described, but we also know that behind the decision to run is the belief that one is capable of running and winning. We also know that this decision calculus is gendered.[1] Women are less likely than men to possess the desire to run for political office or to believe themselves a viable candidate. They are also more likely to need additional support systems and encouragement to become candidates. In weighing the pros and cons, they make rational decisions about what is best for their situation.[2]

Women and men both invest time in their communities and sometimes these contributions vary by sex. This civic engagement also has a decision calculus. Most adults in the United States are busy juggling paid work, child and family responsibilities, and hobbies and leisure pursuits. Why do some people also carve out time for volunteering, serving on local boards or committees, or organizing community events? They, too, have to believe they have the skills, must be motivated, and, often, have to be asked by someone to get involved.[3]

This chapter considers the overlap in these two areas of research: running for office and volunteering and civic engagement at the level of school board. We examine the domain of education: volunteering in schools, serving on citizen advisory boards related to school districts, and running for school board trustee. How does the choice to be involved in the community foster ambition among men and women and create opportunities to be recruited to run for school board? Examining the path to school board elections allows us to do several important things. Because this is the level of elected office at which there is near gender equity, understanding women's success at this level may shed light on opportunity structures at higher levels of office. Also, even though outcomes at this level are less gendered, the path to candidacy may be different for women than for men.

Who Volunteers?

Though one might be tempted to view volunteering in the schools or being a member of a parent organization like the PTA as nonpolitical, in fact, participants in these activities are building their civic skills.[4] Research suggests that three conditions are required for people to become active in their communities: people must have the desire or motivation to participate, they must believe they have the necessary skills, and they often have to be asked or recruited.[5] Volunteering and participating in civic organizations has a multiplier effect: the more one engages, the more experienced a volunteer one becomes, and thus more likely to be recruited into other volunteer activities.[6] In other words, volunteering begets volunteering. Volunteering and membership in nonpolitical civic organizations and other institutions of civic life are important for men and women, but important differently.[7] Though women are slightly less likely to be involved in civic organizations, when they are and also have high levels of education, they develop skills necessary to foster ambition. Importantly for our work, though having school-aged children decreases the likelihood of working outside the home in fields where skills are acquired, these family responsibilities increase participation in the school-related volunteer opportunities. Whether women's activity is centered around their conceptions of motherhood[8] or borne out of a desire to invest in their communities, involvement in parent organizations (like the PTA, or music or sports booster groups) and volunteering in the schools (serving as room parent, or working in the school library) build civic skills necessary for participation in more political activities.

Women volunteer at slightly higher rates than men,[9] and this is true of young women as well.[10] Among high-achieving millennials, school board is the only office that men and women consider in almost equal measure; about 35 percent of men and 36 percent of women report the possibility of running for this office. Among Whites, women are more likely (37 percent) than men

(33 percent) to think about running for school board.[11] While more young men of color than young women of color considered running for school board, the proportion of women of color was higher than the proportion of White men who thought about a run for school board. Clearly, women and people of color see greater electoral opportunities at this level of office.

There is also a substantial link between volunteering and civic engagement.[12] Women often become involved in politics through local issues. Senator Patty Murray (D-WA) is an example, as she was motivated to lobby her state legislature when she learned of budget cuts to a preschool program with which she had personal experience. When she was dismissed as "just a mom in tennis shoes," she decided that her experience volunteering in the schools had given her the organizational skills and personal network necessary to run for elected office herself.[13] She was elected to serve on her local school board, then was elected to the Washington State Senate, and finally elected as the first female U.S. senator from Washington. She is now the senior senator and was formerly chair of the Veterans' Affairs and Budget Committees, the first female chair of either body.[14] Chapters 6 and 7 in this volume also document the importance of local issues for enhancing women's ambition. Not only are women socialized into politics through local issues but also they are most successful at the local level.[15] Though women hold 20.6 percent of all seats in Congress, they are 23.8 percent of all statewide elected officials and 25.4 percent of state legislators.[16] Women are a higher proportion of school board members than in other elected venues,[17] constituting 44 percent of school boards.[18]

School Board Trustees as a Path to Candidacy

A great deal of research has been conducted on why fewer women are in elected office than men (see Introduction of this volume), and much of this scholarship has focused on the role of ambition. Progressive ambition, the desire to run for higher office than one holds, is important, and there is some evidence that, at least at the local level, men at one time possessed more of it than women.[19] Lawless and Fox have shown that a critical factor is whether one imagines oneself qualified to run for elected office. There are also significant gender differences in ambition that result in women more often declining attempts to recruit them to run for office and, when they do run, being more likely to make the first foray into elected office at the local level rather than at the state or federal levels. Women are also more likely to run when they have a "network of encouragers." This network often involves family members, a particularly important factor in women's decisions to run for office.[20]

What about school board trustees? While political scientists have not focused as much attention on school boards as they have on mayoral or city councils, previous work found gender differences in motivation for running for school board.[21] Men are more likely to have run for school board to effect policy change and to be motivated out of concerns about morality. Women, in contrast, are more likely to run because of their interest in a particular issue, like the case of Patty Murray, discussed earlier.

Recall from the earlier discussion of volunteering that people need to have the ability or skills to participate, they need to have the desire, and often they need to be recruited. Also recall that, once a person develops skills through volunteering and membership in organizations, she is often recruited to other types of activity and that these processes are gendered (see Chapter 9 by Aldridge, Karpowitz, Monson and Preece, in this volume, for more on the link between volunteering and recruitment for political office). Our study posits a direct pathway from volunteerism, to civic engagement, to running for elected office. Moreover, we expect the combination of types of volunteerism and engagement to vary between men and women. This is especially important given that school board elections are the level of office most accessible to women.

Our study uses in-depth, qualitative data from personal interviews in one case study city (which we are calling Jaytown) and data collected from publicly available sources for the 20 largest cities in the same state as Jaytown. We have conducted a series of in-depth interviews with current and former members of the seven-person Jaytown school board (see the online appendix for more details[22]). Jaytown is a midsize city located near a large metropolitan area in the southwestern United States. We spoke with every current member of the board and interviewed those newly elected in 2015 as well as those who lost their reelection bids. Because we are arguing that participation on citizen boards/committees often serves as an important pool for recruiting candidates for school board, we have also collected data on the kinds of citizen participation in the 20 largest school districts (by student population) in the same state as Jaytown, which is one of these 20 largest districts. Using information about the various citizen committees in each of our 20 cities, we cross reference this with election data, using ballotpedia.org. In this way, we are able to track how these citizen committees might lead to running for elected office.

In previous work, we have shown that school board trustees often follow the path of civic engagement and volunteerism to public office.[23] Male candidates we interviewed spoke in terms of civic mindedness and in their belief in their abilities to be effective in the office. They described their interest in running for office as having a "heart for service" or "desire to serve my country and community." For some, their professional experiences were also factors in their decision to run and in their effectiveness once in office. Trustees described making connections in the business community, which helped them develop networks on which they drew during their campaigns. Some of these male candidates also had school-related volunteer experience, often as athletic boosters or as members of Dads' Clubs.

All of the male candidates with whom we spoke made the decision to run easily and none described needing encouragement. The women, by contrast, were more likely to contextualize their service as a part of their roles as parents[24] or as a function of specific issues motivating their campaigns (see Chapters 6 and 7 for more on this). Each of these women had been active in her child's or grandchild's school, serving on PTAs, as room mothers,[25] or in booster clubs. Some of the women also progressed beyond their child's local school to positions on the citywide and even state-level PTA. The women also spoke about skills such as organizing people, logistic expertise in putting on events, and goal setting and execution as useful to them in campaigning for office and in being trustees. These are precisely the civic and organizational skills we expect based on prior research on volunteering.

There was one type of community service common to both female and male trustees: citizen advisory committees. Many school districts have formal avenues for members of the community at large to provide input and advice on district policies and practices. Often these boards or committees provide fiscal oversight, especially in implementation of bond or levy funds. Other committees are centered on particular types of policies, such as physical fitness or nutrition. Still others are targeted outreach to particular communities, such as peoples of color.

All the trustees we interviewed in Jaytown had experience on one or more of these committees or boards prior to running for office. In Jaytown, these boards are appointed by district personnel with input from the current school board. The committee application process involves describing what previous experiences (professional or volunteer) qualify one for service. We find, at least in Jaytown, that while these oversight/policy boards are an important pool from which potential candidates for school board are recruited, the pathways to them are gendered. For example, a White male described having started a Dads' Club at his child's school as well as his leadership experience in his professional organization that he believed qualified him to serve on the citizen committee and then later to run for school board.

A Black female, by contrast, not only served in leadership in the PTA at all of her children's school campuses but also went on to the city's Council of PTAs. Another woman who is White talked about getting involved in the PTA because someone asked her to and she "wanted to be nice." When her children entered middle school (which was more economically and racially diverse than the elementary school), she became concerned about educational opportunities for low-income children, and her prior involvement in the PTA had provided not only civic skills for her to use when advocating for this population but also the network that would, when her children reached high school, lead to her being recruited to run for the school board.

This is significant because the origin of women's political involvement is often in the nonpolitical, child-centered volunteer activity that is commonly seen as part of motherhood. In a culture of intensive mothering,[26] parents' schedules are taxed. They are overfilled not only with ferrying children to various activities but also with phone calls and visits to local businesses requesting donations for fundraisers, hours at the school making photocopies, helping out in the classroom or sorting supplies, or the Herculean task of finding volunteers for an event. We argue that all of these nonpolitical activities can, among those motivated and recruited to political activity, develop civic capacity to build the kind of resume that makes one attractive as a candidate for office.

Our qualitative data suggested to us that there are pathways from generalized school-related volunteer work (for women) and from business connections and generalized civic volunteering (for men) to these school district community advisory boards and then to elected office, but it is not clear whether what we observe is unique to Jaytown. To test whether our findings reflect a pattern that occurs in other districts, we compared membership to elections for all the large districts in the state for which there are available data (see the online appendix for more information[27]).

What happens to these committee-to-candidates when they run? Of the 37 people, one was a trustee, retired and then tapped to serve on a committee. Of the remaining 36 who ran for trustee, about half (19) won (see the online appendix for more information[28]). While there are few gender differences overall, when the data are stratified by race/ethnicity, small differences emerge. Among females of color, winning is just as likely as losing. White women are more likely to win than not. For men, the biggest racial difference is for Latinos; all of whom won their seats (or were appointed). Among White and African American men, one is just as likely to win as not. (See Figure 6.1.) Among these committee-to-candidates, what was the relationship between their experience in volunteering, civic organizations, PTA, school committees, and winning? Are there different patterns for women from men?

For these committee-to-candidates, the takeaway appears to be that more is more and, by contrast, it appears one cannot win with school committee experience alone (see Figure 6.2). In fact, only one woman tried this route and she was not victorious. Those who engaged in three or more categories of activities were more likely to win than not. For women do-it-all candidates, doing it all often included PTA service (often in leadership roles). This group sees success about 60 percent of the time. Men, while a smaller proportion of this group, win more: 83 percent of men who engaged in all four categories won. Perhaps this points to the still-gendered nature of school-related volunteering; men get more "points" for engaging in this sort of activity whereas this is expected of women, especially mothers.

Men were more likely to be do-it-*almost*-all candidates: those who engaged in all the categories except for PTA. Of the 15 men in this analysis, four fit this description and half of them won. By contrast, only one of the 18 women

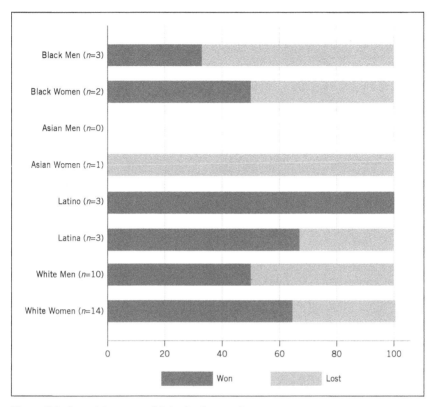

Figure 6.1. Committee-to-candidate election results.

fell into this category. Four women were involved in groups such as neigh-borhood associations, fraternal organizations, or community activism and school district committees, but not any school-related groups (PTA, booster clubs). Half were successful.

This analysis of background supports the qualitative data from Jaytown. Women not only are recruited out of the world of the school volunteer to serve on citizen committees but their volunteering experiences in the schools also lead to success. Women who run for school board with the school district com-mittee experience but who do not have or tout school volunteer experience, in PTA, boosters, or some other domain, are not likely to win.

These data do not provide the depth of information that qualitative inter-views would. They are suggestive, though, that only serving on school dis-trict committees is not a path to success (and, interestingly, no males tried this route). The patterns also suggest that there is value added from engaging in school-related activities in several dimensions: volunteering, PTA mem-bership and/or leadership, *and* school district committees. Whether individ-

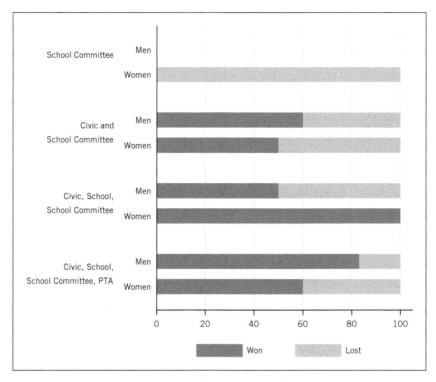

Figure 6.2. Committee-to-candidate election results by activity and gender.

uals were able to hone their civic skills, strengthen networks, or make important connections in preparation for running a campaign for trustee, these activities seem to matter.

We know that these school district community-wide committees can be helpful to a successful bid for a seat on the school board. We also know that, in addition to considering their skill set and available resources, potential candidates consider the opportunity structure. That is, they think about factors such as whether they would be challenging an incumbent or vying for an open seat and whether they have a base of support within the electorate. To assess the importance of these factors on the decision to run for school board, we examine the five races in our sample that pit committee-to-candidates in head-to-head contests. This allows us to hold constant the importance of committee service to examine the other characteristics of the election and of the candidates.

First, we take a look at the factors that may have played a role in the decision to run. Three of the five races were open races and in two a committee-to-candidate challenged an incumbent. Given the difficulty in unseating incumbents, one could argue that the choice to challenge required greater ambition.

TABLE 6.1. HEAD-TO-HEAD RACES BETWEEN COMMITTEE-TO-CANDIDATES

Winner	Loser	Nature of district	Characteristics of election	
White female incumbent Parent volunteer, community activist	Latina challenger Community activist, staffer for city councilman	Urban, working class, primarily Latino	Incumbent	Single member
White female challenger Parent volunteer, civic organizations	White male Committee only Finished 3rd in a field of four	Predominantly White, upper-middle-class suburban district	Incumbent — At large; Incumbent finished 2nd in field of four	
Latino male Committee and civic experience	White male Finance executive	Urban, working class, racial diversity with Latinos and upper-middle-class Whites	Open seat	Single member
African American male Endorsed by outgoing trustee on basis of race Higher education professional	White male Neighborhood association leader	Urban, historically African American, underresourced	Open seat — Single member; Both candidates-to-committee made runoff in a field of four	
White female PTA, Chamber, civic and professional organizations	White female School volunteer	Predominantly White, upper-middle-class suburban district	Open seat	At large

Indeed, in both cases, committee-to-candidate challengers took on established school board trustees. In one of these cases, the incumbent, who was not a committee-to-candidate, was somewhat vulnerable as he drew three opponents, two of whom were committee-to-candidates. As the second row in Table 6.1 indicates, the successful challenger was a "do-it-all" candidate. In addition to the school committee, she had served as a school volunteer and was active in the community. This suggests that her civic skill–incubating experiences provided her with the foundation necessary to turn latent ambition into progressive ambition. This conclusion is further supported as, in subsequent election cycles, the same person also challenged a sitting state legislator in the Republican primary.

In the second case of a committee-to-candidate challenging an incumbent, the challenger also acquired the necessary skills to develop ambition in school committees, in community activism, and by working for a city councilmember. The committee-to-candidate incumbent to whom she lost had done a better job of positioning herself for reelection, touting her record as a parent volunteer, invested member of the community, and problem solver. Still, her challenger took the risk of running and it will be interesting to see if she runs again in the future.

In the previous discussion of what becomes of the committee-to-candidates, we learned that many of the dynamics typical of municipal elections (the power of incumbency, appealing to a coalition of likely voters) remain true even when a candidate has the experience of having served on a citizen committee. So, while this service perhaps places one in a network of encouragers or in a position to be recruited and/or allows one to develop the requisite skills to run for office, success is not guaranteed. What happens when we step back and examine the dynamics within a single city, comparing across cities? Do patterns emerge where citizen committee service matters? Are there places where this type of service does not matter?

We tackle these questions by examining in greater detail the political nuances in two cities beyond our original case study. One, which we will call Riverside, is similar to our original case in size (toward the middle of our list of largest cities) and racial and ethnic makeup of the students, with Hispanics making up the majority of the students, yet holding very little of the political power. It is also similar in the degree to which incumbents are challenged (not often). As a point of comparison, we also look at one of the largest districts in the state, which we will call Danielton. As Figure 6.3 illustrates, Danielton is a much larger city with the accompanying problems of poverty and lower graduation rates.

Riverside school board consists of seven trustees, four of whom are men and three are women. Of the current board, three (two women and one man) are committee-to-candidates. Of the whole board, two are men of color: one is African American and one is Latino. All of the women are White. Four of the seats were up for reelection most recently and two of the incumbents, both women, drew opponents. Both incumbent women won. In one race, a fiscal conservative who has held the seat for almost two decades won handily in a three-person race. The closest challenger, a committee-to-candidate, garnered about a third of the vote. The other race involved an incumbent committee-to-candidate, who beat a male social conservative former teacher.

This school district is a suburban district with an increasing proportion of Latino students, though this region is one that originally was one in which Anglo residents resided (in contrast to other areas of the larger urban area). This is similar to Jaytown, which has also experienced increasing diversity, especially within the school population that is more racially diverse than the city as a whole.

In both Jaytown and Riverside, the school district citizen committees are selected by district staff in consultation with current trustees. The makeup

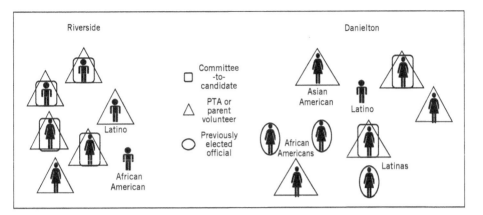

Figure 6.3. Comparison of characteristics of school board trustees.

of the committees appears to include parents and other stakeholders in the community (e.g., business owners, accountants, engineers, realtors), some of whom are community and civic leaders. Neither selection nor membership appears to be politicized in the traditional sense of having a formal endorsement process by an elected official. However, this does not preclude there being a screening process at work to determine who is chosen for these committees.

Both cities' election outcomes are driven by factors that we might expect: the power of incumbency and the lack of power of communities who wish to challenge existing governing structures. In Riverside, unlike Jaytown, not all trustees are committee-to-candidates. Future research is needed to uncover whether Jaytown is, indeed, an outlier in this regard.

Riverside and Jaytown are situated in larger metropolitan areas and both the school district politics and the municipal politics are dominated by a well-established political power elite. Contrast this dynamic with Danielton, one of the largest cities and school districts in the state. Like other large urban centers, Danielton is typified by racial politics and a lively political environment.

In Danielton, unlike in Riverside and Jaytown, the selection process for citizen boards appears to be driven by the prestige of potential members. For example, the committee's description states a desire to have building and construction experts, community members, and district parents. However, in the brief descriptions of the members, none of the parents are "just parents." One Asian male also serves on other city and school district committees. Another male (race unknown) is a parent and "education advocate." A White woman is described as a community volunteer and philanthropist, though further investigation reveals she is one of the city's leading figures in both social and civic circles. Most municipal elections in Danielton, including those for school board, are contested. In the most recent election, all six of the nine seats with elections are contested, most with more than two candidates. One of these six seats is a special election, in the remaining five districts two incumbents are not running for reelection.

On the current board of nine, two are men (an Anglo and a Latino) and seven are women (three African Americans, an Asian, a Latino, a White woman married to a Latino, and another White woman). Two of the nine members have previous experience on district committees. One, a White male, previously served on one of the finance-related committees. The other person, a Latina, previously served on a committee related to the Hispanic community. In one of the open seats, which we will call Place A, where a White female incumbent chose not to run for reelection, three women (two Latinas and a White woman) ran for the position. One of the Latinas is a committee-to-candidate who is an attorney and community leader. The other Latina ran as a "teacher's board member." The White woman in the race has not served on a citizen committee but has been an active school volunteer and community leader and touts her public policy background. The area represented by this trustee is interesting; the wealth of households varies considerably from block to block. This is not particularly unusual in large cities in this state where low house prices have attracted wealthy buyers and gentrification (and economic stratification) follows. The race came down to a runoff between the White woman and the Latina, but not the one who is a committee-to-candidate. In this particular race, the winning candidate used an appeal that combined the "I'm from here" message we have seen previously with a fighter/advocate stance.

The other district without an incumbent running, Place B, was also heavily contested; four candidates ran, three women and a man, all of whom are White. The winner was one of the women, a committee-to-candidate, having served on a generalized (not racially based) community-wide committee. She is highly involved as a parent volunteer and ran as an advocate for the community in a largely affluent, well-educated area of the city. Of the other two women, one is a teacher and the other a parent volunteer who placed emphasis on the needs of special education children. The White man in the race ran as a fiscal conservative and, interestingly in a nonpartisan race, touted his Republican Party experience. The part of the school district these candidates would represent is home both to pockets of working-class residents of various races/ethnicities and to areas that are less racially diverse and where there are many dual-income households as well as ones with stay-at-home moms.

The trustee in Place C represents a largely African American part of the city. Here two Black people (a man and a woman) unsuccessfully challenged the Black female incumbent. The Black male challenger is a committee-to-candidate, having served on a committee focusing on the African American community. He was described in press accounts as a racial and social justice activist. The Black female challenger had a very low profile and press accounts described her as passionate but too inexperienced for the job.

It is clear from our analysis that Danielton's school trustee elections are affected by the fact that there are single-member districts in a city that is segregated by race and class and expected forces of incumbency and coalition-building are at work. In Place A (an open seat), the contest came down to the committee-to-candidate (a Latina who is from the do-it-all background) and the White woman who has not served on a school board committee but otherwise has a do-it-all resume, with the Latina winning because she was able to mobilize the Latino community. In Place B, also an open seat, race was not a factor as all candidates were White. Our analysis of background characteristics accurately predicted that the woman who is a parent volunteer, who is highly civically engaged, and who has held up her public policy experience was successful. The quality of challengers to incumbents also matters, a dynamic that most likely played out in Place C where the incumbent won over a weak challenger.

Concluding Thoughts on Who Runs

Throwing one's hat into the ring for school board trustee is relatively accessible to a would-be candidate. It is less expensive than state legislative or congressional races and the barriers to entry may seem less insurmountable. Our work suggests, though, that service on citizen committees not only increases the likelihood of being recruited but also, when combined with other school-related volunteering, translates into victory, especially among women. Starting with talking to current and former school board trustees, we learned that membership on district citizen committees was important in their recruitment to run for school board. There are gender differences in the pathways that led these individuals to be selected for the committees in the first place. As we broadened our scope to the other large cities in the state, we discovered that, while there are many committee-to-candidates, not all school board trustees have this on their resumes. We find more women when we explored this group of committee-to-candidates, but being a committee member alone is not sufficient. Those committee-to-candidates who become trustees are the do-it-all types. For women, doing it all almost always includes some kind of school volunteering, often PTA leadership.[29] This supports the findings from the original qualitative interview data that, in the domain of the school board trustee, electorally successful women have school volunteering backgrounds.

By combining in-depth qualitative interview data with quantitative data gleaned from public sources, we have painted an interesting picture of the relationship among volunteering, engagement, ambition, and public service (see Chapter 7 by Mo and Anderson-Nilsson, in this volume, for more information on other nontraditional sources of political ambition). The image that emerges is one where the volunteer experience is important for women, but where the politics of place, race, and class still matter.

NOTES

We thank the people who have helped make this chapter stronger and more interesting. We appreciate the editors of this volume for bringing scholars together to talk about this important topic, first at the "Good Reason to Run" conference hosted by University of Pennsylvania in the fall of 2017. We are grateful for the thoughtful comments from fellow conference participants. We thank Shauna L. Shames especially for sharing her data from her book, *Out of the Running: Why Millennials Reject Political Careers and Why It Matters* (New York: New York University, 2017), and the anonymous reviewers for their suggestions.

1. Jennifer Lawless and Richard Fox, *It Still Takes a Candidate: Why Women Don't Run for Office* (Cambridge: Cambridge University Press, 2010).

2. Shames, *Out of the Running.*

3. Sidney Verba, Nancy Burns, and Kay Lehman Schlozman, "Knowing and Caring about Politics: Gender and Political Engagement," *Journal of Politics* 59 (November 1997): 1051–1073; Sidney Verba, Kay Lehman Schlozman, and Henry Brady, *Voice and Equality* (Cambridge, MA: Harvard University Press, 1995).

4. Verba, Schlozman, and Brady, *Voice and Equality*; Rebecca Deen and Beth Anne Shelton, "Bake Sales for a Better America: The Role of School Volunteers in Civic Life," *International Journal of Interdisciplinary Social Sciences* 6, no. 7 (2012): 25–38; Rebecca Deen and Beth Anne Shelton, "Motherhood and Public Service: An Exploration of School Board Trustees," in *Mothers in Politics and Public Life* (Toronto: Demeter, 2017), 30–50.

5. Verba, Schlozman, and Brady, *Voice and Equality.*

6. Verba, Schlozman, and Brady, *Voice and Equality.*

7. Nancy Burns, Kay Lehman Schlozman, and Sidney Verba, *The Private Roots of Public Action: Gender, Equality and Political Participation* (Cambridge, MA: Harvard University Press, 2001).

8. Deen and Shelton, "Bake Sales."

9. Burns, Schlozman, and Verba, *Private Roots.*

10. Krista Jenkins, "Gender and Civic Engagement: Secondary Analysis of Survey Data," Center for American Women and Politics, July 2005, accessed March 7, 2018, available at http://www.cawp.rutgers.edu/sites/default/files/resources/gendercivicengagmnt.pdf.

11. Shames, *Out of the Running.*

12. Burns, Schlozman, and Verba, *Private Roots.*

13. Barbara Mikulski and Catherine Whitney, *Nine and Counting: The Women of the Senate* (New York: William Morrow, 2000).

14. "About Patty," U.S. Senator Patty Murray, accessed March 7, 2018, available at https://www.murray.senate.gov/public/index.cfm/aboutpatty.

15. "Facts and Historical Data on Women Candidates and Officeholders," Center for American Women and Politics, accessed October 29, 2019, available at https://cawp.rutgers.edu/facts.

16. "Facts and Historical Data on Women Candidates and Officeholders," Center for American Women and Politics, accessed October 29, 2019, available at https://cawp.rutgers.edu/facts.

17. Deen and Shelton, "Motherhood and Public Service"; Frederick M. Hess, *School Boards at the Dawn of the 21st Century* (American School Boards Association 2002).

18. "Frequently Asked Questions," National School Boards Association, accessed March 7, 2018, available at https://www.nsba.org/about-us/frequently-asked-questions.

19. Timothy Bledsoe and Mary Herring, "Victims of Circumstances: Women in Pursuit of Political Office," *American Political Science Review* 84, no. 1 (March 1990): 213–223.

20. Lawless and Fox, *It Still Takes a Candidate.*

21. Melissa Deckman, "Gender Differences in the Decision to Run for School Board," *Journal of Women, Politics and Policy* 35, no. 4 (July 2007): 87–117.

22. The online appendix can be found through the Harvard Dataverse, available at https://doi.org/10.7910/DVN/BJTB1W.

23. Rebecca Deen and Beth Anne Shelton, "Intensive Mothering in the Public Sphere: The Case of the School Volunteer," paper presented at American Sociological Association Meeting, Montreal, Canada, August 2017.

24. Deen and Shelton, "Motherhood and Public Service."

25. While the term *room parent* is often used, all in our sample are mothers.

26. Sharon Hays, *The Cultural Contradictions of Motherhood* (New Haven, CT: Yale University Press, 2002).

27. The online appendix can be found through the Harvard Dataverse, available at https://doi.org/10.7910/DVN/BJTB1W.

28. The online appendix can be found through the Harvard Dataverse, available at https://doi.org/10.7910/DVN/BJTB1W.

29. As Deen and Shelton's "Bake Sales" points out, one can be a PTA member without actually doing any work. PTA board leadership (serving on a committee, chairing events, or being part of the executive board) is where one develops civic skills.

7

Youth National Service and Women's Political Ambition

The Case of Teach For America

CECILIA HYUNJUNG MO AND
GEORGIA ANDERSON-NILSSON

Women are woefully underrepresented in all major political offices in the United States. While many reasons account for why over half of the population holds only about a quarter of the country's elected offices, one explanation comes up again and again: an insufficient number of women choose to pursue elected office.[1] The 2018 midterm election was dubbed by political pundits as the "pink wave" because an unprecedented number of women ran for political office. But the surge in female candidates still translated to fewer than a third of congressional candidates and nominees being women.[2] It turns out that drafting more women to run for political office is not a simple endeavor. Even women at the highest levels of professional accomplishments, who we would most expect to be politically ambitious, are much less likely than their male counterparts to consider entering the political arena.[3] Women officeholders often describe having been repeatedly asked to run for office before even considering to take the plunge.[4] Even when they have more years of experience than their male counterparts running for office, women often question their own qualifications to hold office. In fact, women cite the "realization that I was just as capable" significantly more often than men as a factor in the decision to run.[5] Gender and politics scholars have established that there is a worrisome political ambition gender gap and have uncovered many factors that constrain and limit women's political ambition. What is less known is whether particular experiences are more likely to predispose women to being more politically ambitious and more responsive to political recruitment efforts.

In this chapter, we argue that the answer to this question is "yes." We present evidence that national service programs have the potential to galvanize political ambition in their female participants. We focus specifically on Teach For America (TFA), a prominent youth national service program that recruits some of the most promising young leaders in the country to serve in some of the most struggling schools in the United States. Studying nine cohorts of TFA applicants between 2007 and 2015, we find that women who participate in TFA emerge with higher levels of political ambition than otherwise similar women who do not. While our study focuses on only one civilian national service program, these findings suggest that national service programs may contain ingredients that are important in activating political interest among underrepresented populations. In many ways, this makes intuitive sense. National service programs are specifically designed to cultivate democratic norms and values, explicitly aiming to create more civically engaged citizens.[6] Moreover, civic participation is generally associated with higher levels of political participation because engaging in programs that aim to address public problems gives citizens an opportunity to build civic skills and increases opportunities to be recruited into politics.[7] The connection between national service and interest in running for political office is a natural extension of this linkage between national service and civic engagement.

Why Youth National Service?

Why might youth national service activate political ambition in women? There are two main reasons we expect this to occur. First, national service programs typically integrate individuals into networks and provide resources that help to foster continued civic participation.[8] In other words, national service programs can offer organizational support in the form of formal programming, partnerships with other organizations, and connections with other participants and alumni, which can act as resources for overcoming some of the central challenges potential candidates will likely face in running for office. Individuals who have sources of support for building their capacity as leaders as well as their social capital are more likely to run for office, and these support networks are especially important for women. Previous research has found that organizational affiliations are more important in predicting women's legislative candidacies than men's, and, even among women who are already activists, those who are more integrated into social networks express more political ambition.[9] Digging into this connection showed that organizational support can help women overcome important impediments to political ambition that are unique to female candidates. For example, political parties are less likely to target women for recruitment than men, and service organizations can help fill this lack of formal party support.[10] Service organizations can also spark political ambition by directly encouraging their participants to be politically engaged and to consider political leadership, which they often do. This is not trivial, as women are less likely than men to receive the suggestion to run for office. For example, while familial encouragement is an important predictor of political ambition for both men and women, women are much less likely than men to report having received parental encouragement to run for office.[11]

Second, by design, national service programs provide participants with exposure to specific public policy issues, which can catalyze an interest in influencing public policy through political office. The opportunity to develop expertise in a policy area is particularly important to women in their calculus to run for office. Women are much less likely than men to think they are qualified to run for office, and a deep immersive experience could help women overcome some of their self-doubts. Moreover, frustration with policy failures appears to be a stronger motivator to become politically involved for women than for men. In a survey of American mayors, women were more likely than men to cite specific experiences with public policy problems as a motivating factor in deciding to run for office.[12] Often, women's attention to these public policy issues stems from direct experiences: one U.S. congresswoman first decided to run for municipal office when her daughter was hurt while playing on neglected public playground equipment and her local government failed to make the necessary repairs. Relatedly, previous research has found that women express more interest in running when political office is viewed as a mechanism to fulfill community-oriented goals rather than power-related, individualistic goals.[13] To the extent that national service makes a social ill salient and provides participants with direct experience and expertise with it, women who participate in these programs may feel greater motivation to run for office than those who do not.

In sum, the seeds of policy exposure and support structures planted by national service can grow into greater political ambition among women. National service experiences typically involve a deep exposure to a set of public policy issues, which could ignite a desire and sense of efficacy for addressing specific policy problems. They also aim to offer a supportive and formal structure for their participants and alumni to become agents of social change with respect to these policy issues. Youth national service programs like the Peace Corps and AmeriCorps are designed with an intention to develop active and engaged citizens. Indeed, national service programs in the United States are rooted in the notion that their participants emerge better equipped and motivated to actively improve their communities. As such, these programs invest in activities that specifically aim to cultivate civic and political participation. For example, TFA actively maintains structured alumni networks focused on cultivating participants' activism and inspiring "a diverse set of leaders with classroom experience to engage civically and politically."[14] TFA and other national service programs also often lower many of the costs associated with running for office, as they integrate participants into networks of support and provide them with public experience and training in relevant policy areas. For example, the White House Project, a nonprofit organization aiming to increase female representation in American institutions, businesses, and government, has a formal partnership with TFA.[15]

Another consideration is the gender makeup of non-military national service programs in the United States. Women make up the majority of participants of large civilian national service programs. When we examine the demographic characteristics of some of the most prominent civilian national service programs in the country, we see that, of the membership in these programs, women constitute 70 percent of TFA, 63 percent of the Peace Corps, and 68 percent of AmeriCorps.[16] As such, pursuing a strategy to tap civilian national service participants to run for political office leads recruiters to a pool of potential officeholders that are overwhelmingly female. Looking at non-military national service as an on-ramp to elected public service roles would thus lead to a field of candidates that is not so dominated by men.

The Case of TFA

We examine the case of TFA, a prominent and prototypical civilian national service program. TFA was established in 1990 with the explicit aim of recruiting and developing future leaders, and its highly selective application process reflects this goal, annually attracting a pool of over 50,000 applicants composed of high-achieving college graduates predominantly drawn from high-status socioeconomic backgrounds. TFA recruits participants with the explicit claim that the organization brings people into "the civil rights movement of our time," addressing the issue of educational inequality.[17] Indeed, part of TFA's stated mission is to motivate its participants to become leaders in affecting systemic change both within their own classrooms and beyond.

The TFA classroom experience immerses participants in issues of education inequality and education policies and provides them with a community to reflect on the issues they witness. Participants teach in the poorest schools in the United States; TFA partners with schools that have a minimum of 60 percent of students qualifying for free or reduced-price lunch. TFA members are assigned to serve in some of the toughest classrooms in the country; very often, they are in schools that struggle to attract and retain teachers.[18] For at least two years, participants are fully immersed in these schools as full-time classroom instructors, witnessing firsthand that "many children lack the education, support, and opportunity to learn and to thrive."[19] One TFA alumna describes a deep sense of frustration with the lack of resources in her school: dysfunctional or nonexistent phones and copiers, and limited or no access to basic resources like copier paper.[20] Another recounts, "Some of my tenth graders read their first book ever in my classroom." Participants have ample opportunities to reflect upon these experiences, regularly interacting with other TFA teachers and TFA alumni, both formally and informally, as mentors, colleagues, and friends. Moreover, TFA provides its teachers with regional support to deliver structured feedback and coaching throughout the program.

TFA provides a strong organizational support network before, during, and after service and makes an explicit effort to inspire alumni to remain politically involved. After their service, TFA recruits interested alumni into its Capitol Hill Fellows program, which provides participants with experience in the legislative process and encourages corps members and alumni to join nonpartisan organizations like Leadership for Educational Equity, which, in turn, focuses on recruiting and supporting "leaders with classroom experience to engage civically and politically."[21] Moreover, TFA's alumni network includes a legion of education leaders, including principals, school district and charter school leaders, as well as state education chiefs.

Two features of TFA may make it a particularly fertile environment for women's political ambitions to grow: (1) TFA operates within the female-dominated field of education and (2) women serve as important, high-profile members of TFA's leadership team.[22] Extant gender and politics scholarship has found that women are more likely to run for offices that correspond with issue areas that are stereotypically associated with women, such as those specializing in education and health care.[23] Moreover, providing visible examples of effective female leaders can encourage women to recalibrate their aspirations. In fact, one impediment scholars have identified to women's political ambition is a lack of role models. The presence of female leadership can reduce harmful gendered stereotypes and increase the expectation among women that they too can be successful as leaders.[24] While these qualities suggest that TFA may be a special case among national service organizations, these features are such that, if we do not see a relationship between TFA participation and political ambition among women, it is unlikely that we would observe a relationship between national service participation and women's political ambition in general. As such, the TFA case is a strong case to start with. Moreover, TFA is an ideal case to consider from a methodological perspective. As we establish in our discussion of our study approach below, we are able to causally identify the connection between national service and women's political ambition in a meaningful way given some unique features of TFA's admissions process.

Our Approach

Does the TFA experience increase political ambition in women? To answer this question, we leveraged an original survey of TFA applicants during the 2007–2015 application cycles. Over 380,000 applied to TFA during this study period. However, we restricted our focus to the 120,417 applicants who made it to the final stage of the TFA admissions process and, hence, were competitive candidates for admission. Among this target population, we achieved an overall response rate of 33 percent among TFA participants (13,745 individuals) and a 24 percent response rate among nonparticipants (18,872 individuals). Approximately 70 percent of survey respondents are women, which reflects the gender breakdown of the overall TFA applicant pool for the 2007–2015 application cycle (71 percent women). Of the 13,745 TFA participants who at least began the survey, 10,098 are women (73 percent). And of the 18,872 nonparticipants who at least started the survey, 13,577 are female (72 percent). Given our interest in women's political ambition, the focus of our analyses was on these female applicants, specifically.[25]

Our measures of political ambition are derived from a survey module that asked respondents about their political ambition, interest, and participation. The module began with the following statements: "The following are some forms of political action that people can take. For each action, please indicate whether you have done it, you have not but might do it, or you have not and would never under any circumstances do it." Respondents were then asked about the following eight activities: (1) running for political office; (2) participating in a political campaign; (3) attending a government or community meeting; (4) contacting a government representative; (5) writing for a blog, newspaper, or magazine about a cause; (6) signing a petition; (7) joining boycotts, strikes, and/or demonstrations; and (8) becoming a member of a political party.

Respondents were provided with three options to choose from: "I have done," "I have NOT done, but WOULD do," or "I have NOT done, and WOULD NEVER do." Eight binary political participation measures were constructed based on these questions, where those who answered "I have done" or "I have NOT done, but WOULD do" were categorized as being interested in the given political activity and those who answered "I have NOT done, and WOULD NEVER do" as being uninterested in the given activity. Our primary measures of interest in examining political ambition are the first two measures that ask about running for elected office and participating in political campaigns, which is necessary when running for political office.

Many studies of political ambition have focused on women who have already run for office. Here, we examine a population of women who have generally *not* made the decision to run, allowing us to say something more meaningful about what predisposes women to consider running for office in the first place. Moreover, the design of the survey module allows us to ask about self-reported interest in both running for office and participating in political campaigns.

A potential problem with estimating the actual effect of participating in TFA is that the types of people who participate in TFA are likely to be different along a variety of dimensions from the general population, particularly in terms of those characteristics that also predict political ambition. For instance, TFA applicants are all college graduates, typically have college-educated parents, and, as reflected in their interest in participating in a national service program focused on education inequality, are more politically engaged than the average citizen. Indeed, survey respondents, including those who were not admitted to TFA, report extremely high levels of interest in various forms of political participation. Over 90 percent of applicants report an interest in attending government and community meetings, contacting a government representative, writing for a cause, and signing a petition, and over 80 percent report an interest in joining a political party and participating in boycotts, strikes, and/or demonstrations. Hence, it would be incorrect to say that the difference in the average TFA alumna's political ambition and that of women in the general population is the effect of participating in TFA. The difference would, in large part, reflect differences in the population that is attracted to apply to TFA and the population that would never apply to TFA in the first place. It is also incorrect to simply compare the political ambition levels of TFA participants and TFA nonadmits, as applicants who are admitted may be systematically different from applicants who are rejected in ways that would also predict political ambition.

To address this inferential problem, we take advantage of a threshold rule used in TFA's admissions process. We are able to employ what researchers call a quasi-experimental regression discontinuity design to estimate the effect of TFA. In 2007, TFA implemented a selection process in which they assigned scores to each applicant, with an acceptance threshold score. This enables us to know which applicants barely scored above the threshold as well as which applicants scored just below the required score. Identifying these two groups is extremely useful, as these two groups are, on average, virtually identical on every dimension that would affect political ambition aside from TFA participation. We confirmed this by assessing differences in the survey response rate and a number of demographic characteristics that should not be affected by TFA participation (e.g., age, race, parental education, college selectivity, etc.). As such, we can infer that any differences we see in political ambition between these two groups are due to TFA participation.

Importantly, although female TFA applicants express high levels of interest in political participation on average, female applicants are far less keen to express political ambition. Whereas an overwhelming majority of female applicants who responded to our survey are interested in the seven other political participation questions we asked about, a minority (about 40 percent) of female respondents express interest in running for office, with 1.2 percent having actually done so. Moreover, much like the general population, women who applied to TFA are much less likely than men who applied to TFA to express interest in running for office or participating in political campaigns. Hence, although TFA applicants are, on average, quite exceptional in their political engagement, women who apply to TFA look very much like the general population of women in terms of their political ambition being notably lower than that of their male counterparts.

In estimating the effect of TFA participation on women's political ambition generally, we also considered how this effect is impacted by a variety of background characteristics that may be relevant in predicting political ambition. In general, individuals who run for office tend to be those with access to resources such as time and money.[26] As such, individuals with high socioeconomic status (SES) are more likely to run for office than low SES-individuals, despite the fact that less affluent and less privileged individuals are no less qualified and no less preferred by voters.[27] For both men and women, family obligations such as being married and having children are also associated with lower levels of political ambition, although the effect of family responsibilities on ambition are more pronounced for women due to socialized expectations surrounding gender roles.[28] These demographic characteristics—SES, marital status, having children—that constrain or boost individuals' ability to engage in political activism can be thought of as "biographical availability" for political participation.[29]

In our analysis, respondents who are either married or in a civil union were categorized as being married. Although we asked respondents about the number of children they had, for our analyses we constructed a binary variable for whether or not they had any children. To measure a respondent's SES, we used a question that asked them to categorize their family's class while they were growing up, ranging from lower class to upper class. We labeled respondents as High SES if they selected "upper class," "upper middle class," "middle class," or "lower middle class," and Low SES as "upper lower class" and "lower class."

National Service Participation Increases Women's Political Ambition

National service can spur increased political ambition in women. We find that participation in TFA has a causal impact on political ambition in women. As summarized in Figure 7.1 (top), on average, women who participated in TFA are 10.2 percentage points ($p = 0.05$) more likely to express interest in running for political office than women who did not.[30] Generally, the effects of participation in TFA on political ambition are higher among those from relatively higher SES backgrounds (11.5 percentage points; $p = 0.04$). Among single women with no children from high-income backgrounds, the effect increases to 14.6 percentage points ($p = 0.05$). These effects are statistically significant at standard levels of statistical significance and substantively meaningful. To put these effects into context, another study of political ambition found that

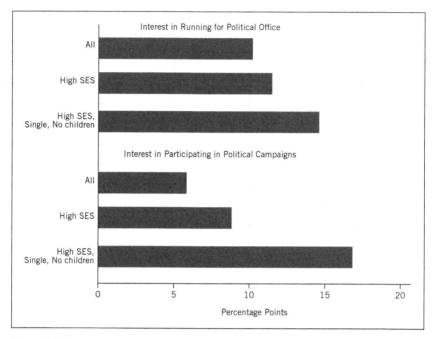

Figure 7.1. Interest in running for political office (*top*) and interest in participating in political campaigns (*bottom*).

a one-unit increase in a candidate's self-assessment of qualification on a seven-point scale—from "qualified" to "very qualified"—is associated with a 4 percentage point increase in the likelihood that she would consider running for office.[31] Our main finding of 10.2 percentage points is more than twice this effect.[32]

The pattern of effects is similar when we look at interest in participating in political campaigns, as Figure 7.1 (bottom) depicts. The effect of TFA participation on interest in participating in political campaigns is 5.8 percentage points ($p = 0.06$). When we consider effects among those who have more biographical availability stemming from being in a high-SES family, effects increase to 8.8 percentage points ($p = 0.04$). Effects are larger among those who are single (12.4 percentage points; $p = 0.02$) and those who have no children (6.4 percentage points); $p = 0.09$. When considering those with the most biographical availability with regard to both income and family responsibilities, the effect nearly triples to 16.8 percentage points ($p = 0.007$).

Our results are further supported when we consider individuals who were admitted into TFA but did not actually matriculate. If the effect we observe is truly a result of participation in TFA, we should see that the effect is stronger when we exclude admitted nonparticipants. This is indeed what we observe: excluding admitted nonmatriculants from each of the analyses we conducted above systematically results in effect sizes that are larger by up to 2.0 percentage points.

Interestingly, when we compare the effects for women of color to effects among White women, we observe stronger effects among women of color. Among White women, the average causal effect of participating in TFA on interest in pursuing political office is 5.9 percentage points, while, for women of color, it is 22.7 percentage points. When we examine interest in participating in political campaigns, we observe an identical pattern. The effect of TFA participation among White women on political campaign interest is 4.5 percentage points, whereas the effect of TFA participation on this metric among women of color is 15 percentage points. However, because women of color make up less than a third of our sample, we do not have enough statistical power to detect a statistically significant effect. We find this result worthy of noting all the same, as it suggests that national service programs may have a particularly large effect on the political ambitions of women of color.

When we evaluate the impact of TFA on the six other forms of political participation we asked about, we find virtually no effect. This is consistent with our expectations and with past scholarship. For example, in a study investigating the effects of participation in the Mississippi Freedom Summer Project on participants' levels of political activism later in life, Doug McAdam found that the women who participated in the program did not become more active after the program, as women who participated in Freedom Summer were already highly active.[33] Much like Freedom Summer participants, the women who apply to and participate in TFA already have very high levels of political interest and participation generally.

Recall that over 90 percent of female applicants report an interest in attending government or community meetings (96.6 percent, with 59.1 percent having done it already), contacting a representative (94.5 percent, with 53.0 percent having done it already), writing for a cause (91.2 percent, with 29.7 percent having done it already), and signing a petition (98.4 percent, with 87.6 percent having done it already). And over 80 percent report an interest in joining boycotts, strikes, and/or demonstrations (82.7 percent, with 34.3 percent having done it already) and joining a political party (84.3 percent, with 48.5 percent having done it already). Moreover, female applicants who did not participate in TFA have similarly high levels of interest in all forms of political engagement we inquire about, apart from our political ambition measures. There is very little room to be more interested on these six activities, whereas we have not hit the ceiling on interest in the activities connected to political ambition. Only 41.3 percent of female applicants report an interest in running for political office (with only 1.2 percent having done it already) and 79.4 percent report an interest in participating in a political campaign (with 32.1 percent having done it already). Given the high amounts of interest in political activities at the outset, it is not surprising that participating in TFA has no meaningful effect on our political engagement measures that are not related to political ambition.

With that said, this null finding on these six political participation measures does not necessarily mean that participation in national service programs has no effect on other forms of political participation. Our measures were simple binary interest measures. While the presence of interest may not change, the *degree* of interest may change due to TFA participation.

Recruit Women with Service Histories

In a political environment in which women are underrepresented and often hesitant to run for office, we find that national service is one mechanism that can ignite women's political ambition. Compared to applicants for TFA who are otherwise highly similar, women who participate in TFA are more politically ambitious.

Of course, these findings are naturally limited in scope. We examine here a group of highly educated people who have selected to enter youth national service programs and who are disproportionately drawn from middle- and upper-class economic backgrounds. However, past research has shown that political ambition is difficult to find even among women from white-collar professions, such as law and business, and among women who already have prior political experience.[34] Here, we present evidence of an experience that sparks political ambition in women who already possess many of the characteristics associated with political ambition. Another limitation is that, because TFA is focused on a policy domain that is stereotypically female, it may be a proverbial snowflake in terms of its impact on political ambition for women specifically. However, rather than jeopardizing the validity of these findings, in our view, this concern only paves the way for questions that test the effects of other national service organizations on the political ambitions of their female alumni.

Understanding what experiences do and do not catalyze political ambition in women is a critical step in crafting effective recruitment strategies for those hoping to mobilize future women candidates. If national service experiences increase women's interest in running for political office, then organizations and individuals seeking to recruit women into politics might look for women who have a history of national service. Our findings suggest that alumnae of these programs might be more likely to respond favorably to political recruitment. Moreover, our findings indicate that TFA and similar organizations might be fruitful organizational partners in the effort to recruit motivated female candidates.

While there is no guarantee that national service alumnae will be good candidates for political office, alumni of TFA are a population with great promise. For example, TFA participants have been shown to empathize with disadvantaged communities and be more attuned to the injustices faced by low-income and minority communities.[35] As such, this pool of potential candidates may facilitate greater political representation of the perspectives of underrepresented communities. The women who apply to TFA express high levels of political participation and interest to begin with, but nonparticipants are more interested in forms of political participation in which other actors play a central leadership role relative to TFA participants. Our results clearly show that the women who go through TFA emerge with a willingness to play a much more agentic role when it comes to participating in politics. As such, alumnae of national service, particularly women who have fewer family responsibilities and greater financial security, may be easier to recruit for political office.

NOTES

1. CAWP, "Current Numbers | CAWP" (New Brunswick, NJ: Center for American Women and Politics, Eagleton Institute of Politics, Rutgers University, 2018), accessed March 1, 2019, available at http://www.cawp.rutgers.edu/current-numbers.

2. Kelly Dittmar, "By the Numbers: Women Congressional Candidates in 2018," CAWP, September 12, 2018, accessed March 1, 2019, available at https://www.cawp.rutgers.edu/congressional-candidates-summary-2018.

3. Christopher F. Karpowitz, J. Quin Monson, and Jessica Robinson Preece, "How to Elect More Women: Gender and Candidate Success in a Field Experiment," *American Journal of Political Science*, March 1, 2017, available at https://doi.org/10.1111/ajps.12300; Jessica Robinson Preece, Olga Bogach Stoddard, and Rachel Fisher, "Run, Jane, Run! Gendered Responses to Political Party Recruitment," *Political Behavior* 38, no. 3 (2016): 561–577.

4. Tamara Keith, "Best Way to Get Women to Run for Office? Ask Repeatedly," NPR, March 4, 2014, accessed March 1, 2019, available at https://www.npr.org/2014/05/05/309832898/best-way-to-get-women-to-run-for-office-ask-repeatedly.

5. Susan J. Carroll and Kira Sanbonmatsu, "Entering the Mayor's Office: Women's Decisions to Run for Municipal Positions," in *Women and Executive Office: Pathways and Performance*, ed. Melody Rose (Boulder, CO: Lynne Rienner, 2013).

6. Cecilia Hyunjung Mo and Katharine M. Conn, "When Do the Advantaged See the Disadvantages of Others? A Quasi-Experimental Study of National Service," *American Political Science Review* 112, no. 4 (November 2018): 721–741, available at https://doi.org/10.1017/S0003055418000412.

7. Scott Keeter, Cliff Zukin, Molly Andolina, and Krista Jenkins, "The Civic and Political Health of the Nation: A Generational Portrait" (Center for Information and Research on Civic Learning and Engagement, 2019), accessed March 1, 2019, available at http://pollcats.net/downloads/civichealth.pdf; Jan Teorell, "Linking Social Capital to Political Participation: Voluntary Associations and Networks of Recruitment in Sweden," *Scandinavian Political Studies* 26, no. 1 (2003): 49–66, available at https://doi.org/10.1111/1467-9477.00079.

8. Doug McAdam, *Freedom Summer* (Oxford University Press, 1990); Doug McAdam and Cynthia Brandt, "Assessing the Effects of Voluntary Youth Service: The Case of Teach For America," *Social Forces* 88, no. 2 (December 1, 2009): 945–969, available at https://doi.org/10.1353/sof.0.0279; Ellen Quintelier, "Who Is Politically Active: The Athlete, the Scout Member or the Environmental Activist? Young People, Voluntary Engagement and Political Participation," *Acta Sociologica* 51, no. 4 (December 1, 2008): 355–370, available at https://doi.org/10.1177/0001699308097378.

9. Kira Sanbonmatsu and Susan J. Carroll, "Poised to Run: Women's Pathways to the State Legislatures" (Rutgers, NJ: Center for American Women and Politics, Eagleton Institute of Politics, Rutgers University, 2009); Edmond Costantini, "Political Women and Political Ambition: Closing the Gender Gap," *American Journal of Political Science* (1990): 741–770.

10. Kira Sanbonmatsu, *Where Women Run: Gender and Party in the American States* (Ann Arbor: University of Michigan Press, 2006).

11. Shirley Rombough and Diane C. Keithly, "Women in Politics: An Analysis of Personal Characteristics Leading to Success in Gaining Local Elective Office," *Race, Gender and Class* 17, nos. 3–4 (2010): 173–188.

12. Lynne A. Weikart, Greg Chen, Daniel W. Williams, and Haris Hromic, "The Democratic Sex: Gender Differences and the Exercise of Power," *Journal of Women, Politics, and Policy* 28, no. 1 (2007): 119–140; Mirya R. Holman, *Women in Politics in the American City* (Philadelphia: Temple University Press, 2015).

13. Monica C. Schneider, Mirya R. Holman, Amanda B. Diekman, and Thomas McAndrew, "Power, Conflict, and Community: How Gendered Views of Political Power Influence Women's Political Ambition," *Political Psychology* 37, no. 4 (2016): 515–531.

14. Teach For America, "The Alumni Network," 2018, accessed March 1, 2019, available at https://www.teachforamerica.org/life-as-an-alum/the-tfa-alumni-network.

15. Bryce Covert, "Teaching Matters: Why It May Put More Women into Public Office," *Forbes*, July 2012, accessed March 1, 2019, available at https://www.forbes.com/sites/brycecovert/2012/07/26/could-teachers-be-a-secret-weapon-in-closing-congresss-gender-gap/#1acbe5265d7e.

16. More information, accessed February 1, 2018, available at https://www.teachfo ramerica.org/alumni/community/alumni-survey-snapshot; "AmeriCorps Alumni Outcomes," AmeriCorps, Corporation for National and Community Service, August 2016, accessed March 1, 2019, available at https://www.nationalservice.gov/sites/default/files/evidenceexchange/FR_AmeriCorpsAlumniOutcomesFinalTechReport.pdf; "Make the Most of Your World: 2019 Factsheet," Peace Corps, accessed March 1, 2019, available at https://files.peacecorps.gov/multimedia/pdf/about/pc_facts.pdf.

17. Eric Westervelt and Anya Kamenetz, "Teach For America at 25: With Maturity, New Pressure to Change," December 1, 2014, NPR, accessed March 1, 2019, available at https://www.npr.org/sections/ed/2014/12/01/366343324/teach-for-america-at-25-with-maturity-new-pressure-to-change.

18. Molly Ness, *Lessons to Learn: Voices from the Front Lines of Teach For America* (Routledge, 2013).

19. Teach For America, "The Challenge," 2018, accessed March 1, 2019, available at https://www.teachforamerica.org/what-we-do/the-challenge.

20. Donna Foote, "Two Teach For America Recruits Share Their Stories," *US News and World Report*, April 11, 2008.

21. Available at educationalequity.org.

22. TFA's current CEO and former CEO are female, its founder is a woman, its chief operating and program officer is female, and the chair of TFA's national board of directors is female.

23. Richard L. Fox and Zoe M. Oxley, "Gender Stereotyping State Executive Elections: Candidate Selection and Success," *Journal of Politics* 65, no. 3 (2003): 833–850.

24. David E. Campbell and Christina Wolbrecht, "See Jane Run: Women Politicians as Role Models for Adolescents," *Journal of Politics* 68, no. 2 (2006): 233–247.

25. More details on our data, estimation strategy, response rates, and measures can be found in the archived in *Politics, Groups, and Identities*, available at https://www.tandf online.com/doi/suppl/10.1080/21565503.2019.1630288/suppl_file/rpgi_a_1630288_sm8 559.pdf.

26. Sidney Verba, Kay Lehman Schlozman, and Henry E. Brady, *Voice and Equality: Civic Voluntarism in American Politics* (Cambridge, MA: Harvard University Press, 1995).

27. Nicholas Carnes, *The Cash Ceiling: Why Only the Rich Run for Office—and What We Can Do about It* (Princeton, NJ: Princeton University Press, 2018).

28. Rachel Silbermann, "Gender Roles, Work-Life Balance, and Running for Office," *Quarterly Journal of Political Science* 10, no. 2 (2015): 123–153; Sarah A. Fulton, Cherie D. Maestas, L. Sandy Maisel, and Walter J. Stone, "The Sense of a Woman: Gender, Ambition, and the Decision to Run for Congress," *Political Research Quarterly* 59, no. 2 (2006): 235–248.

29. Doug McAdam, "Recruitment to High-Risk Activism: The Case of Freedom Summer," *American Journal of Sociology* 92 (1986): 64–90.

30. The "p.p." in the figures stand for percentage points.

31. Richard L. Fox and Jennifer L. Lawless, "Gaining and Losing Interest in Running for Public Office: The Concept of Dynamic Political Ambition," *Journal of Politics* 73, no. 2 (2011): 443–462.

32. Note that all reported effects are statistically meaningful at all standard levels of statistical significance. The precise estimates and statistical significance are reported in the online appendix, archived *Politics, Groups, and Identities*, available at https://www.tandf online.com/doi/suppl/10.1080/21565503.2019.1630288/suppl_file/rpgi_a_1630288_sm 8559.pdf.

33. Doug McAdam, "Gender as a Mediator of the Activist Experience: The Case of Freedom Summer," *American Journal of Sociology* 97, no. 5 (March 1, 1992): 1211–1240, available at https://doi.org/10.1086/229900.

34. Nicholas Carnes, *The Cash Ceiling: Why Only the Rich Run for Office—and What We Can Do about It* (Princeton, NJ: Princeton University Press, 2018).

35. Cecilia Hyunjung Mo and Katharine M. Conn, "When Do the Advantaged See the Disadvantages of Others? A Quasi-Experimental Study of National Service," *American Political Science Review* 112, no. 4 (November 2018): 721–741, available at https://doi.org/10.1017/S0003055418000412.

PART III

Why Not Run?

I n the previous part, the chapters examined some good reasons that women want to run for office. This part looks at the flip side—what structural and institutional factors might make women rationally not as interested in being candidates? We argue (here and elsewhere) that political activity is the result of a rational costs-versus-rewards comparison (even if such a calculus is not fully conscious).[1]

Running for political office involves interest: an individual must want to serve in political office, to spend resources and time in the course of campaigning, and to endure an invasion of privacy, not just of oneself but of one's family and friends.[2] It is thus quite rational that many people would see political office as unappealing. At the same time, what makes the office unappealing may be, in itself, gendered. That is, women may see some factors as far less of a barrier than men do, while other barriers that are inconsequential to men may be a major obstacle to women.[3] As a result, women may look at the same opportunity and context as men yet come to a different decision about whether to throw their hat into the ring.

While Part I examined which women run, with an eye to the individual-level characteristics that might deter running, Part III asks whether environmental and institutional factors might play an important role in suppressing women's political ambitions. After all, if women's ambition is relational and contextual,[4] we might expect women to be much more sensitive to the political environment around them and how that environment impacts her and her family. Earlier research, for instance, finds that women are much less likely to run when they live further away from the state capitol, while men are unaffected by the distance that they must travel to serve in office.[5] Newly elected congresswomen have further pointed to the gendered nature of political service. For example, Senator Tammie Duckworth recently had a baby, but Senate rules forbid her from bringing her child to the floor, even when she needed to be there for a vote; a subsequent rule change highlighted the unique experiences of being a new mother in politics.[6] Or, Katie Porter, a new congresswoman from California has noted the challenges associated with being a single mother who now lives more than 2,000 miles from her home district. Representative Porter stated, "Congress wasn't built for members like me. . . . There is no template for how to do this in my situation as a single mom."[7] The chapters in this part pursue this logic, offering good (as in evidence-based) reasons why women, or certain subgroups of women, might be deterred from candidacy by factors not under their control.

Chapter 8, "The Uneven Geography of Candidate Emergence: How the Expectation of Winning Influences Candidate Emergence," by Ondercin, starts this part with a discussion of the role of political geography in women's ambition. Although Tip O'Neill famously told us decades ago that "all politics is local," scholars have not always taken seriously geographic differences as a variable of interest, particularly in thinking about political ambition.[8] Ondercin finds that the proportion of women running in—and winning—elections varies dramatically across states, and that this variation can be best explained by women's strategic choices to run when they are in "women-friendly" districts, which are more diverse, not just more liberal. However, she finds that Democratic women are more likely to make such strategic choices than Republican women, all else being equal.

In Chapter 9, "How Political Parties Can Diversify Their Leadership," Gimenez Aldridge, Karpowitz, Monson, and Preece shine a light on a different aspect of candidacy decisions: the role of party gatekeepers, which has only begun to be examined by other scholars.[9] In this study, Gimenez Aldridge et al. consider the effects of encouragement—and its lack—on whether women are likely to step forward into political positions (in this case, party leadership). If women (even those who are well qualified) need more encouragement than men, then party chairs have a special role to play in recruiting and supporting women. The authors find that the lack of such support amounts to another deterrent. Women were much more likely to run when explicitly recruited by caucus leaders than when no effort at recruitment was made. This suggests that parties might be able to quickly and substantially increase the number of women in politics simply by changing internal party procedures.

In Chapter 10, "Late to the Party: Black Women's Inconsistent Support from Political Parties," Brown and Dowe also consider political parties, but turn their attention to a specific subgroup of would-be candidates, Black women, who run at much lower rates than other subgroups of women despite being among the most politically engaged citizens.[10] Black women, they find through elite interviews conducted between 2014 and 2016, typically do not enjoy the support of either major political party. There are, however, non-profit training and support organizations that the authors have found to be supportive of Black female candidates, and they urge such potential candidates to use these as resources while also expressing hope that parties will become more supportive as well.

Concluding this part, Chapter 11, "Women's Political Ambition and the 2016 Election," by Bonneau and Kanthak, examines the immediate impact of the 2016 election on women's political ambition. Although eventually a record number of women came forward as candidates for the 2018 elections, Bonneau and Kanthak find evidence that Hillary Clinton's loss in the 2016 presidential contest *decreased* rather than increased women's political ambition (and the ambition of the men who voted for Clinton). They offer an intriguing analysis to explain why more female candidates emerged, despite the lower levels of political ambition they document; women and men, they suggest, run for office for different reasons. The women running in 2018 seem to be running not out of innate ambition for office but out of anger or policy-oriented concerns. General ambition to run, especially right after Clinton's loss, showed a marked and fascinating decrease.

These chapters provide a clear and broad view of the rationality of *not* running for office. Through the lens of women's reluctance to put themselves forward, we can identify some key problems in our political system more generally. Uneven political geography, strategic behavior by political leaders, the dominance of a two-party system designed to favor White candidates, and negativity and sexism in the media are features—not bugs—of the American political context. We thus argue that it is essential to accept the rationality of the noncandidacy of women in such settings rather than depicting women as the more politically timid or fearful sex. When we fail to account for these real environmental and institutional constraints on women's candidacies, we run the risk of labeling the problems as women's failings instead of systemic issues that require intervention from policy-makers and parties to address. In turn, this shifts resources and attention away from relatively "cheap" important changes, like recruiting women through caucuses, and toward costly and informal interventions like nonprofit recruitment.

NOTES

1. Shauna L. Shames, *Out of the Running: Why Millennials Reject Political Careers and Why It Matters* (New York: New York University Press, 2017).

2. Edmond Costantini, "Political Women and Political Ambition: Closing the Gender Gap," *American Journal of Political Science* 34, no. 3 (1990): 741–770; Malliga Och and Shauna L. Shames, eds., *The Right Women: Republican Party Activists, Candidates, and Legislators* (Santa Barbara, CA: Praeger, 2018); Shauna L. Shames, "American Women of Color and Rational Non-Candidacy: When Silent Citizenship Makes Politics Look Like Old White Men Shouting," *Citizenship Studies* 19, no. 5 (July 4, 2015): 553–569.

3. Jill S. Greenlee, Mirya R. Holman, and Rachel VanSickle-Ward, "Making It Personal: Assessing the Impact of In-Class Exercises on Closing the Gender Gap in Political Ambition," *Journal of Political Science Education* 10, no. 1 (2014): 48–61; Jennie Sweet-Cushman, "Where Does the Pipeline Get Leaky? The Progressive Ambition of School Board Members and Personal and Political Network Recruitment," *Politics, Groups, and Identities* (2018): 1–24; Jason Windett, "Differing Paths to the Top: Gender, Ambition, and Running for Governor," *Journal of Women, Politics, and Policy* 35, no. 4 (October 2, 2014): 287–314, available at https://doi.org/10.1080/1554477X.2014.955403.

4. Susan J. Carroll and Kira Sanbonmatsu, *More Women Can Run: Gender and Pathways to the State Legislatures* (New York: Oxford University Press, 2013).

5. Rachel Silbermann, "Gender Roles, Work-Life Balance, and Running for Office," *Quarterly Journal of Political Science* 10, no. 2 (2015): 123–153.

6. Susan Serfaty, "Babies Now Allowed on Senate Floor after Rare Rule Change—CNNPolitics," CNN, April 18, 2018, accessed November 20, 2019, available at https://www.cnn.com/2018/04/18/politics/tammy-duckworth-senate-baby-rules/index.html.

7. Rachael Bade, "Congress Wasn't Built for Members Like Me," *POLITICO*, November 26, 2018, accessed November 20, 2019, available at https://www.politico.com/story/2018/11/26/congress-new-members-women-1014696.

8. Silbermann, "Gender Roles, Work-Life Balance, and Running for Office."

9. Melody Crowder-Meyer, "Gendered Recruitment without Trying: How Local Party Recruiters Affect Women's Representation," *Politics and Gender* 9, no. 4 (2013): 390–413; Yann P. Kerevel, "(Sub)National Principals, Legislative Agents: Patronage and Political Careers in Mexico," *Comparative Political Studies* 48, no. 8 (July 1, 2015): 1020–1050.

10. Nadia E. Brown, *Sisters in the Statehouse: Black Women and Legislative Decision Making* (New York: Oxford University Press, 2014); Mirya R. Holman, "The Differential Effect of Resources on Political Participation across Gender and Racial Groups," in *Distinct Identities: Minority Women in U.S. Politics*, ed. Nadia E. Brown and Sarah A. Gershon (New York: Routledge, 2016); Emily M. Farris and Mirya R. Holman, "Social Capital and Solving the Puzzle of Black Women's Political Participation," *Politics, Groups, and Identities* 2, no. 3 (July 3, 2014): 331–349.

8

The Uneven Geography of Candidate Emergence

*How the Expectation of Winning
Influences Candidate Emergence*

HEATHER L. ONDERCIN

W hen deciding to run for office, female candidates ask themselves a variety of questions that influence their decision to run. Am I qualified? What effect will this decision have on my career and family? Can I raise enough money? Are there organizations that can help me? In this chapter, I argue that female candidates also ask themselves how likely they are to win the election. The answer to this question fundamentally shapes the probability that women will emerge as candidates. I demonstrate that female candidates act strategically and are more likely to emerge as candidates in races where they are more likely to succeed. To advance the number of women in elected office, we need to consider the varied terrain that female candidates face and how the variation in the likelihood of winning shapes the decision to run.

Reflecting on the early electoral opportunities of women, Diane Kincaid commented that "statistically at least, for women aspiring to serve in Congress, the best husband has been a dead husband, most preferably one serving in Congress at the time of his demise."[1] Political ambition is still influenced by family situation (although in a less morbid fashion) (see Bernhard, Shames, Silbermann and Teele, in this volume). But most studies of political ambition focus on individual characteristics of potential candidates. In Chapter 1, O'Connor and Yanus find that women are less interested in running for office and view themselves as less qualified for elected office.

The editors of this volume challenged us to think about women's candidacies and political ambitions as contingent, malleable, and relationally embedded. I argue that we need to look beyond the individual and examine how the geographic location affects the expression of political ambition. By examining where women candidates are likely to win, we can understand how context can help shape the expression of political ambition. Moreover, we are able to identify the conditions most likely to lead to advancing the number of women in elected office. This information can help female candidates make calculated decisions about where and when to run for elected office. Additionally, political organizations and parties can use this information in developing both short-term and long-term strategies for advancing women in elected office.

Political scientists argue that when deciding to run for elected office, potential candidates think about the costs and the potential benefits. Potential candidates use simple cost-benefit analysis and are more likely to decide in favor of running when the benefits outweigh the costs. When potential candidates engage in these calculations, political scientists refer to this as strategic behavior.[2] Potential candidates who identify electoral opportunities where they have a higher probability of winning are, therefore, more likely to obtain the benefits of office and pay lower costs. Thus, Gertzog postulates that candidates are "calculating and rational. The chances of securing their party's nomination are carefully considered, and entry into a race is based on the likelihood of success."[3]

The likelihood of winning either the primary or the general election varies considerably across different geographic locations in the United States. Figure 8.1 depicts the probability of a female candidate winning her party's nomination in 2014 by congressional district. Darker colors on the figure represent a higher probability of winning the primary election, and lighter colors indicate a lower probability of winning the primary election. The uneven geography of success for female candidates in primary elections is apparent in top image of Figure 8.1. Women are much more likely to secure their party's nomination in congressional districts in the Northeast and the West Coast. Women have the lowest probability of securing their party's nomination in the Southern part of the United States. There is also considerable variation within states. For example, significant variation exists across districts within the state of Florida. Women have a low probability of winning the primary election in the northern part of the state. In the Fourth Congressional District that contains Jacksonville, women have a probability of only 0.10 for winning the primary election. Women experience a much higher probability of winning the primary election in the southern part of Florida. For example, female candidates have a probability of 0.53 for securing their party's nomination in the 23rd Congressional District, containing Weston.

We see similar uneven geography when it comes to women winning the general election. The bottom image of Figure 8.1 reports the probability of a woman winning the general election across congressional districts in 2014. Overall, the probability of women winning the general election is lower than the probability of women winning the party's nomination. Similar to the primary elections, women are more likely to win the general election on the West

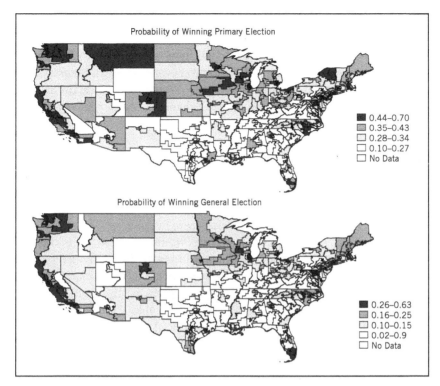

Figure 8.1. Probability of a woman candidate winning the primary election and general elections in 2014 by congressional district.

Coast and in the Northeast, with the lowest probability of winning found in the Southeast. There is also considerable variation in the probability of a woman winning within states. Even though it is located in the Northeast, the state of Pennsylvania has historically elected very few women to Congress. One reason this may be the case is that women do not have a high chance of winning the general election. Women have only a 0.08 probability of winning the general election in the 9th (Altoona) and 10th (Williamsport) Congressional Districts. However, the chances of a woman winning increases if we move east in the state to the 13th Congressional District, which includes parts of Philadelphia, where women have a 0.36 probability of winning the general election.

The chances of women winning either the primary or the general election, therefore, vary considerably across the United States and within states. Districts where women have a lower chance of winning represent the districts that are going to be costlier for women to run in. Additionally, the lower likelihood of winning indicates that there is a lower probability that a woman will receive the benefits from running for elected office. In contrast, districts where women have a higher probability of winning, represent contests with lower costs and a higher likelihood of receiving the benefits associated with winning.

How does the chance of winning the primary and general elections influence the likelihood that women emerge as candidates? I argue that women minimize the higher perceived and actual costs associated with being a female candidate by behaving strategically and choosing to run in congressional districts where they are more likely to win elected office. Certain district characteristics appear to increase women's chances of running and winning elections.[4] These "women-friendly districts" tend to be located outside the South, are smaller in geographic size and more urban, have higher relative incomes and a lower percentage of residents occupied in blue-collar jobs, and have a higher percentage of each of the following: foreign-born residents, college-educated residents, Black residents, and Hispanic residents. While many of these district characteristics also favor Democratic candidates, Palmer and Simon find that these features also help explain where Republican women run and win.[5] In addition to district characteristics, women are also more likely to emerge in open seat races, which, despite the increased competition, represent the best opportunity for a nonincumbent to win elected office.[6] Strategic behavior by female candidates in choosing where and when to run should be associated with women emerging as candidates in winnable, less costly races and contribute to a decline in women's status as sacrificial lambs in electoral politics.

Parties fundamentally structure the electoral opportunities of candidates. Female candidates particularly feel the influence of parties. The eligibility pool of potential female candidates varies based on sex, with Republicans having a considerably smaller pool than Democrats.[7] The parties shape the pathways to elected office, and Democratic and Republican women respond to the polarized electoral context differently.[8] Further, some scholars suggest that the relatively small number of female Republicans in elected office is due to a lack of strategic behavior on their part.[9] Consistent with this, Stambough and O'Regan find that the Republican Party is more likely to nominate women in governor races that are unwinnable.[10] The cumulative effect of these processes is that most female candidates and elected officials are members of the Democratic Party.[11] Due to the ways party and candidate sex interact in electoral politics, it is important to examine the behavior of female Democratic and female Republican candidates separately.

I assess the argument that potential female candidates behave strategically in where they run for office using a two-stage probit model.[12] The first stage of the model estimates the probability of a female candidate winning the primary and the general elections in a given district. The second stage uses the linear expectation of a female candidate winning an election from the first stage to estimate the likelihood of a female candidate emerging in a given district. I examine all congressional elections between 1992 and 2014 in this analysis. Details about the model specification and results tables are in the online appendix.[13] Here, I report my main findings using a series of graphs.

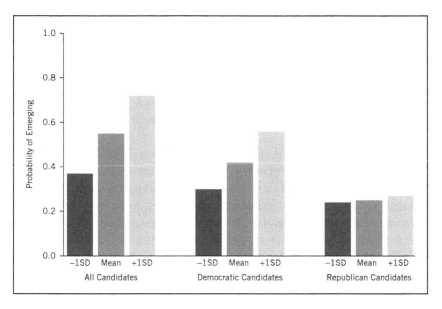

Figure 8.2. Probability of a woman candidate emerging given the likelihood of winning the primary election. Note: A standard deviation (SD) is a measure of how closely clustered data are around the mean: 34.1 percent of observations are found one standard deviation on each side of the mean.

Figure 8.2 reports the probability of a female candidate emerging at the mean and one standard deviation above and below the mean of the linear expectation of a woman winning a primary for all candidates, female Democratic candidates, and female Republican candidates. The mean represents districts with the average chance of a female candidate winning the primary. A standard deviation is a measure of how closely other districts are clustered around the mean and provide a useful way to make standardized comparisons across the different analyses. Roughly 68 percent of all observations in the data set are located in one standard deviation above or below the mean. Consistent with my argument, female candidates, especially Democratic women, demonstrate strategic behavior by emerging in races where they are more likely to win. The expectation of women winning the primary is a positive and significant predictor of a female candidate emerging in a congressional district. In districts with the average probability of a woman winning the primary, there is a 0.55 chance that a woman will emerge as a candidate. In districts one standard deviation below the mean, the probability of a female candidate emerging drops to 0.37. In districts where the chance of winning the primary is one standard deviation above the mean, the probability of a woman emerging increases to 0.72.

The probability of a Democratic woman emerging in the primary is also positive and significantly related to the expectation of a Democratic woman winning the primary election. At one standard deviation below the mean expectation of a Democratic woman winning the primary, the likelihood of a Democratic woman emerging is 0.30. Moving to districts where the expectation of winning the primary is one standard deviation above the mean expectation of winning the primary, the probability of a female Democrat emerging as a candidate increases to 0.56. The expectation of winning the primary election does not have a significant influence on Republican women emerging as candidates.

Figure 8.3 illustrates the effect of the expectation of winning the general election on the probability of emerging in the primary election for all female candidates, Democratic candidates, and Republican candidates. As expected, the likelihood of a female candidate emerging in the primary election increases as the probability of winning the general election increases. The increases in the likelihood of emerging are not as large as the relationship between emerging and success in the primary election. The probability of a female candidate emerging increases from 0.63 in districts where the expectation of winning the general is one standard deviation below the mean to 0.76 in districts where the expectation of winning the general election is one standard deviation above the mean. Across all congressional districts, then, there is consistent evidence that female candidates behave strategically by entering races where they are most likely to win.

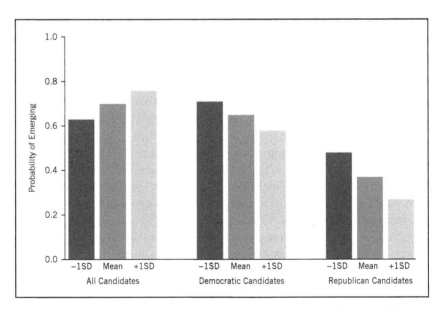

Figure 8.3. Probability of a woman candidate emerging given the likelihood of winning the general election. Note: A standard deviation (SD) is a measure of how closely clustered data are around the mean: 34.1 percent of observations are found one standard deviation on each side of the mean.

Figure 8.3 also includes the relationships between a female Democrat emerging in the primary election given the expectation of a Democratic woman winning the general and the relationship between a female Republican emerging in the primary given the expectation of a Republican woman winning the general election. Surprisingly, Democratic and Republican women are less likely to emerge in congressional districts where their chances of winning are higher. Instead, there is a negative relationship, with Democratic and Republican women being less likely to emerge in districts where they have higher chances of winning.

Discussion and Conclusion

Female candidates face an uneven terrain when running for elected office in the United States. In some locations, female candidates encounter level ground in their pursuit of elected office. For a woman with political ambition, the likelihood that you act on those ambitions and run for elected office are constrained by where you live. Conditions in some districts make it more likely that women will win elected office, and, as a result, female candidates are more likely to emerge. In other locations, female candidates encounter uneven ground, or even mountains they must scale, to be successful in running for elected office. Here, female candidates are less likely to win elected office and are thus less likely to emerge as candidates for elected office.

Despite a record number of women emerging as candidates and winning in the 2018 midterm elections, women still must act strategically about when and where to emerge as candidates. Democratic women were so successful in 2018 because they chose to run in places where they were likely to win. Compared to the success of Democratic women in 2018, Republican women had fewer opportunities to emerge in districts where they are likely to win. The 2018 midterms serve to illustrate how female candidates face uneven opportunities and how those opportunities are enhanced or limited by political party.

What can a politically ambitious woman do with this information? One thing is that women could move locations to find the best electoral chances. Being a carpetbagger may be viewed negatively but may be the strategic thing to do for women with political ambition. Notably, Hillary Clinton and Elizabeth Dole made calculated moves to New York and North Carolina, respectively, in their runs for the Senate. Women who have the desire to run for elected office and have the ability to move should pay careful attention to how smooth the roads are in different locations.

Female candidates act strategically at the first stage of the election process by emerging in primary elections where they are most likely to secure the party's nomination. This behavior will increase women candidates' chances of advancing to the general election. Analysis of the general elections suggest that women do not act as strategically at this stage. Democratic and Republican women are more likely to emerge in races where their chances of winning the general election are lower. These findings illustrate that the process of increasing women in elected office is not straightforward. Rather, we have to consider how both stages of the electoral process shape female candidates' behavior.

This finding may be particularly discouraging to potential candidates, parties, and organizations attempting to increase the number of women in elected office. Increasing the number of women in elected office is not just about getting more women to run but also about identifying the places where female candidates will be successful in both the primary and the general election. In the short term, parties and organizations working to increase women's representation should focus their energies and resources in the locations where women can be the most successful. In the long term, these groups should identify the places where the narrow canyons women are now navigating can be widened and offer more opportunity.

Party recruitment plays an essential role in encouraging candidates to run for elected office.[14] Recruitment may be even more critical to the decision to run for elected office for women than for men.[15] We should expect parties also to act strategically, recruiting candidates in locations where they are most likely to win. Strategic party behavior, therefore, would reinforce the patterns identified above for female candidates. However, as Crowder-Meyer finds that the sex of the party recruiters and the networks they use influence the likelihood of recruiting women candidates.[16] Given the pivotal role that recruitment plays, academics and organizations who desire to increase women's representation should work with parties to help them identify locations where they can win elections and increase women's representation and integration into existing political networks.

Further work is needed to understand more about what makes a congressional district receptive or hostile toward women. In this project, I have used the demographic characteristics of a district. Palmer and Simon originally identified these "women friendly" features based on where women have been successful in the past.[17] But there could be many more factors that increase the openness of a district to women candidates. Academics and practitioners need to work together to more clearly identify these features. Because once we have a better understanding of these obstacles, we may be able to change them, opening up greater opportunities for women to run for office.

NOTES

1. Diane Kincaid, "Over His Dead Body: A Positive Perspective on Widows in the U.S. Congress," *Western Political Quarterly* 31, no. 1 (1978): 96–104, 98.

2. David W. Rohde, "Risk-Bearing and Progressive Ambition: The Case of Members of the United States House of Representatives," *American Journal of Political Science* 23, no. 1 (1979): 1–26; Jeffrey Lazarus, "Buying In: Testing the Rational Model of Candidate

Entry," *Journal of Politics* 70, no. 3 (2008): 837–850; Walter J. Stone and L. Sandy Maisel, "The Not-So-Simple Calculus of Winning: Potential US House Candidates Nomination and General Election Prospects," *Journal of Politics* 65, no. 4 (2003): 951–977.

3. Irwin Gertzog, "Women's Changing Pathways to the U.S. House of Representatives: Widows, Elites, and Strategic Politicians," in *Women Transforming Congress*, ed. Cindy Rimon Rosenthal (Norman: University of Oklahoma Press, 2002), 95–118, 103.

4. Heather L. Ondercin and Susan Welch, "Comparing Predictors of Women's Congressional Election Success: Candidates, Primaries, and the General Election," *American Politics Research* 37, no. 4 (2009): 593–613; Barbara Palmer and Dennis Simon, *Breaking the Political Glass Ceiling: Women and Congressional Elections* (New York: Routledge, 2008).

5. Palmer and Simon, *Breaking the Political Glass Ceiling*.

6. Ondercin and Welch, "Comparing Predictors"; Tiffany D. Barnes, Regina P. Branton, and Erin C. Cassese, "A Reexamination of Women's Electoral Success in Open Seat Elections: The Conditioning Elect of Electoral Competition," *Journal of Women, Politics, and Policy* 38, no. 3 (2016): 1–20.

7. Melody Crowder-Meyer and Benjamin Lauderdale, "A Partisan Gap in the Supply of Female Potential Candidates in the United States," *Research and Politics* 1, no. 1 (2014): 1–7.

8. Kira Sanbonmatsu, *Where Women Run: Gender and Party in the American States* (Ann Arbor: University of Michigan Press, 2010); Danielle M. Thomsen, "Why So Few (Republican) Women? Explaining the Partisan Imbalance of Women in the US Congress," *Legislative Studies Quarterly* 40, no. 2 (2015): 295–323.

9. Barbara Burrell, *Gender in Campaigns for the U.S. House of Representatives* (Ann Arbor: University of Michigan Press, 2014).

10. Stephen J. Stambough and Valerie R. O'Regan, "Republican Lambs and the Democratic Pipeline: Partisan Differences in the Nomination of Female Gubernatorial Candidates," *Gender and Politics* 3, no. 3 (2007): 349–386.

11. Sanbonmatsu, *Where Women Run*; Kira Sanbonmatsu, "Political Parties and the Recruitment of Women to State Legislatures," *Journal of Politics* 64, no. 3 (2002): 791–809; Kira Sanbonmatsu, *Democrats, Republicans and the Politics of Women's Place* (Ann Arbor: University of Michigan Press, 2003).

12. Giacomo Chiozza and Hein E. Goemans, "Peace through Insecurity Tenure and International Conflict," *Journal of Conflict Resolution* 47, no. 4 (2003): 443–467.

13. The online appendix can be found through the Harvard Dataverse, available at https://doi.org/10.7910/DVN/BJTB1W.

14. Daniel M. Butler and Jessica Robinson Preece, "Recruitment and Perceptions of Gender Bias in Party Leader Support," *Political Research Quarterly* 69, no. 4 (2016): 842–851; Melody Crowder-Meyer, "Gendered Recruitment without Trying: How Local Party Recruiters Affect Women's Representation," *Politics and Gender* 9, no. 4 (2013): 390–413.

15. Richard L. Fox and Jennifer L. Lawless, "Entering the Arena? Gender and the Decision to Run for Office," *American Journal of Political Science* 48, no. 2 (2004): 264–280.

16. Crowder-Meyer, "Gendered Recruitment without Trying."

17. Palmer and Simon, *Breaking the Political Glass Ceiling*.

9

How Political Parties Can Diversify Their Leadership

ALEJANDRA GIMENEZ ALDRIDGE, CHRISTOPHER F. KARPOWITZ,
J. QUIN MONSON, AND JESSICA ROBINSON PREECE

Party leaders across the United States have vastly different perspectives about what constitutes appropriate action to increase female representation and whether these actions are even needed. The individuals below all serve as precinct chairs in a Republican Party caucus system in the same conservative state. They were asked by the state party chair to participate in an initiative to increase women's representation in local party leadership. However, their views on increasing women's representation and opinions about their authority to do so vary widely.

These local party officials are not an anomaly. This chapter takes an in-depth look at what happens when party leaders encourage more women to run for party leadership positions. We find that when state party leaders ask precinct chairs to recruit women to run for higher offices, precinct chairs generally comply with this request. They often do so by recruiting women from an existing pool of people active in the local party organization. Specifically, they tend to target women serving as party precinct secretaries or treasurers—offices in which women are overrepresented. These women generally respond quite well to recruitment. We found a significant increase in the number of women in party leadership positions in the precincts targeted for the recruitment intervention.

The implication of our findings is that the easiest way for parties to increase women's leadership is to identify women who are already engaged in party service and encourage them to shift their contributions toward party leadership. Chapter 6 by Deen and Shelton also probes this connection between being in a service position and running for office. They find that civic service builds skills and knowledge in candidates and that the connection is

John* is a 66-year-old in his second term as precinct chair for his neighborhood Republican Party. When asked by the state Republican Party chair to personally recruit a few women to run for local precinct offices, he supported the idea and worked to comply with the request. Looking back on it, he said, "I met with the [precinct] cochair [and] we discussed contacting each household. He has much more free time so he called each household and either talked to them or left a message."

Ann is a 58-year-old in her third term as a precinct chair for her neighborhood Republican Party. When asked by the state Republican Party chair to read a paragraph to caucus meeting attendees encouraging women to run for party leadership positions, she declined to do so. She said, "I didn't feel right about using my position of authority to influence the nominations."

Edward is a 40-year-old three-time precinct chair for his neighborhood Republican Party. When asked by the state Republican Party chair to personally recruit a few women to run for local precinct office, he declined to do so. He elaborated: "It is not a problem and it is not my place. We want the most qualified, not just those who are a particular gender. Gender has nothing to do with being qualified to run to be a delegate or officer."

Mark is a 51-year-old in his first term as a precinct chair for his neighborhood Republican Party. When asked by the state Republican Party chair to read a paragraph to caucus meeting attendees encouraging women to run for party leadership positions, he fulfilled the request. When asked why he recruited women, he remarked that he was "just trying to help the party keep some balance."

Eleanor is a 63-year-old serving for the second time as a precinct chair for her neighborhood Republican Party. When asked by the state Republican Party chair to read a paragraph to caucus meeting attendees encouraging women to run for party leadership positions, she fulfilled the request. She explained that one of the women she recruited to run as a state delegate "wanted to do something to get started by being involved at the neighborhood level."

* Names have been changed to protect privacy.

different for women and men. While Deen and Shelton show that service positions help to build skills and knowledge in candidates, Mo and Anderson-Nilsson (Chapter 7) show that youth service programs ignite political ambition in women who already possess many of the characteristics associated with political ambition. Both of these works complement our findings— service positions serve as natural pipelines into higher office. Together, our results suggest that when political party leaders recognize service-oriented experience as good preparation for officeholding, they will be more effective in identifying women to recruit.

The Setting and Context

In this chapter, we discuss the results of a successful attempt by a state Republican Party chair in a conservative state to diversify party leadership—specifically, the gender composition of the party's state nominating convention. We hope that this can serve as a blueprint for other party leaders who wish to bring more women into party leadership. While our data were collected from Republicans, it seems likely that a similar intervention among Democrats might also be successful, especially because there is broader ideological support for interventions to increase women's representation among Democrats. Further, we suspect—but cannot be sure—that the kinds of interventions we discuss in this chapter could also be used to increase women's representation in other types of political activity.

The conservative state that we studied has a caucus system that functions very similarly to the well-known Iowa presidential caucuses. Redlawsk, Tolbert, and Donovan[1] describe the Iowa caucuses as "lengthy local party meetings used to conduct party business and select delegates." Party caucus meetings provide a regular environment for people to interact and express their political opinions and voice their concerns. Smaller precincts may have as few as 10 people attending while some precincts have over 100 people in attendance.

Given the relatively small number of attendees, caucus proceedings tend to be fairly informal. Though the process varies slightly depending on the state and party, caucus meetings typically have a few similar elements: precinct informational reports and business, nominations for party offices, candidate speeches for those running for party offices, and then the voting. Nominations happen the night of the caucus, and many people decide to run on the spot. Attendees often prod their family members or friends at the meeting to run.

The most influential party office elected at the meetings we studied is delegate to the state party nominating convention ("state delegate"). A few weeks after the caucus meetings, state delegates from each precinct attend the state party convention to choose candidates for statewide and federal offices. Consequently, state delegates can be very influential if there is a competitive intraparty race. Further, because the state is overwhelmingly conservative, the Republican intraparty fight is often more important than the general election. In fact, longtime incumbents have been defeated at the nominating convention by delegate support for an intraparty challenger.

Because of their influence, statewide and federal candidates (or their staff) typically call delegates individually to answer policy questions and ask for their support in the weeks leading up to the party convention. Candidates hold dozens of delegate-only town hall meetings and conference calls, in addition to sending mailers and emails to delegates. On top of this, the party hosts several meet-and-greet events for delegates and candidates, and there is anecdotal evidence that once politicians are in office, they remain especially attentive to delegates' positions on issues.

Historically, although attendance at the neighborhood caucus meetings tends to be roughly equally divided between men and women, only 20–25 percent of the state delegates elected at those caucus meetings were women. This means that Republican candidates in the state have been selected by a pool of party activists who are overwhelmingly male. Hence, diversifying the composition of delegates to the state nominating convention could have a significant impact on important party decisions. It could also influence the public's perception of the legitimacy of convention decisions—in fact, bolstering public perceptions of the convention process was the party chair's primary motivation for trying to increase women's representation with the interventions described below.

The Intervention

The state party chair sent a signed letter to each precinct chair on party letterhead about a week before the 2014 caucus meetings.[2] The letter contained a basic reminder about the upcoming caucus night. In addition to receiving a reminder about the upcoming caucus night in the letter, a subset of precinct chairs was randomly assigned to receive an additional request to increase women's representation and participation at these meetings. Because some precinct chairs were given this additional statement and others were not, we can compare outcomes between the groups and measure the effect of the intervention. It may be helpful to think of this study design like a medical drug trial in which participants are randomly assigned to receive the drug being tested or a placebo sugar pill and then monitored to see the outcome in each group. Because the types of people in the treatment and control groups are, on average, otherwise similar to each other, any difference in the average outcome between the two groups can be attributed to the treatment. In other words, in a randomized controlled trial like this, we can isolate the impact of getting the intervention from party leaders versus not getting it.

In our study, we assigned one-quarter of the precincts to serve as a "Placebo," or control group. Their letter had the generic reminder about the upcoming caucus night but no further information. This group serves as the baseline in our analysis. It tells us what the world would look like without the intervention. (See Figure 9.1.)

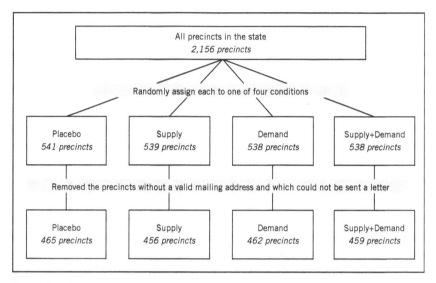

Figure 9.1. Flowchart of the study conditions.

The other three quarters of the precincts were randomly assigned to one of three possible messages. One version asked precinct chairs to recruit two to three women to run as state delegates. We call this the "Supply" intervention because it sought to increase the supply of women running. Another version asked precinct chairs to read a statement at the meeting that encouraged caucus attendees to elect more women as state delegates. We call this the "Demand" intervention because it sought to increase voter demand for women candidates. The final version asked precinct chairs to both recruit women *and* read the statement to caucus attendees. We call this the "Supply + Demand" intervention.

We worked closely with the state party leadership to draft the specific language for each letter. This was important because the language needed to authentically represent the views of the state party chair who was sending the letter. For example, at one point, we suggested some language that sounded too much like a formal quota to party leadership. It was important to them, and to us, that the request feel appropriate for an ideologically conservative party. In the end, the intervention letters included variations on the following statement: "One of the things that you, as precinct chair, can do to help is to foster an environment in which women feel comfortable running for positions as precinct leaders or delegates. The party needs good delegates—both women and men—who can bring the concerns or our families, neighborhoods, and communities to the state convention."

With about 2,000 total precincts in the state, there were over 500 precincts assigned to each condition. However, the party did not have updated contact information for some of the precinct chairs. In the end, 1,842 precinct chairs had working mailing addresses, so those were the precincts included in the study results.

Overall Results

After the caucus meetings, the party sent us the results of the elections from each meeting so we could determine whether the intervention had an effect on who was elected. There was a significant increase in the number of women who won a seat as a state delegate in the precincts that were assigned to the Supply + Demand intervention. In the Placebo precincts, only 37.5 percent of precincts elected any women at all to a state delegate position. In the Supply + Demand precincts, that number increased dramatically to 45.4 percent. Further, in the Placebo precincts, women comprised just under 24 percent of state delegates; that number rose to almost 30 percent in the Supply + Demand precincts. There were also notable increases in women's representation in the separate Supply + Demand precincts, though those increases were not statistically significant.[3] What is remarkable about these effects is that they are the result of a single letter from the state party chair. This modest effort had a significant impact on the composition of the state delegates. To illustrate the magnitude of the effect, we estimate that if all of the precincts had been assigned to the Placebo condition, about 920 of the 3,839 delegates (approximately 24 percent) would have been women; if all of the precincts had been assigned to the Supply + Demand condition, about 1,150 of the delegates (approximately 30 percent) would have been women. That would mean an additional 230 women participating in party leadership and developing the kinds of political knowledge, experience, and networks that often prepare and motivate individuals to run for other offices.

How Did Precinct Chairs Respond to the Intervention?

While the overall results show that there was a significant effect of the intervention, it is also important to understand how this result happened and what the reactions of local precinct chairs were. To explore this, we sent an online survey invitation to all precinct chairs less than two months after the caucus meetings. While the interventions were conducted through official party communications, this survey was conducted by us as third-party researchers.[4] We asked the precinct chairs a number of questions about their caucus experience and offered them a chance to provide feedback on the caucus system generally. Toward the end of the survey, we reminded them that a letter was sent to all precinct chairs by the state party chair and asked them to identify some items that were in this letter. If a precinct chair remembered one or both of the interventions being in the letter, then we asked them if they complied with the request, along with some follow-up questions.

Level of Cooperation with Recruitment Request

In total, 604 of the approximately 1,800 precinct chairs responded to the survey. Two-thirds of those precinct chairs remembered receiving a letter (400 out of the 604 respondents) from the state party. About half of those chairs recalled being asked to complete the relevant task. Although these numbers are fairly low, it is important to remember that the party only sent a single letter. It is likely that repeated messages from the party would have been more memorable.

For precinct chairs who remembered being asked to recruit women in the letter, we asked how many women they recruited. Of those assigned to the Supply or Supply + Demand interventions (both of which asked the precinct chair to recruit a few women to run for party leadership positions), 78 percent reported that they reached out to at least one woman: 16 percent of precinct chairs reported reaching out to only one woman, and 62 percent reached out to two or three women. This suggests that most precinct chairs were willing to comply with the request of the state party chair, even with just a single request.

What Reasons Did Some Precinct Chairs Give for Not Recruiting?

While most precinct chairs reached out to recruit women, there were some precinct chairs that said they read the letter and explicitly stated that they did not reach out. We asked precinct chairs in the Supply and Supply + Demand conditions, who were asked to recruit women but told us that they did not, why they did not reach out, and the results are presented in Table 9.1.

The most common answers were that the precinct chair felt electing enough women delegates is not a problem in their precinct (39 percent) and that the party should not be telling the precincts who to elect (29 percent). This is a reminder that not all local party leaders are receptive to party diversity initiatives. Still, the number of precinct chairs who were not willing to participate is lower than what one might expect, given that these were overwhelmingly conservative individuals.

Several respondents also selected the "Other" option and included comments. Though the comments in the "Other" section varied, they reflected the general sentiment that extra efforts based solely on gender were not needed and that it was not appropriate to recruit more women. For example, one precinct chair said, "Women are adults, if they want to run for an office they can step up and run without me holding their hand." Another precinct chair added, "It is not a problem, [nor] is it my place to do so. We want the most qualified, not just to fill a specific number of women." Another commented, "Simply because I don't believe that being a particular gender qualifies you to be a better precinct officer." But there were other kinds of objections. For

TABLE 9.1. WHY PRECINCT CHAIRS DID, AND DID NOT, REACH OUT TO WOMEN	
Reasons precinct chairs decided NOT TO reach out to women	
Electing enough women delegates is not a problem in my precinct	39%
I didn't want to because the party should not be telling us who to elect	29%
I didn't know of any women who would be interested and/or qualified	16%
I didn't plan on attending the caucus meeting	13%
Inviting other women to the caucuses is not my place	13%
I didn't have time	10%
I forgot	3%
Other	16%
N	31
Reasons precinct chairs decided TO reach out to the women they recruited **She is . . . (multiple responses allowed)**	
Actively involved in her neighborhood or community	68%
An active member of the party	65%
Someone who knows the issues well	59%
An acquaintance from church	46%
A skilled homemaker	31%
An active volunteer at a local school	31%
A leader in her local congregation	20%
An accomplished professional	17%
An acquaintance from work	1%
Other	17%
N	112

example, one person remarked, "Affirmative Action is interesting but I don't need to apply more guilt to more women to do more things."

These responses reflect an important, if not particularly common, viewpoint—some local party leaders do not think that party leadership should be involved in recruitment. They believe that candidates should self-select into the experience. From a practical perspective, though, it's important to keep in mind that this represents a minority viewpoint. The bottom line is that nearly 80 percent of Republican precinct chairs who were asked to do so followed the recommendation of the state party chair to recruit women to run.

Whom Did Precinct Chairs Recruit?

We asked precinct chairs who reported recruiting at least one woman about the reasons they chose to reach out to each woman they recruited. Their responses provide important insights into what local Republican Party leaders look for when seeking out potential candidates for party leadership positions after being asked to diversify party leadership. Table 9.1 (bottom) shows these results; party chairs could select multiple reasons.

Being involved in the party and the neighborhood or community were the most commonly selected answers. When thinking about the first woman they recruited, 65 percent of precinct chairs said the woman was an active member of the party, and 68 percent said she was active in the neighborhood or community. The next most common reason was being someone whom the precinct chair thought knew the issues well: 59 percent were considered to know the issues well. Precinct chairs are invested in the party and justifiably see investment in the party as an important prerequisite for party leadership.

Party chairs almost never recruited a woman because she was an acquaintance from work. Similarly, they recruited only 17 percent of women because they were an accomplished professional. This is likely because workplaces tend to draw from a larger geographic area than a neighborhood precinct. It could also be because workplaces remain quite sex segregated; most precinct chairs are men, and their professional interactions may mostly be with other men.

On the other hand, 46 percent of precinct chairs reached out to a woman because they were an acquaintance from church. This seems unusually high, but this state is heavily religious, making it possible that a precinct chair's most frequent interactions with women in the community come through a local church congregation. While the state does enjoy higher than average church involvement, this phenomenon may still be applicable to Republicans in other states. Nationally, Republicans (including those that lean toward the Republican Party) report higher levels of religiosity with 44 percent saying they attend services at least once a week versus 29 percent of Democrats. Furthermore, among Republicans, only 14 percent are religiously unaffiliated, or religious "nones," compared to 28 percent of Democrats.[5] Higher levels of religiosity and religious affiliation among Republicans means that Republicans have more opportunities to build connections through church networks. More research would be helpful for understanding how common political and religious networks overlap around the country, and how these networks work to benefit recruitment. Additional research could also address the non-religious networks Democrats tend to rely upon.

Interestingly, nearly a third of precinct chairs said they selected the first woman at least in part because she was a skilled homemaker. Further, nearly a third of precinct chairs selected the first woman because she was an active volunteer at a local school. These highly gendered qualifications suggest that precinct chairs often turn to "feminine spaces" to find women to serve in party leadership positions when asked to recruit women. Because existing political networks tend to be dominated by men, explicitly turning to feminine spaces to recruit women is a common suggestion in the academic literature for increasing women's representation.[6] Our data reinforce that this is an important and effective tactic. In other words, Mitt Romney's awkwardly phrased tactic of compiling "binders full of women" is, in fact, a best practice for recruiting candidates from underrepresented backgrounds. Those involved in recruitment should make a practice of explicitly considering those outside of their male-dominated professional and political networks.

How Did Women Respond to Recruitment?

How did the women who were recruited respond to these interventions? Specifically, did the rate at which women and men ran for state delegate positions change as a result of the intervention? In this section, we show that the gender composition of the elected party positions overall did not change much as a result of the interventions. However, the distribution of which offices women ran for changed dramatically because of the intervention. Thus, though the intervention did not fundamentally alter the mix of men and women standing for local party positions, it did result in fewer women running for behind-the-scenes service positions and more women running for more comparatively prestigious leadership positions.

Observing the Elections

To collect data on candidate behavior during the caucuses, we sent trained student observers to 130 precincts to take structured notes during the caucus meeting, including gathering information about each candidate. These precincts were approximately representative of the state as a whole.[7] To maximize accuracy and information collection, we sent two observers to each meeting. To avoid any biases in the note-taking process, the students did not know the purpose of the study; they were simply told we were interested in learning more about caucus proceedings generally.

In most precincts in this state, there are six party offices: precinct chair, precinct vice-chair, secretary, treasurer (sometimes combined into one position with the secretary), state delegate, and county delegate. While there is typically only one precinct chair, vice-chair, secretary, and treasurer per precinct, precincts may be allotted multiple delegate positions for state and/or county delegates, depending on the size of the precinct. The elections for each office normally proceed in the order the offices were mentioned above. If the order changes, it is often to elect the state delegates earlier, an indication of its relative importance.

The six precinct roles can be broken down into three categories: leadership, service, and consolation. The leadership positions are the precinct chair and state delegates. While the precinct chair is an obvious fit for the leadership category as the leader of the precinct, the state delegate position is also perceived as a leadership position because of its decision-making power at the state convention, as described above. The county delegate and the precinct vice-chair are generally seen as consolation offices. In fact, the county delegate position is usually decided *after* the state delegate position as a deliberate consolation for those who ran but did not win a seat as a state delegate. The vice-chair is seen as the other consolation office because it serves to support the precinct chair but has few specific duties of its own. Tellingly, in some precincts, the precinct chair is automatically given the option of also serving as a state delegate and the vice-chair is automatically given the option of also serving as a county delegate. Finally, the secretary and treasurer positions are the service positions. These party officers work hard behind the scenes to keep things moving. Responsibilities include keeping track of precinct finances, maintaining membership records, and organizing meetings. In smaller precincts, these two positions are often combined into one.

The Gender Balance among the Offices

In the 2012 caucuses (the cycle before the intervention we discuss in this chapter), women made up 33 percent of precinct officials across all offices. The bulk of the women were in service positions; 69 percent of all secretaries and 64 percent of all treasurers were female. On the other end of the spectrum, the leadership precinct offices tended to be male. Women made up just 23 percent of state delegates and 25 percent of precinct chairs statewide.

In the Placebo precincts in 2014, these patterns remained. Figure 9.2 shows the proportion of women running for office in both the Placebo and the Supply + Demand conditions. As previously explained, the precincts in the Placebo condition were not given any special instructions related to representation. This means that we can use them as a control group to see how things would have been if the intervention had not happened. We can compare outcomes in the Placebo precincts to outcomes in the intervention precincts to measure the impact of the intervention.

As Figure 9.2 shows, more than 80 percent of all candidates for secretary were women in the Placebo precincts. Only 21 percent of precinct chair candidates and 25 percent of state delegate candidates were women in the Placebo condition. In other words, the patterns from previous years remained in these precincts. However, the Supply + Demand condition had a dramatic effect on the offices that women ran for. Figure 9.2 shows that the proportion of candidates for the service positions—secretary and/or treasurer—significantly decreased from 81 percent in the Placebo precincts to 57 percent in Supply + Demand precincts. Where are these women going? Our data suggest that they ran for more prestigious offices. In particular, there was a 7 percentage point increase in the number of women who ran for state delegate

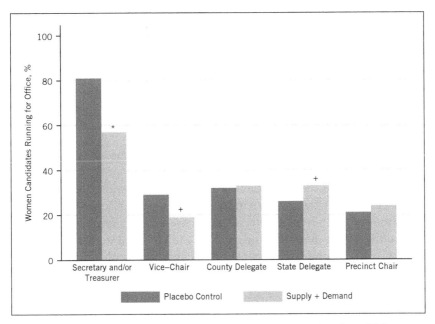

Figure 9.2. Proportion of women running for each office, by condition (*$p < 0.05$, +$p < 0.2$).

positions—the position precinct chairs were asked to recruit women to run for. There was also a small increase in the proportion of women candidates for precinct chair.

We have shown that our intervention substantially decreased the proportion of women running for service positions and modestly increased the proportion of women running for leadership positions. But what effect did this have on the overall number of women running? Interestingly, the total number of candidates and their gender is essentially the same in all conditions, as shown in Table 9.2. The large drop in women running for service positions was compensated by the increase in women running for leadership positions—and because there are several state delegate positions in each precinct, the total number can remain equal despite a much larger percentage drop in service positions. Although we do not have conclusive individual-level data on this, these results suggest that the interventions did not actually bring more women into the political world. Rather, it appears that many of the women who would have run for secretary, treasurer, or precinct vice-chair instead ran for precinct chair and state delegate. This is consistent with the responses from the precinct chairs that they chose to recruit women who were already active in the party.

We believe this is a very important finding from a practical perspective. For a variety of reasons, politically engaged women may initially gravitate

TABLE 9.2. TOTAL NUMBER OF CANDIDATES RUNNING FOR ALL OFFICES

	Average number of candidates	% Male	% Female	N
Placebo	16.5	66	34	543
Supply	15.1	67	33	475
Demand	16.4	67	33	494
Supply + Demand	14.1	67	33	477

toward service and support positions like party secretary or campaign volunteer rather than leadership positions. Left to their own devices, they frequently remain in those positions. But for parties interested in increasing women's representation, women in service and support roles are an excellent pool from which to recruit. After all, they have already shown a track record of commitment to the party. And contrary to claims that women prefer to be in service and support roles, our results suggest that with a little bit of encouragement, many are more than happy to step into leadership roles. If you ask them, they will run.

Looking Forward

While the data for this chapter were collected in 2014, the lessons to be learned are still relevant for current and future political parties. And while the data we offer in this chapter are from local races, this recruitment effect from party elites is not limited to local races. The 2018 election cycle saw a surge of women candidates, most notably for the U.S. Congress. Overall, there were 23 women candidates for Senate and 235 women candidates for the House of Representatives, more than any previous year.[8] However, both of those pools were overwhelmingly Democratic. Of the 23 women Senate candidates, 15 were Democrats and 8 were Republicans. Of the 235 women House candidates, 183 were Democrats and only 52 were Republicans. Combining both houses, 78 percent of all women candidates for U.S. Congress in 2018 were from the Democratic Party. This stark lack of women Republican candidates as compared to the supply of women Democratic candidates should motivate the Republican party to engage in more party-based recruitment efforts at all levels of government.

Following the message of this chapter, the Democratic Party or other influential party members likely played a role in encouraging those women to run for office at some point in their political journey. For example, consider the story of Representative Rashida Tlaib—she was part of the wave of new women elected to the U.S. House of Representatives in November 2018, as a result of an influential party member encouraging her to run. She first entered the political arena in 2004 when she interned in the Michigan House of Representatives, and later was brought on as a staffer. In 2008, the representative she worked for had reached his term limits and encouraged her to run for his seat. Because of his encouragement, she ran for and won her district's seat in the Michigan House, her first political office. She served in the Michigan House for as long as her term limits would allow, and shortly after leaving office she ran for and won a seat in the U.S. House of Representatives.

This chapter has shown that when party leaders identify women involved in partisan service and encourage them to run for office, it can be an effective method of diversifying who runs. Representative Tlaib's story follows this pattern and suggests that our findings are not just limited to the Republican Party or local offices. Her story is perfectly illustrative of the power that influential individuals within the party have to recruit individuals who are closely linked to the political process but might otherwise be looked over.

Conclusion

This chapter has outlined how party leaders can increase women's representation in party leadership by explicitly endorsing the goal of greater women's representation and actively recruiting women to run for these offices. We show that most Republican precinct-level party officials were willing to participate in these efforts when asked to do so by party leadership. The combination of the requests coming directly from the state party chair and the ideologically authentic phrasing of the request were likely important factors in the success of the intervention.

Our deep dive into who precinct chairs recruited and how those women responded yielded several interesting results. First, party chairs understandably turned to women who were already active in the neighborhood or party. Women in service and support positions are a frequently untapped resource that parties should turn to when diversifying their leadership. Further, many precinct chairs sought out women because of their involvement in stereotypically feminine activities like volunteering at a school or homemaking. This highlights the importance of being prepared to not just accept women as leaders but also accept stereotypically feminine activities as leadership training. Diversifying party leadership means diversifying the acceptable pathways to party leadership.

Further, contrary to some assumptions about women's preferences, when encouraged to do so, women left service and consolation roles and ran for leadership roles. This reinforces a great deal of other scholarship on the disproportionate role that recruitment and community support play in women's decisions to run for office[9] and echoes the findings of other chapters in this volume about the role community service often plays in women's pathways to office.

Most important, we show that parties do have levers to increase women's representation in their ranks. Our study involved a single letter sent from a state party chair to precinct chairs. This very modest intervention had a significant impact on women's representation in the party. More sustained efforts are likely to have an even greater impact. Party leaders can promote women's leadership by strategically reaching out to those who are already contributing to the party in less visible ways. This intervention works especially well when party leaders are simultaneously reminding voters of the value of women's voices. Though seemingly simple, this is an effective route toward increasing female political leadership.

NOTES

1. David P. Redlawsk, Caroline J. Tolbert, and Todd Donovan, *Why Iowa? How Caucuses and Sequential Elections Improve the Presidential Nominating Process* (Chicago: University of Chicago Press, 2011), 24.

2. Exact treatment of the letters can be found in the online appendix, available at https://doi.org/10.1111/ajps.12300.

3. C. F. Karpowitz, J. Q. Monson, and J. R. Preece, "How to Elect More Women: Gender and Candidate Success in a Field Experiment," *American Journal of Political Science* 61 (2017): 927–943.

4. We identified ourselves as researchers interested in that state's recent elections.

5. Calculated by the authors from the Pew Research Center's 2014 Religious Landscape Survey. See also Pew Research Center, "U.S. Public Becoming Less Religious," November 3, 2015, accessed October 12, 2018, available at http://www.pewforum.org/2015/11/03/u-s-public-becoming-less-religious/.

6. Melody Crowder-Meyer, "Gendered Recruitment without Trying: How Local Party Recruiters Affect Women's Representation," *Politics and Gender* 9, no. 4 (2013): 390–413.

7. While our observed precincts did not cover the whole state, nearly 75 percent of the state's population lives within the region we randomly selected precincts from, thus making it plausible that these precincts represent the state fairly well. Additional analyses comparing descriptives of the precincts show that there is balance across the conditions.

8. "Summary of Women Candidates for Selected Offices: 1970–2018 (Major Party Nominees)," Center for the American Women and Politics, available at http://www.cawp.rutgers.edu/sites/default/files/resources/can_histsum.pdf.

9. Susan J. Carroll and Kira Sanbonmatsu, *More Women Can Run: Gender and Pathways to the State Legislatures* (New York: Oxford University Press, 2013).

10

Late to the Party

Black Women's Inconsistent Support from Political Parties

NADIA E. BROWN AND PEARL K. DOWE

A
s we write this chapter, there is an ongoing celebration on social media of the political #BlackGirlMagic[1] that was witnessed in 2018. At least 428 Black women across the nation ran for office, including women such as Ayanna Pressley, who became the first Black women elected to Congress from Massachusetts, and Lucy Mcbath, who was a political newcomer who decided to run after losing her son to gun violence. Prior to the 2018 midterm election, Black women held only 3.7 percent of state legislative seats and just five mayoral positions in the United States' 100 largest cities. Less than 20 seats in the House of Representatives were held by Black women, while a single Black woman was in the Senate. The 2018 election cycle brought a wave of women that would change these numbers. In Maryland, 10 women were elected to the legislature and 8 Black women were reelected; in Minnesota, 2 new women were elected to the legislature, including Ilhan Omar, who is the first Somali American woman elected to Congress.

The successes of 2018 extended the celebration of political Black Girl Magic that occurred in 2017 on the local level, in which African American women were elected to mayoral seats in seven of the nation's largest cities.[2] In 2017, Keisha Lance Bottoms became the mayor of Atlanta. Her campaign gained national attention as pundits wondered if Atlanta, the bastion of Southern Black Democratic power for the past 44 years, would be led by Mary Norwood, a White female independent. The state Democratic Party poured $100,000 into the race and, as the race tightened, support came from national Democratic figures such as New York mayor Bill de Blasio, who endorsed Bottoms, and Black senators Kamala Harris and Cory Booker, who held a campaign rally during the last weekend of the race.

The Black Girl Magic that we witnessed in the recent election cycles is highly unusual because, we argue, Black women candidates typically do not enjoy support from their political parties. The Atlanta mayoral race saw an increased level of attention from the Democratic Party because of the unusual politics surrounding this election. The last White mayor of Atlanta was Sam Massell in 1969, and the city is overwhelmingly Democratic. Many people felt that Republicans just cannot win in Atlanta. However, the race was contentious, and Bottoms did not easily win the seat. She failed to receive the endorsement of high profile (Black) politicians, and Bottoms was tied to the ethical scandals of the outgoing mayor. Indeed, Democrats were divided in their support of Bottoms. However, the Democratic Party of Georgia fully supported Keisha Bottoms, drawing the ire of high-profile Democratic figures.

While political drama ensued, Bottoms nevertheless enjoyed resources from her party by drawing on her personal strength and support from allies outside of traditional political networks. Bottoms was sworn in on January 2, 2018, at the Martin Luther King Chapel on Morehouse College's campus, and local dignitaries, community leaders, and celebrities were in attendance.

Although some Black women have been successful in high-profile campaigns, Black women across the country have expressed a growing frustration with the dynamics of the political parties that have devalued their electoral strength and viability as candidates. Drawing on the experiences of Black women candidates as reported in elite interviews,[3] we show how these women compensate for the lack of party support with their personal networks and resources. Unlike Mayor Lance Bottoms, countless other Black women candidates and those with nascent political ambition find the Democratic Party to be inconsistent or absent in their campaigns. In what follows, we present several detailed narratives of Black women candidates who shared their frustrations with their political party. We conclude with a set of recommendations to political parties for better engagement with Black women candidates as well as useful steps for potential candidates to follow to mount a successful campaign in the absence of party support.

Black Women, Political Marginalization, and the Democratic Party

Black women have shown themselves to be a significant political actor as both voters and candidates. In 2008, Black women had the highest voter turnout rate among all groups of eligible voters (70 percent of eligible Black women voted). Black women again exceeded expectations in 2012 as they led all other groups again in voter turnout, casting 11.4 million votes.[4] In 2016, there was less investment in voter mobilization of African Americans and this was evident in an overall decrease of Black voter turnout. However, of Black women who voted, 94 percent voted Democratic, which was in direct contrast to the voting pattern of White women during that election cycle.

Despite the underrepresentation of Black women, they continued to be a critical contributor to the growth of the overall number of African American elected officials. Since 1990, there have been consistent increases in the aggregate amount of elected Black officials nationwide. During this same period, Black women exceeded the number of Black male elected officials.[5] Currently, there are 1,840 women serving in state legislators and 272 are Black. Of the 75 women serving in statewide executive offices only two are Black. It has also been shown that African American women are more likely to be politically ambitious than their White counterparts,[6] which is evident in the fact that African American women account for a greater proportion of Black elected officials than White women do of White elected officials.[7] Black women have found success in majority-minority districts,[8] and recently they have shown the potential to be successful in non-majority-minority districts, which presents the possibility for increased Black women's representation.[9] The substantive and descriptive forms of participation have been sustained and are evident in the 115th Congress. Of the 105 women, 18 are Black. Also, one Black woman and one Caribbean American woman serve as nonvoting delegates.

In general, Black women are typically more likely to be discouraged from running for political positions and are less likely to be recruited by their White counterparts. The lack of recruitment has an extensive impact on political advancement, and it serves as a key factor indicating that they have fared better than expected as candidates.[10]

Carroll and Sanbonmatsu argue that recruitment for female candidates is more influential in the outcome of political success than it is for male candidates.[11] This hesitancy by party leadership reflects the limited idea of what type of candidate is electable. Limited recruitment impacts the ability of Black women to secure campaign resources necessary to establish a viable campaign early, especially resources outside of their districts.[12] It has been shown that Black candidates are more likely to raise less money, rely heavily on small donations, and depend on donations outside of their districts.[13] Party leaders doubts about candidate electability are problematic for Black women seeking election in majority White districts. This hesitancy poses difficulty in launching a successful campaign due to the challenges in securing resources to launch a campaign.[14] It has been argued that party competition is an avenue for advancing inclusion and promoting the needs of the disadvantaged.[15] However, Frymer[16] notes that African American scholars see the two-party system as limited and exclusionary in nature.[17] This exclusionary pattern is evident when looking at the positionality of Black women as candidates within the Democratic Party. Throughout much of the era in which African Americans began

to fully engage in the electoral process, the Democratic Party has often perceived the support of Black voters as a means to victory while viewing it as a
destabilizing force that pushed away White voters. However, these voters were
needed in order for Democrats to mount any type of viable campaign for
local and state offices where there were large populations of African Americans and during presidential elections.

African American voters were also needed by the Democratic Party to
broaden the electoral base to increase its chances of winning presidential
elections.[18] This strategy by the Democratic Party has contributed to the marginalization of African American voters and African American women in
particular. It is worth noting the irony in this strategy. White women with
few exceptions have been consistent voters for Republican presidential candidates since the collection of data on voting preference began in 1948.[19]

In May 2017, more than two dozen African American women, including
political activists and elected officials, submitted an open letter to Democratic National Committee chairman Tom Perez criticizing him for seeming
to take for granted the party's most loyal base of support. The letter spoke to
the frustration Black women have developed and maintained throughout the
journey of being loyal to the Democratic Party. In addition to this, the letter
also spoke to the neglect of Black women from party leadership. This frustration grew following the 2016 election in which it appeared the Democratic
Party attempted to solve its electoral problem by developing strategies to attract White voters who had left the party decades ago.

The letter stated: "We have voted and organized our communities with
little support or investment from the Democratic Party for voter mobilization efforts. We have shown how Black women lead, yet the Party's leadership from Washington to the state parties have few or no Black women in
leadership. More and more, Black women are running for office and winning
elections—with scant support from Democratic Party infrastructure."[20]

In addition to this open letter, Black women have begun to state their
frustration in other places. According to a recent survey by *Essence Magazine* and the Black Women's Roundtable, Black women support for the Democratic Party is in decline. Seventy-four percent of the respondents felt that
the Democratic Party best represented the group. This is a drop from 85 percent in the previous year. In an interview with Black Women's Roundtable
member Dr. Elsie Scott, she explained this drop in support: "Black women
feel that they are being taken for granted. The Democratic Party seems to
assume that Black women have no place else to go, but they can stay at home
as many did in 2016. They can stop taking Black women for granted. They
can actively recruit Black women candidates and once they are recruited,
support them with resources, including money. Black women who run for
Congress have better success records than White women who run for Congress."[21]

In spite of the lack of support by the Democratic Party, Black women have proven their electoral strength as voters and candidates. However, as African American women aspire to move beyond the local level, they face greater challenges in winning office. In many ways, statewide offices are more difficult for African American women to secure. No state has ever elected a Black woman to a governorship, and only 12 Black women have held statewide elected executive office. Without the sustained support of a political party, it is easy to understand why Black women face challenges in seeking office. In spite of this obstacle, African American women are situated in communities that provide resources that spur ambition while mobilizing voters is evident in the following testimonials.

The election of several Black women to a multiplicity of local, state, and federal positions, as well as Kamala Harris's and Stacey Abrams's high-profile bids for the presidency and governorship of Georgia, respectively, demonstrates that perhaps the Democratic Party may be attempting to rectify its long-standing ambivalence toward Black women. Or, as we demonstrate, perhaps it is that Black women's success is not dependent on the party at all. Instead, this group is not waiting for the Democratic Party to embrace them and, rather, is taking it upon themselves to be the change they wish to see with or without institutional support from their political party.

Data and Methods

As prototypical intersectional subjects—doubly marginalized by race and gender and whose narratives are used to expose the undertheorized categorization of identity[22]—Black women candidates warrant rigorous study, specifically with respect to how they experience and manage race and gender in American politics. To be sure, the need to look at intragroup differences within a single case study is guided by shortcomings within the extant literature on Black women political candidates. As previously noted, much of the literature on women candidates or minority candidates does not focus on the unique subject positions of Black women. We seek to move beyond cross group analysis among women or minority men to look within Black women candidates as a group to examine the distinct and/or analogous narratives of party involvement in their campaigns for political office.

This study draws on elite interviews with Black women candidates for political office and elected officials. In person, one-on-one interviews were conducted between 2014 and 2016 with Black women candidates. The data for this study come from 10 in-depth, semi-structured, and open ended interviews that one of the coauthors conducted with Black women in Maryland, Virginia, Illinois, and Missouri. Interviews lasted between 45 and 90 minutes. All interviews were on the record. These interviews were recorded and transcribed and organized into themes. These states were selected because

the researcher had access to this population as she had built professional relationships with these candidates and lawmakers during her previous academic research projects. These women were candidates for political offices
ranging from the state legislature, to the county prosecuting attorney, city
treasurer, or mayor. None of the races was nonpartisan. All the women in
the study were asked, "How active are your party's leaders at recruiting diverse candidates" and "Were you recruited to run for any office?" These questions serve as the bases for the analysis of this chapter. However, the larger
interview protocol asked questions about the woman's political priorities,
how her appearance may or may not impact her political experiences, and
her understanding of how race and gender influence political behavior.

Because this study relies solely on the self-reports on the perception of
the role of political parties in Black women's candidacies, it is difficult to measure the veracity of claims. These women are, after all, politicians who have
had some degree of success in a system that relies heavily on political parties.
They may not feel as if the party has been useful or aided in their successes
or that the party has been detrimental to their candidacies, but, nevertheless,
political parties are important in all of the races that these women ran in.
Again, the races in which the woman sought elected office were all partisan
and required them to engage with a party structure in some fashion. To be
sure, self-reports on the perception of the political party in their races is subject to memory and may be biased. It is important, therefore, to review the
responses of the candidates and lawmakers as a representation of their understandings of the usefulness of political parties. Also, candidates and elected officials may seek to play up their own agency and personal abilities to
portray a sense of independence and being an autonomous actor. Despite these
limitations, exploring Black women candidates' articulations of the role of
political parties in their elections should benefit scholars who work in understanding how race and gender influence party involvement.

The remaining sections of this chapter present Black women candidates
and elected officials' perception of political parties in their races. These women
do not indicate that they feel powerless in the face of a large political ma-
chine—such as a political party. Instead, they discuss how they have navi-
gated politics with or without the help of their political party. They also note
that they draw from other networks, when necessary, to mount successful
political campaigns. Last, they show that despite obstacles that they encounter due to racism and sexism, Black women candidates are optimistic that
they can win elected office.

Party Support for Black Women Candidates

The Black women candidates in our studies forcefully note that political parties overwhelmingly ignored them. These women used their own networks

and resources to advance their candidacies. State Representative Cora Faith Walker (D-MO) detailed that when she decided to run for office, the Democratic Party did not contribute in any meaningful way to her campaign because she was well networked and known in her community. State Representative Walker noted: "I knew a lot of people already, that I worked with already. So, while the party itself didn't bring resources, they didn't give me money. . . . I felt that it was because I already had established relationships with people."[23] Because State Representative Walker ran using her own networks, she referenced how being a Black woman impacted her entry into politics. She shared that part of the difficulty was "knowing that I'm a female and a Black female, that I have to go that extra step so that I'm thoroughly prepared."[24] The decision to run for office, albeit without much support from her political party, was seen as something that she was prepared to do because of her identity. Namely, the adversities faced by being Black in a society that undervalues this population and the agency that Black women exude in spite of these handicaps provided State Representative Walker with the tenacity to run for a seat in the Missouri State Legislature without the institutional backing and support of her party.

Similarly, Leslie Broadnax, a candidate for St. Louis County prosecuting attorney responded, "not at all!" when asked how active her party's leaders were at recruiting diverse candidates. She further elaborated that the Democratic Party in St. Louis "is very non-supportive of minorities and the fact of the matter is that St. Louis County in particular is diverse and been cut off from the Democratic party farm system. I still have access to some of it because I'm an elected official, but I don't have full access. There is still an unspoken rule that you do not file and run against an incumbent."[25] When asked if this was something specific to Black women or if the unspoken rule was in place for all would-be candidates regardless of race/gender, Broadnax forcefully stated, "This is something I have dealt with from the local African American officials of the local municipalities. You know that county is a beast. We have 90 municipalities, each has their own mayor and board. Many of whom are not minorities. I have gotten 'we find you to be disrespectful because you did not ask permission to run nor did you wait your turn.' Quite frankly, my turn was never going to come."[26] According to Broadnax, there is a "gentleman's agreement" between good ol' boys about who is going to run for political office. The Democratic Party as an institution supports that structure and rewards these men—often White men—with political seats. In Leslie Broadnax's case, she lost to Bob McCullough (the White male incumbent) on August 5, 2014, just nine days before Mike Brown was murdered by Officer Darren Wilson in Ferguson, Missouri. McCullough oversaw the grand jury that failed to indict Wilson. Broadnax's depiction of the Democratic Party supporting and rewarding the good ol' boys seems to be the case in this particular election.

While the vast majority of Black women identify with the Democratic Party and those in our studies ran as Democrats, one candidate shared that Blacks need to think about the Republican Party. Dianne Harris, a Black woman Republican from the Chicagoland area, was running for Congress in 2014. She noted that "Democrats, they will recruit more diverse candidates. . . . And the African American community is always there, helping them get signatures, and petitions, and helping them register voters. But then, when seats come up, they're not reached out to. And some African Americans are seeing that. And they think that they are being used."[27] State Representative Jamilah Nasheed (D-MO) reified Harris's sentiments and shared that "the relationship with not just female politicians but African Americans within the Democratic party is a problem. People are afraid to talk about that. The fact that you have a base of people that are so loyal to one particular party knowing that they take them for granted."[28] As a response, candidate Harris recommended that Blacks should explore the Republican Party as an option. While Harris did not comment on the differences in policy positions or the historical legacy of race-baiting that was/is prevalent within the GOP, she did urge other Blacks to look outside of the Democratic Party to see if the Republican Party would be an option for them. For her, the party's platform was more in line with her traditional social beliefs and conservative economic priorities. Harris readily admitted that the "Republicans have not reached out. And that's one reason why African Americans say that they are not interested in becoming Republicans."[29] When asked how she became interested in running for office, Dianne Harris replied, "I was recruited. The Republican party now is becoming more inclusive, trying to be more inclusive."[30] When asked how supported she felt by her party, she shared similar stories to other Black women candidates of feeling as if the party could do more to assist her. For example, Harris believed:

> I've come to the conclusion that I've overspent my money. And I'm tired of spending my money. There are times that I will get it back and there are times that I don't. This time around, being recruited, I feel that I should have had more contributions. But I'm told that when I win the primary, but I will need to get to that point, that I will have more contributions. But, I've spent more than I've collected. . . . For example, I have a very very good campaign manager. He's good. He's getting paid for being good. And he's being paid out of my pocket, but I know that needs to be done. A lot of times people need to hire people to do a lot of things, and if you need to do that, that's why you have to be rich to be a politician. But, I'm told, if I win the primary, I will have more support. I will have more backing. I believe that.[31]

Dianne Harris decries the need for deep financial pockets in order to run for political office, something she does not have. She's not alone. Research indicates that Black women candidates often have less personal capital to invest in their campaigns and do not have a wealthy inner circle from which to draw contributions. As such, this group holds more fundraisers to generate substantially less funds than their male and White counterparts.[32] Regardless of party, Black women candidates do not feel as economically supported in their campaigns. What is telling, however, is that, when a candidate is recruited by her party, she does not receive financial benefits that would cover more of the costs associated with the campaign. Turning our attention back to Dianne Harris, ultimately, she lost the primary and did not recoup her investment into her campaign. The Republican Party supported another (White) woman candidate for a seat from Cook County in the Illinois House of Representatives. This candidate lost in the general election, and the seat is currently held by a White male Democrat.

Like Harris, another Black woman candidate shared the difficulties in raising money for her campaign. State Representative Bonnaye Mims (D-MO) believes that the Democratic Party does a good job of recruiting Black candidates in Kansas City, however, they "only recruit what they want then they decide from that pool."[33] She was a participant in a candidate training program and that drew the attention of the Democratic Party power brokers in Kansas City, Missouri. Mims noted that the party saw how hard she worked and that she was able to motivate people. These skills were tremendously useful because "I didn't see the Democratic party doing much for me. They asked me to help canvas. But, I have 15 people canvassing and helping me. But that was my race, not some of the other races."[34] State Representative Mims stated that she would have used the money to pay the canvassers. "I hired 2 drivers to cover my polls. My own union gave me $5000. The White Republican males got 3 times that, but they only gave their canvassers $50, $75 for them to be in that hot sun all day. I felt good. Mine got $15 per day. I paid all my workers a decent salary. I made sure that they had lunch, a breakfast, snacks and water all day long."[35] State Representative Mims was immensely proud of her ability to pay her workers. She was only able to do this because of the support she received from her union. She did not, however, get much financial support from the Democratic Party. State Representative Mims was grateful to her union because she found it difficult to raise money on her own.

While the narratives of Mims, Harris, Nasheed, and Walker are representative of the other women interviewed for this study, others note that their political party has been supportive. For example, Tishaura Jones reported that her party leaders have been "okay" at recruiting diverse candidates "because I have been recruited."[36] This interview was conducted when Jones was recruited to serve as the treasurer of the City of St. Louis. She later ran an unsuccessful campaign for the mayor of St. Louis in 2016. But Jones noted that there is a small pool of candidates, namely Black candidates, because of the perception that politics is for Whites. Because Jones comes from a family of politicians, she said, "I grew up in it, so I'm used to all the nuances and kind of craziness that could happen. I don't know if it's a lack of interest in our part as African Americans wanting to get involved. Because we see here in places like Ferguson, 76 percent Black, only one Black school board member, only one Black councilmember, out of a 53 member police department that only has 3 African Americans—it's just lopsided. The demographics have recently changed in the city. We can't necessarily represent anyone either."[37] Jones further noted that if residents saw politicians that looked like them then they may have more trust in their elected officials. This was particularly telling in the aftermath of the fatal shooting of Mike Brown. This interview was conducted two days after the murder and tensions were high in St. Louis, Black elected officials were struggling to respond to the incident. At this time, elected officials had yet to address the protesters or join in the civil unrest. Therefore, Jones's comments were rather telling. She believed that there was a special calling for Black politicians to enact change or at least be seen as responsive to the residents' outcry for political transparency. Jones surmised that "having more Black women elected officials, someone to be a face for the community, may draw out others."[38] When asked if political parties are doing enough to mobilize and reach out to Black women, Jones forcefully stated "absolutely not."[39] She continued:

> When I look at the number of Black women that entered politics just as I did in 2002, when I first became a committeewoman, we didn't see a lot of women entering. Men are, you know the reason. Basically, men just wake up one day and say "this is what I am doing." But, women have to be asked. So, I tried to put that in anytime I'm talking to a group of women or a group of girls. Women have to be asked. So, I'm asking you today, therefore, you cannot say that nobody ever asked you. With women, it takes a lot for us because we feel like we have to be the best, have the most experience, or have the education, basically, we have to have everything right for us to take the next step. And I will be totally honest, I didn't have everything in line. I got knocked up right before I filed. It was a shaky for me at that point. I just have this belief that this is the work that God choose me to do. And that if made the first step, then He would be with me to make sure that all of the other things fell into place. And He did. Thank you, Jesus.

Much of Tishaura Jones's comments are reflexive of women in politics and are not specific to Black women. Yet, her words are instructive to Black women, in particular, who are living in localities without politicians who look like them. If you want to see a change in your community, you need to be that change agent and run for political office. Stepping out on faith and having a belief in your own abilities are key for women with nascent political ambitions. Regardless of party involvement in your campaign, women should stand firm on their desires to make their communities better by running for office. If Black women want their elected officials to reflect their values and political priorities, particularly in Black cities that lack Black political leadership, then they should run for office. According to Jones, this is the call for action for Black women.

Conclusion and Recommendations

Black women candidates and elected officials uniformly express a belief that their political party can and should do more to recruit diverse candidates.

Practical Recommendations for Backing Black Women Candidates and Incumbents Seeking Reelection

- Political parties should foster positive relationships with Black women in three meaningful ways:
  - Develop and invest in Black women political leaders through candidate training programs.
  - Provide Black women candidates with seed money early in their campaigns.
  - Work with political action committees (PACs) that explicitly support Black women candidates such as the Black Women's PAC and Higher Heights for America PAC.
- Take an active and sustained interest in districts where Black women are likely to run and win. Parties should move away from transactional elections in which they only come into certain communities to ask for votes but disappear once the election is over.
- Include more Black women in key leadership positions within the party at various levels, and allow Black women to help set the political agenda for the party.
- Black women who are interested in running for office should consider the following resources:
  - She Should Run.
  - IGNITE.
  - Collective PAC.
  - Black Women's PAC.
- Parties, allies, and supporters of Black women with nascent political ambition, and Black women political candidates themselves, should consider utilizing social media to connect with other like-minded individuals. For example, #DeclareYourAmbition is a popular hashtag created by IGNITE to encourage young women to run for office.

The narratives shared by the women in the study forcefully underscore that they are not supported by their party. This is a telling feature of American politics in local elections primarily because Black women are reliable voters and often strong candidates. As such, it would behoove political parties to be attentive to this group of voters and candidates. However, the data from this study indicate that Black women are perfectly capable and well equipped to win elected seats without significant assistance from their political party. This research demonstrates that if political parties even minimally supported Black women candidates, this population may mount stronger campaigns. At least, we see that if Black women candidates had more money for their campaigns they would be able to afford the necessary staff to assist in their electoral pursuits.

In conclusion, we urge political parties to fully support viable Black women candidates—particularly in the primary elections. Following are practical recommendations for backing Black women candidates and incumbents seeking reelection.

We believe that these recommendations will foster more inclusive political parties. It is our contention that electoral successes, seen most notably by women such as Ilhan Omar, Lucy McBath, and Keisha Lance Bottoms, will be accessible to other Black women candidates if the party supports this group of election seekers. Mayor Lance Bottoms was successfully able to leverage party resources and relied on her network of Black women to secure election. Given our study and the victories of 2018, we are convinced that other Black women candidates can and will use this model if party support is afforded to them. Black women candidates take a dual approach—one that is situated with an understanding of community and a desire to have party resources—to make electoral gains.

NOTES

1. Coined by CaShawn Thompson in 2013, the phrase "blackgirlsaremagic" was first used to combat negative media and personal critiques of Black women on Twitter. It was shortened to "Black Girl Magic" to celebrate Black women's resilience in the face of multilayered and intersectional oppressions. Aria S. Halliday and Nadia E. Brown, "The Power of Black Girl Magic Anthems: Nicki Minaj, Beyoncé, and 'Feeling Myself' as Political Empowerment," *Souls* (2018): 1–17.

2. Yvonne Spicer was elected as the first Black women mayor in the 317-year history of Framingham, Massachusetts. Vi Lyles will serve as the first black female mayor of Charlotte. She served for 30 years as a city administrator before running for office. Mary Parham-Copeland will become the first black mayor of Milledgeville, Georgia. Andrea Jenkins, the first openly transgender black woman elected to office, won a seat on the Minneapolis City Council and LaToya Cantrell will become the first Black female mayor of New Orleans.

3. All interviews were approved by the Institutional Review Board at Purdue Univerity.

4. "U.S. Census: Blacks Voted at a Higher Rate Than Whites in 2012 Election—A First, Census Bureau Reports," available at https://www.census.gov/newsroom/press -releases/2013/cb13-84.html.

5. See Carol Hardy-Fanta, Pei-te Lien, Dianne M. Pinderhughes, and Christine Marie Sierra, "Gender, Race and Descriptive Representation in the United States: Findings from the Gender and Multicultural Leadership Project," *Journal of Women, Politics, and Policy* 28, nos. 3–4 (2006): 7–41; Byron D. Orey, Wendy Smooth, Kimberly S. Adams, and Kisha Harris-Clark, "Race and Gender Matter: Refining Models of Legislative Policy Making in State Legislatures," *Journal of Women, Politics, and Policy* 28, nos. 3–4 (2006): 97–119; Wendy Smooth, "African American Women and Electoral Politics: Translating Voting Power into Office-holding," *Gender and Elections: Shaping the Future of American Politics* (2014): 167–189. Cambridge University Press, New York.

6. R. Darcy and Charles D. Hadley, "Black Women in Politics: The Puzzle of Success," *Social Science Quarterly* 69, no. 3 (1988): 629–645.

7. Linda Faye Williams, "The Civil Rights-Black Power Legacy: Black Women Elected Officials at the Local, State, and National Levels," in *Sisters in the Struggle: African American Women in the Civil Rights-Black Power Movement*, ed. Bettye Collier-Thomas and V. P. Franklin (New York: New York University Press, 2001): 306–331; Smooth, "African American Women and Electoral Politics."

8. Becki Scola, "Women of Color in State Legislatures: Gender, Race, Ethnicity and Legislative Office Holding," *Journal of Women, Politics, and Policy* 28, nos. 3–4 (2007): 43–70.

9. In 2016, Black women were 3 of the 14 nonincumbent women elected to the U.S. House or Senate. Senator Kamala Harris (D-CA) became the second Black woman ever to serve in the U.S. Senate, Representative Lisa Blunt Rochester (D-DE) was the first woman elected to Congress from Delaware, and Representative Val Demings (D-FL) joined Florida's congressional delegation. Both Rochester and Demings won open seats in non-majority-minority districts.

10. Susan J. Carroll and Kira Sanbonmatsu, *More Women Can Run: Gender and Pathways to the State Legislatures* (New York: Oxford University Press, 2013).

11. Kira Sanbonmatsu, "Electing Women of Color: The Role of Campaign Trainings," *Journal of Women, Politics, and Policy* 36, no. 2 (2015): 137–160.

12. Kira Sanbonmatsu, "State Elections: Where Do Women Run? Where Do Women Win?" in *Gender and Elections: Shaping the Future of American Politics*, ed. Susan J. Carroll and Richard L. Fox (New York: Cambridge University Press, 2006), 189–214.

13. G. S. Thielemann, "Minority Legislators and Institutional Influence," *Social Science Journal* 29, no. 4 (1992): 411–421.

14. Sanbonmatsu, "State Elections."

15. Robert A. Dahl, *Pluralist Democracy in the United States: Conflict and Consent* (Chicago: Rand McNally, 1967); V. O. Key Jr., *Southern Politics in State and Nation* (New York: Alfred A. Knopf, 1949).

16. Paul Frymer, "Race, Parties, and Democratic Inclusion," in *The Politics of Democratic Inclusion*, ed. Christina Wolbrecht and Rodney E. Hero (Philadelphia: Temple University Press, 2005), 122–142.

17. H. Walton, *Black Political Parties: An Historical and Political Analysis* (New York: Free Press, 1972); L. Guinier, "The Triumph of Tokenism: The Voting Rights Act and the Theory of Black Electoral Success," *Michigan Law Review* 89, no. 5 (1991): 1077–1154; Paul Frymer, *Uneasy Alliances* (Princeton, NJ: Princeton University Press, 1999).

18. Frymer, "Race, Parties, and Democratic Inclusion"; Raphael J. Sonenshein, "Can Black Candidates Win Statewide Elections?" *Political Science Quarterly* 105, no. 2 (1990): 219–241; Katrina Gamble, "Young, Gifted, Black and Female, Why Aren't There More Yvette Clarkes in Congress," in *Whose Black Politics? Cases in Post-racial Black Leadership*, ed. A. Gillespie (Routledge, 2010).

19. J. Junn, "The Trump Majority: White Womanhood and the Making of Female Voters in the US," *Politics, Groups, and Identities* 5, no. 2 (2017): 343–352; Charles Tien, "The Racial Gap in Voting among Women: White Women, Racial Resentment, and Support for Trump," *New Political Science* 39, no. 4 (2017): 651–669.

20. "Open Letter to DNC Chair: There's Too Much at Stake to Ignore Black Women," 2017, available at https://www.nbcnews.com/news/nbcblk/open-letter-dnc-chair-tom -perez-there-s-too-much-n764221.

21. Pearl K. Dowe, personal interview with Dr. Elsie Scott, October 31, 2017.

22. Black feminists have long advanced the claims that multiple identities—such as race, gender, class, and sexual orientation—are mutually reinforcing and interlocking, thus calling on feminist scholars to complicate the view of a "universal woman," for example Gloria T. Hull, Patricia Bell-Scott, and Barbara Smith, *All the Women Are White, All the Blacks Are Men, but Some of Us Are Brave: Black Women's Studies* (New York: Feminist Press, 1982); Kimberle Crenshaw, "Demarginalizing the Intersection of Race and Sex: A Black Feminist Critique of Antidiscrimination Doctrine, Feminist Theory and Antiracist Politics," *University of Chicago Legal Forum* 1, no. 8 (1989): 139; Evelyn Brooks Higginbotham, *Righteous Discontent: The Women's Movement in the Black Baptist Church, 1880–1920* (Cambridge: Harvard University Press, 1994); J. C. Nash, "Re-thinking Intersectionality," *Feminist Review* 89, no. 1 (2008): 1–15; Angela Davis, *Women, Race and Class* (New York: Vintage Books, 1981).

23. Nadia Brown, personal interview with State Representative Cora Faith Walker, 2017.

24. Brown, interview with State Representative Cora Faith Walker.

25. Nadia Brown, personal interview with Leslie Broadnax, 2014.

26. Brown, interview with Leslie Broadnax, 2014.

27. Nadia Brown, personal interview with Dianne Harris, 2014.

28. Nadia Brown, personal interview with State Representative Jamilah Nasheed, 2014.

29. Nadia Brown, interview with Dianne Harris, 2014.

30. Brown, interview with Dianne Harris, 2014.

31. Brown, interview with Dianne Harris, 2014.

32. Nadia E. Brown, *Sisters in the Statehouse: Black Women and Legislative Decision Making* (New York: Oxford University Press, 2014).

33. Nadia E. Brown, personal interview with State Representative Bonnaye Mims, 2014.

34. Brown, interview with State Representative Bonnaye Mims, 2014.

35. Brown, interview with State Representative Bonnaye Mims, 2014.

36. Nadia E. Brown, personal interview with Tishaura Jones, 2014.

37. Brown, interview with Tishaura Jones, 2014.

38. Brown, interview with Tishaura Jones, 2014.

39. Brown, interview with Tishaura Jones, 2014.

11

Women's Political Ambition and the 2016 Election

Chris W. Bonneau and Kristin Kanthak

In April 2016, Hillary Clinton was the front-runner for the Democratic Party nomination for president. Her closest competitor, Bernie Sanders, was addressing the crowd at a campaign rally in Philadelphia. There, he leveled the following criticism at Clinton, a former U.S. senator and secretary of state: "I don't believe she is qualified." Although Clinton later won the nomination, she lost the presidential election to Donald Trump. A year prior to Sanders's rally, Trump himself had tweeted that Clinton's husband's infidelity was an indication that she was unqualified to be president: "If Hillary Clinton can't satisfy her husband what makes her think she can satisfy America?"

A few months later, in November 2016, Alyson Leahy, a 30-year-old Wisconsin graphic designer, watched as Trump was declared the winner of the presidential election. "I felt that Trump's win was the quintessential example of an unqualified man winning over an incredibly qualified woman," Leahy told CNN. "And the idea that people I knew, that I was related to, voted for that man . . . it made me sick." But rather than just staying mad, Leahy responded to the election by attending rallies and then running for office for the first time, unseating an incumbent to win a seat on her local county board. And exactly two years after she cried as she watched Trump elected to the highest office in the land, Leahy's name appeared on the ballot for a Wisconsin State Assembly seat in the 2018 election.

And, indeed, Leahy lost her first foray into politics, but her candidacy is not an unusual one; it is part of a larger trend: A record number of women appeared on the 2018 midterm election ballot. Many American women who had never considered running before did so as a result of Clinton's loss. In some sense, this is not surprising. Political scientists have known for years that observing women candidates for office has a number of benefits,[1] including increasing women's political ambition.[2] Clinton's 2016 run for the White House was the first time Americans had experienced a woman running for the highest office in the nation. Certainly, Clinton as candidate could have served as a role model for other women to run.

Yet women did not experience the first woman major party candidate in a vacuum. Rather, they experienced it within a profusion of viciousness hurled at the most politically ambitious woman most of them had ever seen. Clinton's unprecedented run for the presidency stirred up a similarly unprecedented level of sexism.[3] The Clinton candidacy may have decreased women's political ambition, especially because women often cite their perceived lack of qualifications when they say they do not want to run for office[4] and because women's perceived likelihood of winning plays into their decision about whether or not they will run.[5] Why should they run when the most qualified woman who has ever run cannot even win?

The 2016 election, then, provided us with the opportunity to see both of these phenomena in real time. To tease out these effects, our project draws on a unique data set of panel responses to questions about politics and political ambition, asked just before the election, just after the election, and just after the inauguration of Donald Trump as the 45th president of the United States. This design allows us to take account in real time of the effects of the election and of the inauguration on women's political ambition. Notably, the inauguration spurred a series of Women's marches, in which more than one million people marched in the U.S. capital and around the nation on the days after the inauguration in resistance to Trump, events that may have actually increased women's political ambition.

Specifically, we conducted a study on Amazon's Mechanical Turk that asked subjects to rate their levels of political ambition on a seven-point scale (from "strongly agree" to "strongly disagree" on the question, "I have plans to run for political office in the future"). The initial survey took place just before the election of 2016. We then returned to the subjects for a follow-up study twice—once just after the election and once just after the inauguration. We found that the political events of 2016–2017 *did* have an effect on women subjects. Specifically, willingness to run for office declined significantly both for women voters and for women nonvoters just after the 2016 election. After the 2017 inauguration—and the concomitant "Women's marches"—the political ambition of women voters rebounded, but political ambition of women nonvoters remained significantly lower than it was prior to the election. Interestingly, political ambition among *men* who voted and felt warmly toward Clinton experienced a significant decline after the election but rebounded to earlier levels by the inauguration. Political ambition among nonvoting men saw no change, after either the election or the inauguration.

In other words, the political events of 2016–2017 in toto likely decreased political ambition among women but only among those least involved in politics in the first place.

Tracking Ambition across Time

To better understand how the events of the 2016 election affected political ambition, we asked a set of Americans how likely they were to run for office someday at three separate periods: just before the election, just after the election, and just after the inauguration. We found our subjects on Mechanical Turk,[6] a marketplace for work in which people can perform simple tasks for small amounts of money. In our case, the task was providing answers to a series of survey questions. For the first wave, we recruited 765 subjects and paid them $0.50 each. We asked the subjects a series of questions about themselves and their attitudes toward politics. Most important, each subject was asked whether they agreed with the statement, "I have plans to run for political office in the future." Subjects were asked to rate how much they agreed with that statement on a seven-point scale from "strongly disagree" to "strongly agree." Subjects were asked to provide their email addresses if they wanted to be recontacted in the future. We used those email addresses to contact subjects again twice, once just after the election and once just after the inauguration.

In our analysis, we hope to explain the difference between the answer to the political ambition question before the election and the answer to the political ambition question after the election in the second wave and after the inauguration of Trump in the third wave. The difference we measure, then, for both of the last two waves is the difference between the value in that wave and the value *in the first wave*. In other words, if a subject chose seven ("strongly agree") in the wave prior to the election, then six ("moderately agree") in the wave after the election, she would have a value of –1 for the second wave. If the same subject then responded in the third wave (postinauguration) by choosing five on the same question, she would have a value of –2 for the third wave.

We also asked subjects a series of questions, including the gender with which they identify, their feelings about Clinton on a 100-point feeling thermometer scale, the political party with which they identify, and whether or not they voted. It is important to note that all subjects who responded in the first wave were invited again in the second and third waves. It was possible to respond only to the first and second, only to the first and third, or to all three waves. The number of observations, then, varied for each wave. The observations included here, then, are for subjects who responded to the first and second waves (for the second wave) and subjects who responded for the first and third waves (for the third wave).

This chapter's figures depict how differences in views of Clinton affected political ambition after the election and after the inauguration. To construct the figures, we estimated a regression with the difference in political ambition as the dependent variable. Results of the regression appear in the online appendix for this chapter.[7] The graphs presented here are based on those regressions.

Figure 11.1 (left) depicts the change in willingness to run for office from just before the election to just after the election. As is clear, women's views of Clinton mitigate the effect of her candidacy. Notably, the postelection change in statistical significance occurs near the 40-point mark in the 100-point feeling thermometer scale. In other words, as women begin to feel more positively toward Clinton, the election is more likely to have a deleterious effect on their willingness to run for office in the future. Those women, both voters and nonvoters, who rate Clinton at 40 or higher are significantly less willing to run for office just after the election than they were just before the election.

Figure 11.1 (right) shows the same effect for the change in willingness to run just before the election and just after Trump's inauguration. Again, women who esteem Clinton are more likely to see a change in their willingness to run once the 2016–2017 election cycle was complete. But notably, among voters, there is no value at which the effect is statistically significant. This contrasts with nonvoters, where the effect is significant for *every* value of the Clinton feeling thermometer. In other words, women who voted were *not* significantly less likely to be willing to run at the end of the election as they were at the

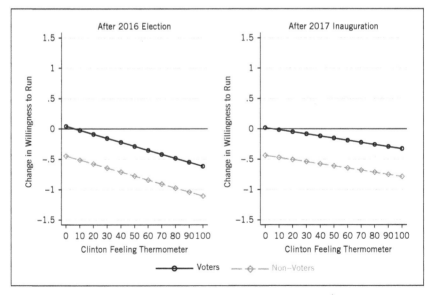

Figure 11.1. Change in women's political ambition after the 2016 election (*left*) and after the 2017 inauguration (*right*).

beginning. Yet women who did not vote ended the election period significantly less likely to run than they were before the election, and this was true even for those nonvoters who disliked Clinton the most.

Taken together, we can conclude that seeing Trump win the election over Clinton had a significantly deleterious effect for all women on their willingness to run, save those who felt the coldest about Clinton herself. Yet voting and nonvoting women seemed to react differently to seeing Trump inaugurated. For women who voted, the strength of the effect weakened after the inauguration. Perhaps the marches or their own anger prompted them to increase their political ambition. But it is important to note that, even if true, those levels of ambition increased only to their preelection levels. According to these results, seeing Trump inaugurated did not prompt greater ambition, at least not greater than had already been ignited from the primary election.

For nonvoters, however, the result is even more striking. Women nonvoters, even those who dislike Clinton very much, came out of the election season with significantly less ambition than they did when they entered it. Furthermore, for those women who are somewhat cool to Clinton (they rate their feelings about her around 30–40 on the 100-point scale), nonvoting women show a significant decline in their willingness to run, even when compared to women who voted. It is possible that these women, who do not have enough interest in politics to vote, may be the least likely to run in any event. But the results of these regressions make clear that there was certainly no jump in political ambition, at least among those women in our sample.

What about Men?

Our main question of interest is about women's political ambition, but men are included in our sample and in the regression we estimated (see the online appendix[8]). Because of this, we can consider how the 2016 election affected their political ambition. We can see the change from just before the election to just after the election in Figure 11.2 (left). The result for men who voted is nearly flat: Their views of Clinton had little to do with how the election affected their political ambition. Notably, for both women and men, those whose feelings about Clinton range from about 50 to about 80 saw a significant decline in their political ambition from preelectoral levels.

Figure 11.2 (right) shows the change in ambition from before the election to after the inauguration. While the effect of the view of Clinton remains flat for men and for both men and women voters, the effect of the election is no longer significant. Most voters, both men and women, came out of the election cycle with no significant change in their willingness to run for office.

Figure 11.3 (left) shows the change in political ambition for nonvoters from just before the election to just after the election. Again, feelings about Clinton are flat for men. And although the predicted value is positive for men

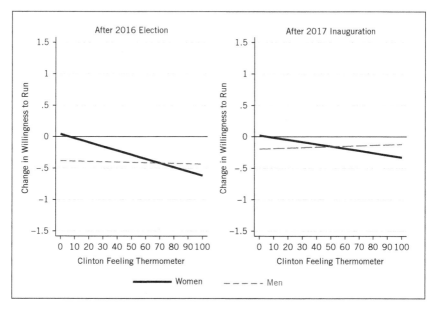

Figure 11.2. Gender differences in change in voters' political ambition after the 2016 election (*left*) and after the 2017 inauguration (*right*).

nonvoters (indicating an *increase* in political ambition for men who did not vote), it does not approach statistical significance for any value of the Clinton feeling thermometer. And, as noted above, this is different for women nonvoters, who experienced a decrease in political ambition at values of the Clinton feeling thermometer above 40 or so.

Figure 11.3 (right) shows the by-now-familiar flat effect of esteem for Clinton on the political ambition of men who are nonvoters. Here, however, even the predicted values for men are below zero, although not significantly so. And as noted above, women nonvoters are significantly less likely to run after the election than before, an effect that is not only significantly different from zero but also significantly different from that of men for some values in the center of the Clinton feeling thermometer.

It should not be ignored that this election increased virtually no one's political ambition. Given these results, we should not have expected women to flock to get on the ballot (which makes what happened in 2018 very interesting), but we should not expect that of men, either. No one came out of the election significantly *more* ambitious than they were prior to it, and no one has even a predicted value that is positive. The election of 2016, then, was harmful to political ambition in general, even if that harm was most obvious for some.

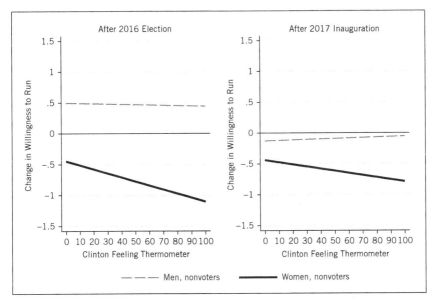

Figure 11.3. Gender differences in change in nonvoters' political ambition after the 2016 election (*left*) and after the 2017 inauguration (*right*).

Concluding Thoughts

Depictions of the 2016–2017 election cycle being the most divisive on record are myriad. Citizens—men and women, voters and nonvoters, alike—are angry and frustrated. In many ways, the results depicted here reflect that. It should be unsurprising that no one came out of this election cycle with significantly more political ambition than he or she had at its start.

Of course, we will never know what effect a Clinton electoral win would have had on women's political ambition. But now that we have experienced a Clinton electoral loss, we can draw upon this unique data set to explore in real time the effects of this election on political ambition. Seeing Trump beat Clinton decreased political ambition for Clinton supporters, save men who did not vote. Indeed, we show that men who voted saw decreases in political ambition that mirrored those of women who voted.

So how do we square these results with the record number of women who ran for office in 2018, just two years later? The answer perhaps lies in what we already know about why women run. Simply stated, women run for different reasons than men do. A rise in political ambition, our results indicate, is *not* the reason more women ran. Rather, they ran despite the fact that their ambition remained unchanged. They did so because they saw running as a decision that may be tied more closely to policy preferences than to political ambition as we have traditionally understood it.[9] The answer to seeing more women run, then, may not be to try to increase the number of women who answer "yes" to the question "I have plans to run for political office in the future" but rather to increase the number of women who believe that the political environment requires them to run *today*.

NOTES

1. Lonna Rae Atkeson, "Not All Cues Are Created Equal: The Conditional Impact of Female Candidates on Political Engagement," *Journal of Politics* 65, no. 4 (2003): 1040–1061; Kim L. Fridkin and Patrick J. Kenney, *The Changing Face of Representation* (Ann Arbor: University of Michigan Press, 2014), available at https://www.press.umich.edu/6200859/changing_face_of_representation; David E. Campbell and Christina Wolbrecht, "See Jane Run: Women Politicians as Role Models for Adolescents," *Journal of Politics* 68, no. 2 (2006): 233–247; Christina Wolbrecht and David E. Campbell, "Leading by Example," *American Journal of Political Science* 51, no. 4 (2007): 921–939; Susan Hansen, "Talking about Politics: Gender and Contextual Effects on Political Proselytizing," *Journal of Politics* 59, no. 2 (1997): 73–103; Jeffrey A. Karp and Susan A. Banducci, "When Politics Is Not Just a Man's Game: Women's Representation and Political Engagement," *Electoral Studies* 27 (2008): 105–115.

2. Lori Beaman, Esther Duflo, Rohini Pande, and Petia Topalova, "Female Leadership Raises Aspirations and Educational Attainment for Girls: A Policy Experiment in India," *Science* 335, no. 6068 (2012): 582–586; Jill S. Greenlee, Mirya R. Holman, and Rachel VanSickle-Ward, "Making It Personal: Assessing the Impact of In-Class Exercises on Closing the Gender Gap in Political Ambition," *Journal of Political Science Education* 10, no. 1 (2014): 48–61; Fabrizio Gilardi, "The Temporary Importance of Role Models for Women's Political Representation," *American Journal of Political Science* 59, no. 4 (2015): 957–970.

3. Clare Foran, "Will Hillary Clinton's Defeat Set Back Women in Politics?" 2016, accessed August 15, 2017, available at https://www.theatlantic.com/politics/archive/2016/11/hillary-clinton-donald-trump-women/508340/; Peter Beinart, "Fear of a Female President," 2016, accessed August 15, 2017, available at https://www.theatlantic.com/magazine/archive/2016/10/fear-of-a-female-president/497564/.

4. Jennifer L. Lawless and Richard L. Fox, *It Still Takes a Candidate: Why Women Don't Run for Office* (New York: Cambridge University Press, 2010).

5. See Ondercin, Chapter 8, in this volume.

6. See Adam J. Berinsky, Gregory A. Huber, and Gabriel S. Lenz, "Evaluating Online Labor Markets for Experimental Research: Amazon.com's Mechanical Turk," *Political Analysis* 20, no. 3 (2012): 351–368, for the validity of using Mechanical Turk.

7. The online appendix can be found through the Harvard Dataverse at https://doi.org/10.7910/DVN/PJNOVP.

8. The online appendix can be found through the Harvard Dataverse at https://doi.org/10.7910/DVN/BJTB1W.

9. See Thomas and Wineinger, Chapter 5, in this volume.

PART IV

How Nonprofits Help Women Run for Office

This part offers a closer look at the world of not-for-profit women's candidate recruitment and training programs, both in the United States and around the world. In the United States, idiosyncratic features of the political system mean that nongovernmental actors play an essential role in politics. The rules that govern the political system, the sheer scale and diversity of the country, and an insistence on the importance of individual participation all encourage the formation of nongovernmental actors and increase their influence.[1] American not-for-profit organizations thus have a critical role to play in helping women move toward political parity with men.[2] Such organizations abound, covering every part of the political pipeline from the early stages of identifying women who might be good candidates, through recruitment and training; from policy education to campaign funding and organization, and even beyond the first win to reelection.[3] Moreover, by using their unique position between political parties and the media to build popular narratives about the need for more women in office, these organizations often have the ability to set political agendas.[4] If academics have turned in recent years to studying women's ambition, it is at least in part due to the massive time, energy, and money that nongovernmental organizations have plowed into advancing women's candidacies.[5] Yet empirical questions remain: in which domains have these organizations been most successful and what are the most effective methods of increasing the substantive and numerical representation of women?

Outside the U.S. context, the need for not-for-profit intervention is less obvious. In many countries, parties, not citizens, control the nomination, selection, and funding of candidates for office, which might suggest to a naive observer that nonprofits have little role to play in training or funding women. Nevertheless, nonprofits and organizations targeting women candidates have proliferated, due, in part, to the need for many countries to prove to either foreign donors or domestic constituents that women's parity is being taken seriously.[6] In particular, they share with their American cousins an ability to agenda-set, promoting the need to elect more women. Still, it remains unclear whether these nonprofits are effective actors, or whether they simply provide a way for parties to shift the burden of achieving parity for women onto entities outside the typical nomination process.

Despite the importance of these questions, we know very little to date about the role that nonprofits play in relation to women's candidacies.[7] This is in part because political scientists have traditionally denigrated "program evaluation." Ambitious researchers—like potential women candidates—often turn their gaze elsewhere.[8] This is unfortunate, as novel areas of research need more attention to theory, not less; and, more pointedly, nonprofits will not stop developing new strategies to get women running simply because academics ignore them. What it means instead is that nonprofits are forced to develop these strategies in a void. They rarely even learn, for instance, whether the trainings they provide inspire or discourage women.[9] This scholarly inattention ensures that many organizations lack the information necessary to redesign their approaches to be more effective.

In Chapter 12, "Women Candidate Recruitment Groups in the States," Kreitzer and Osborn conduct a census of women's campaign training organizations in the United States, identifying the activities and spread of such groups over time, particularly at the local and state levels of office. While more than six hundred such groups have existed in the history of the United States, Kreitzer and Osborn find that many women who might otherwise consider a run for office have little access to such groups. For some, this is based on their policy stances: nearly 75 percent of women's training organizations have an abortion litmus test, and, of those, nearly 75 percent require women to be pro-choice. This means that the vast majority of training organizations are for pro-choice women. There is also a spatial dimension of access to campaign training organizations: some states have many dozens of groups, while others have few, and the partisanship of these groups may further restrict access. The training these groups provide also varies widely. In illustrating these dramatic differences for the first time, Kreitzer and Osborn show the unevenness of the political landscape women in the United States face thanks to the reliance of parties on informal (non-profit-run) recruitment and training processes.

Sanbonmatsu and Dittmar delve more deeply into the efficacy of these programs in Chapter 13, "Are You Ready to Run®? Campaign Trainings and Women's Candidacies in New Jersey." In this case study, conducted over eight years of training programs, Sanbonmatsu and Dittmar document large changes in women's sense of efficacy and interest in running for office after experiencing the program, even among these already-ambitious women. Moreover, they identify key best practices such as networking receptions that benefit women of color, who have been historically marginalized in their candidacies for political office and so are in greater need of a substitute for the "old boys' clubs" that have sustained so many (White, male) political candidacies in the past. Sanbonmatsu and Dittmar's chapter thus offers an important reminder that apparently mundane programming decisions, such as networking events, may do a great deal to diversify the kinds of women who benefit from these programs, even when the nonprofits themselves are highly successful in increasing the number of women running.

Chapter 14, "Pieces of Women's Political Ambition Puzzle: Changing Perceptions of a Political Career with Campaign Training," by Schneider and Sweet-Cushman, complements Chapter 13 by situating campaign training programs in the mind-sets of the women participating before and after the program. Schneider and Sweet-Cushman examine the effects of one-day training programs on women's longer-term conceptions of politics, finding that women feel more confident and positively about political careers after the training than they did before, in part because they were more likely to see political careers as communally oriented rather than power oriented. However, they do not find overall changes in women's stated political ambitions, perhaps because of ceiling effects (many women already expressed an intention to run upon entering the trainings) and perhaps because women's ambitions are constrained by bigger structural factors. Schneider and Sweet-Cushman, therefore, ask nonprofits to grapple with the "other pieces of the puzzle": one-day trainings may have important effects on self-efficacy and women's willingness to consider careers in politics, but more may be needed to overcome the challenges that women face in mounting a campaign—let alone winning.

Finally, in Chapter 15, "Women Running in the World: Candidate Training Programs in Comparative Perspective," Piscopo examines the benefits and limitations of women's candidate training programs in countries around the globe. Because, in many countries, parties are the gatekeepers of candidacy, Piscopo first summarizes much of the work on party discrimination against women outside the United States and then delves into the two main types of training programs—internationally funded and domestically funded—that exist in such countries. Many of these programs are formally partisan, in contrast to the often nonpartisan landscape in the United States described in Chapter 12, but vary widely in their emphasis on self-empowerment versus skills training versus providing funds. Internationally funded programs, however, place more emphasis on agenda-setting—building the "why women" narrative—than domestically funded programs. Nevertheless, as in Chapter 14, Piscopo questions the "lean in" and "why women" narratives, which can blame women for their own marginalization if not elected and for not saving democracy if they are elected. Parties, not just women and nonprofits, must "lean in" to the problems of candidate recruitment and training, especially, but not exclusively, in those countries where they control the selection of candidates.

The chapters on nonprofit intervention thus fall naturally into two pairs, one examining the candidates themselves, and one the broader political systems. Chapters 13 and 14 offer deep assessments of the structure of candidate training programs and how that structure shapes who benefits from attending. By studying two different state chapters of the same organization, over different periods of time, they illustrate the challenges inherent in drawing conclusions about the program's efficacy. On the one hand, both chapters find positive effects of attending programs on women's confidence and sense of inclusion in politics. Nonetheless, one study finds significant effects of the programs on women's willingness to run, while the other does not. As the authors discuss, this may be evidence of the importance of structural factors within the lives of the candidates themselves: non-White candidates in one study benefited from certain kinds of programming, while the other study containing primarily White candidates found little effect on women's willingness to run, perhaps because of other constraints in their lives. These accounts thus question whether nonprofits can overcome all the obstacles women face in running, including in their personal lives, and even when they can, for which sorts of women they make the biggest difference.

In contrast with each other, Chapters 12 and 15 offer broad examinations of the relationships between the structure of the political system and the role and efficacy of the candidate training organizations within them. Per Chapter 12, the United States, which allows any citizen to throw his or her hat into the political ring, offers fertile ground for nonprofits to contour the ideological bent and diversity of the candidate pool. While this gives them the ability to make large strides in women's representation, it also raises new questions about the power of these organizations to shape what women's representation actually looks like, both descriptively and substantively. In comparison, Chapter 15 suggests that these sorts of programs may not translate well in party-nominated (rather than self-nominated) systems. Such programs may undermine public support for women's candidacies while failing to deliver large gains in electoral seats—not because the programs are poorly designed but because their efficacy depends on the whims of the parties. Both chapters force us to reevaluate our understandings of what, when, and where not-for-profit organizations help women run.

NOTES
   1. Alexis De Tocqueville, "Democracy in America," (New York: G. Dearborn & Co., 1838); Robert Dahl, *Who Governs? Democracy and Power in an American City* (New

Haven, CT: Yale University Press, 1961); Rufus P. Browning, Dale Rogers Marshall, and David H. Tabb, "Protest Is Not Enough: A Theory of Political Incorporation," *PS* 19, no. 3 (1986): 576–581; Peter F. Burns, *Electoral Politics Is Not Enough: Racial and Ethnic Minorities and Urban Politics* (New York: State University of New York Press, 2006); Andrea Benjamin, "Coethnic Endorsements, Out-Group Candidate Preferences, and Perceptions in Local Elections," *Urban Affairs Review* 53, no. 4 (July 1, 2017): 631–657.

2. Rebecca J. Hannagan, Jamie P. Pimlott, and Levente Littvay, "Does an EMILY's List Endorsement Predict Electoral Success, or Does EMILY Pick the Winners?" *PS: Political Science and Politics* 43, no. 3 (2010): 503–508; Chao Guo and Juliet A. Musso, "Representation in Nonprofit and Voluntary Organizations: A Conceptual Framework," *Nonprofit and Voluntary Sector Quarterly* 36, no. 2 (2007): 308–326; Dawn Langan Teele, "How the West Was Won: Competition, Mobilization, and Women's Enfranchisement in the United States," *Journal of Politics* 80, no. 2 (April 2018): 442–461; Dawn Langan Teele, *Forging the Franchise: The Political Origins of the Women's Vote* (Princeton, NJ: Princeton University Press, 2018); Kelly LeRoux, "Paternalistic or Participatory Governance? Examining Opportunities for Client Participation in Nonprofit Social Service Organizations," *Public Administration Review* 69, no. 3 (2009): 504–517.

3. Rebecca J. Kreitzer and Tracy L. Osborn, "The Emergence and Activities of Women's Recruiting Groups in the U.S.," *Politics, Groups, and Identities* 7, no. 4 (2019): 842–852.

4. Pippa Norris and Joni Lovenduski, "Women Candidates for Parliament: Transforming the Agenda?" *British Journal of Political Science* 19, no. 1 (1989): 106–115; Loes Aaldering and Daphne Joanna Van Der Pas, "Political Leadership in the Media: Gender Bias in Leader Stereotypes during Campaign and Routine Times," *British Journal of Political Science*, March 2018, 1–21; Gail Baitinger, "Meet the Press or Meet the Men? Examining Women's Presence in American News Media," *Political Research Quarterly* 68, no. 3 (2015): 579–592.

5. Monica C. Schneider, Mirya R. Holman, Amanda B. Diekman, and Thomas McAndrew, "Power, Conflict, and Community: How Gendered Views of Political Power Influence Women's Political Ambition," *Political Psychology* 37, no. 4 (2016): 515–531; Mirya R. Holman and Monica C. Schneider, "Gender, Race, and Political Ambition," *Politics, Groups, and Identities* 6, no. 2 (April 3, 2018): 264–280; Shauna L. Shames, *Out of the Running: Why Millennials Reject Political Careers and Why It Matters* (New York: New York University Press, 2017); Kelly Dittmar, *Navigating Gendered Terrain: Stereotypes and Strategy in Political Campaigns* (Philadelphia: Temple University Press, 2015); Kelly Dittmar, "Encouragement Is Not Enough: Addressing Social and Structural Barriers to Female Recruitment," *Politics and Gender* 11, no. 4 (December 2015): 759–765; Jennifer L. Lawless and Richard L. Fox, "Girls Just Wanna Not Run the Gender Gap in Young Americans' Political Ambition," policy report by the Women and Politics Institute (Washington, DC: American University, 2013); Melody Crowder-Meyer, "Baker, Bus Driver, Babysitter, Candidate? Revealing the Gendered Development of Political Ambition among Ordinary Americans," forthcoming in *Political Behavior* (published online in September 2018); Katherine Levine Einstein, David M. Glick, Maxwell Palmer, and Robert J. Pressel, "Do Mayors Run for Higher Office? New Evidence on Progressive Ambition," *American Politics Research*, January 25, 2018; Jill S. Greenlee, Mirya R. Holman, and Rachel VanSickle-Ward, "Making It Personal: Assessing the Impact of In-Class Exercises on Closing the Gender Gap in Political Ambition," *Journal of Political Science Education* 10, no. 1 (2014): 48–61.

6. Jennifer M. Piscopo, "The Limits of Leaning In: Ambition, Recruitment, and Candidate Training in Comparative Perspective," *Politics, Groups, and Identities* 7, no. 4 (2019): 817–828.

7. Kira Sanbonmatsu and Susan J. Carroll, "Poised to Run: Women's Pathways to the State Legislatures" (New Brunswick, NJ: Center for American Women and Politics, Eagleton Institute of Politics, Rutgers University, 2009); Kelly Dittmar, Kira Sanbonmatsu, Susan J. Carroll, Debbie Walsh, and Catherine Wineinger, "Representation Matters: Women in the U.S. Congress" (New Brunswick, NJ: Center for American Women and Politics, Eagleton Institute of Politics, Rutgers University, 2017).

8. For a counterexample, see Cecilia Hyunjung Mo, Katharine M. Conn, and Georgia Anderson-Nilsson, "Youth National Service and Women's Political Ambition: The Case of Teach For America," *Politics, Groups, and Identities* 7, no. 4 (2019): 864–877.

9. Jennie Sweet-Cushman, "See It; Be It? The Use of Role Models in Campaign Trainings for Women," *Politics, Groups, and Identities* 7, no. 4 (2019): 853–863.

12

Women Candidate Recruitment Groups in the States

REBECCA KREITZER AND TRACY OSBORN

Efforts to solve the puzzle of how to elect more women to political office in the United States have advanced in recent years with the realization that "the ask"[1] is disproportionately important to bring women candidates to the table. Both women's own views of their qualifications for office and the views of party chairs and other recruiters keep women from pursuing elected office at the same rate that men do.[2] Building a structure of alternative recruiters and trainers for women candidates has the potential to overcome these obstacles to office. The United States also lacks the kinds of policies, namely electoral or party quotas, that serve as an impetus for recruiting women candidates in other countries. Thus, the informal network of women's recruitment groups built around identifying, training, and supporting women candidates fills the void of a more formal policy aimed at increasing women's representation and participation.

As this volume illustrates, however, we lack significant evaluation of how this structure of women candidate recruitment groups operates and, ultimately, whether it succeeds in electing more women to office. In this chapter, we provide such a description and initial evaluation of the nature, tactics, and goals of what we call women candidate groups (WCGs) in the United States. We find there are nearly four hundred active WCGs in the United States today. These groups typically have parameters that define the type of women candidates they recruit and train. WCGs engage in a number of activities to support women candidates; primarily, they recruit, train, and fund them, although most groups specialize in one or two of these activities. Though groups exist in each of the lower 48 states at this time, the availability of a WCG to a woman candidate is not the same for all women.

Our Study

In this chapter, we describe some initial observations from our attempt to catalog every WCG currently operating in the United States. We omit nationally focused groups and focus on groups that operate in only one state (or occasionally a few), since our research focus is on women in state and local office.[3] We used the internet to identify groups initially and record common characteristics across groups from their websites. Assistants then used follow-up phone calls and emails to track down details not available or unclear from websites; we include excerpts from these conversations here to illustrate some of our points. Our census of groups is primarily a tool for us to use to identify groups for a later survey of groups' tactics and successes. However, we can learn a lot from our initial look at what kinds of groups exist in the states and how these groups present themselves to the public.

One point of clarification is necessary before we move to describing the groups, however. We classify the network of WCGs in the states as an "informal" network, but this term might lead to some confusion. Many of the groups we find have existed for decades and have well-established programs and goals for recruiting and training women candidates. Thus, one might describe these groups as formal in their approach to increasing women's representation because of their established organization. We call these groups "informal," though, because they exist outside of the official apparatus for nominating women candidates in the United States. Though some of the groups are affiliated with political parties (e.g., the Federations of Republican or Democratic Women in many of the states), none of the groups is part of the nominating structure. Nominations for state and local office in the United States typically occur through primary elections. Yet, candidates for these primary elections emerge through an informal and/or invisible process of local and state political party recruitment.[4] Party chairs look for potential candidates and try to convince them to run, and, in some cases, they might convince candidates *not* to run by gatekeeping them from office.[5]

The WCG structure operates as a parallel set of groups that encourage, train, and support potential women candidates. This parallel operation means groups may interact with parties, but they are *independent from* them. Many groups, in fact, eschew identification with either party and train or recruit both Republican and Democratic candidates. Even groups that are affiliated with or align with a specific party are not necessarily privy to the decision-making structure of the party itself. These groups might suggest and aid potential women candidates while having little to no control over whether the woman receives the endorsement and support of the party itself for the nomination. Thus, the parallel, independent nature of WCGs in the United States is different from parties themselves adopting policies to promote women candidates, such as the "all woman short list" policy of the U.K. Labour Party.

From our data, we can assess three areas of description for WCGs. The first area is the *who*: what kinds of women do these groups recruit and support? The second area pertains to *where*: which states have WCGs, and what kinds of groups are they? Finally, the third area relates to *how*: how do WCGs attempt to increase women's representation? From these three pieces of evidence, we conclude that the informal network of WCGs is large and active, but limited in the types of women they recruit and even in access to women across the country.

The Who: What Kinds of Women Do WCGs Target?

In total, we find over six hundred WCGs in the United States. About one-third of these groups had little to no information online and/or did not respond to our efforts to contact them to obtain information. Thus, we concentrate on the remaining two-thirds, or roughly four hundred, active WCGs across the United States. Our definition of a WCG includes any group that finds, encourages, trains, and/or funds potential women candidates. It is possible that a group that we identify as a WCG does not identify themselves as such; our forthcoming survey will further parse these distinctions. Among these nearly four hundred groups in our initial identification, we find three key points describe the kinds of women WCGs target.

The first point of variation, central to American politics, is partisanship. Of the nearly 400 WCGs, the number of explicitly partisan groups is nearly even between Democrats and Republicans (79 and 80 groups, respectively). Thus, the remaining 238 groups are, at least nominally, nonpartisan or bipartisan in nature. From these initial numbers, we might conclude that WCGs in the states target roughly equal portions of Democratic and Republican women.

The second point of variation precludes such a conclusion of bipartisanship, however. Rather than using partisanship as a selection criterion, it is significantly more common for WCGs to recruit, train, and/or fund candidates based on an abortion opinion litmus test. Nearly three-fourths of the active WCGs in our sample have an abortion litmus test for which potential candidates they will support. Of these nearly 300 abortion-specific groups, 226 are pro-choice, while only 74 are antiabortion groups. Within the current, increasingly polarized American partisan environment, this abortion litmus test appears to provide a de facto partisan criterion for groups to select women candidates. For example, in an email to us, the national organization Electing Women wrote us the following regarding their pro-choice abortion litmus test:

Electing Women is technically not partisan but we only support pro-choice women running for U.S. Senate and Governor's seats and we have yet to find a Republican candidate that we really felt would con-sistently vote pro-choice. We did consider supporting Susan Collins but she supported George W. Bush's Supreme Court nominees who were not pro-choice so we decided not to support her. (email, 8/10/17)

Thus, if we compare groups across both specific partisan criteria and abor-tion opinion criteria, WCGs lean disproportionately to recruiting, training, and supporting pro-choice women, who are largely Democratic women.

A third point of variation across groups is the degree to which they try to recruit a diverse set of women candidates, widely construed. Among ac-tive WCGs, we found only a few groups specialized in recruiting a specific type of underrepresented woman candidate. Two groups explicitly recruit African American women, two groups explicitly seek Latinas, and one group focuses on Asian American women. Twenty-eight additional groups focus specifically on recruiting women of color. Interestingly, however, a signifi-cant number of groups (135) focus on recruiting a "diverse" group of women in a less-defined fashion.

From the information we have, it is difficult to decipher how effectively this generic focus on diversity leads to a deeply diverse group of potential women candidates. Some groups reported significant strides in diverse re-cruiting. For example, the California Issues and Trends (CIT) Program re-ports:

Through stepped-up recruitment efforts, the program has increased in racial and ethnic diversity over time. Results show that nonwhite CIT participants increased from 23% in 2001–2006 to 46% in 2007–2010. In May of 2011, the organization conducted a formal indepen-dent assessment of its signature CIT program. The study found that overall racial and ethnic diversity of its alumnae group closely mirrors the national average, with 66% of study participants self-identifying as white/Caucasian and 34% self-identifying as nonwhite. (Califor-nia's population is 40% white and 60% nonwhite.) (CIT website)

Similarly, Ready to Run® New Jersey, part of the Center for American Women in Politics (CAWP), reports:

CAWP has developed a Diversity Initiative of Ready to Run® to at-tract more women of color into the political process and encourage them to seek public leadership. The Diversity Initiative in New Jersey comprises three separate programs for African American women, Asian American women, and Latinas. Since the creation of the Diver-sity Initiative, fully half of participants in the New Jersey Ready to Run® program have been women of color. (CAWP website)

Diversity, as defined by WCGs, is also not limited to diversity among women of color. Our data reveal groups that focus on Native American, LGBTQ, and low-income women, too. For instance, Carol's List, a Montana group modeled after the national EMILY's List, reports:

> Our president, Carol Williams, was elected by her peers as the first woman Senate Minority Leader in Montana. Founding members Christine Kaufmann and Diane Sands were the first openly lesbian Senator and Representative, respectively. Board member Denise Juneau is the first Native American woman ever elected to a statewide office in the United States. Founding co-chair, Carol Juneau, carried the bill making Montana the first state to implement Indian Education for All. Our legislature needs to look like all Montanans in order to truly represent all Montanans. (Carol's List website)

Similarly, in the wake of HB2 in North Carolina, a contentious bill that restricted bathroom use for transgender people, among other things, the Democratic Women of North Carolina identify an emphasis on including transgender women in the organization. Montana Women Vote advertises on their website that they focus on low-income women. The drawback, however, to these foci on diversity is that for many groups, the target of diversity remains undefined. This could allow WCGs to be flexible in their recruitment goals, but it might also allow groups to push the goal of diversity among women candidates to the side. From our current information, it is difficult to tell whether calls for diversity yield results except for in a handful of cases.

Finally, the goal of diversity is, somewhat surprisingly, *not* disproportionately found in Democratic/pro-choice groups. Fifty-two Republican/antiabortion groups mention diversity as a goal—about 63 percent of the total Republican/antiabortion groups. Seventy-nine Democratic/pro-choice groups mention diversity, which is a larger number numerically but percentagewise is only 33 percent of these groups. Roughly half of nonpartisan or bipartisan groups mention diversity as a goal.

The Where: Access to WCGs across the States

The distribution of WCGs across the states demonstrates that groups are spread across the United States, but they are not ubiquitous, particularly when one considers the type of group. In total number of groups, some states, such as California, Arizona, and New Jersey have between 13 and 28 groups within their state, while others, such as the Dakotas, Wyoming, and Vermont, have only between 2 and 3 groups. Though some of this variation in the overall number of WCGs is surely due to population distribution (i.e., it is not surprising that California has a large number of groups), there are states that appear relatively under- or overserved. For example, Texas has between 7 and 9 groups, while states that are smaller than Texas (e.g., Arizona and New Jersey) have between 11 and 28 groups. Nonetheless, each state has at least 1 or 2 groups, and most have at least 3. This evidence suggests that, generally, the network of WCGs is spread wide enough for women in each of the states to have some access to a candidate group.

However, the picture of WCG distribution changes once one considers the location of groups according to partisanship and/or the prominent abortion litmus test we mention above. Figure 12.1 shows the distribution of all active WCGs by party (explicitly Democrat or explicitly Republican) and abortion litmus test (antiabortion or proabortion rights). Since proabortion rights/Democratic groups are more common, it is not surprising that they are distributed across the states more evenly than anti-abortion/Republican groups. Only four states—Wyoming, Delaware, South Dakota, and New Hampshire—lack a Democratic/proabortion rights group in the state. Alternatively, 21 states lack a Republican/anti-abortion group. Women in most states have access to at least one (but often just one) nonpartisan or bipartisan WCG, if they lack a partisan/abortion-specific one. However, Democratic/proabortion rights women have more options if they seek a WCG in the states.

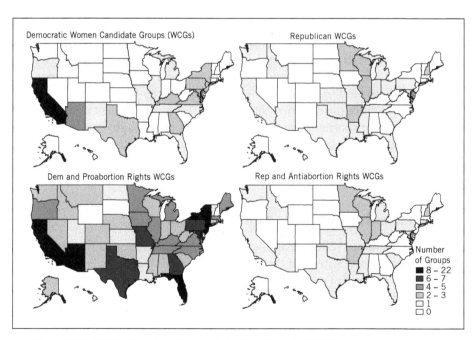

Figure 12.1. Distribution of partisan and abortion litmus test WCGs.

The How: What Do WCGs Do?

Much of the prior two points of variation—diversity and location—hinge somewhat on what skills the WCG at hand can offer potential women candidates. Our data show that WCGs engage in four key activities. First, of our nearly 400 groups, over one quarter (121) of the groups list an explicit goal of appointing more women to boards and commissions in the states. Though we typically think of WCGs as interested in elections exclusively, a strong number of groups also aim to place women in other positions of government power. As this strategy may eventually increase the number of women in positions of electoral candidate recruiting and influence as well, it demonstrates that groups often employ multiple strategies to help women achieve office.

The three most common strategies among groups are recruiting women candidates (286), training women in candidate skills (268), and funding women's campaigns (218). Seventy-six groups in our census engage in all three of these activities simultaneously. As we described above, groups that recruit women largely rely on a partisan/abortion litmus test to determine which women they recruit to office. Few groups specify the types of women candidates they want to recruit beyond this criterion, although a small subset explicitly recruit women of color. Interestingly, groups that fund women candidates do not skew to funding particular types of candidates. We suspected that funding groups would correlate highly with the use of the abortion litmus test, yet this is not the case. Nor are these groups disproportionately Democratic or Republican. Rather, what we find is that groups that fund women candidates do not lean disproportionately toward being pro-choice or anti-abortion, Democrat or Republican. However, it is important to remember that there are *more* Democratic/pro-choice groups, and thus they offer more support generally.

Another key observation is that when groups report that they train women in candidate skills, the definition of a skill is wide. Consequently, the length of the trainings vary significantly: some trainings are just several hours long and others that include dozens of hours are over many months. We find six groups that specifically specialize in training campaign managers (some also run other trainings) to run women's campaigns. Thirty groups specialize in providing leadership training to college students with an eye toward a future pool of women candidates. The best known is probably the units of the NEW Leadership Program, which introduces leadership skills and women in politics information to college students in various states. Nonpartisan groups like Ready to Run® (chapters exist in multiple states) teach a wide curriculum that includes media training, how to fundraise, nominations and party structure, and more.[6] Emerge America, a Democratic leadership program, offers a lengthy six-month program for potential candidates in 22 states. The NFRW's branch chapters in several states run campaign management schools; not all chapters run such programs, however. The emergence of nonpartisan campaign schools in the early 2000s significantly increased the number of in-person training programs for women. Emerge America is also an early 2000s group; we found no such new Republican counterpart across multiple states within this time frame.

One remaining question on which we have little leverage is how groups *recruit* candidates for office. Most groups post information about training sessions on websites, but we are unable from this information to ascertain two key pieces of information. First, we do not know to what extent program cost and time commitment shape the types of women willing to apply for a program. Second, we cannot leverage how many recruits to programs (or simply recruits to run for office) come through an informal network of group members who find participants. One example of this model is Lillian's List, a North Carolina–based pro-choice group. They have a team of one hundred "scouts" whose job it is to identify community leaders and inform the organization. The scouts hold about a dozen meetings over the year to coordinate their efforts. This type of informal network to find participants might bring more women to office, but it might also skew the types of women who participate in directions relevant to those who do the recruiting, similar to the problem of gendered recruiting within party networks. Finally, there are really two types of recruitment to consider. A woman might be recruited to participate in a WCG training session, she might be recruited to run for office (and then possibly trained), or she might be recruited for both.

Conclusion: Are WCGs the Right Way to Increase Women's Representation?

We conclude this overview of WCGs by returning to the reason for their existence: party networks do not do an adequate job of bringing women into American politics, so WCGs rose to fill this void. From our data, we can conclude generally that the network of WCGs in the United States is large and dispersed across the states to access many women. Interestingly, many groups in our census have existed for years; for instance, the Republican Federation of Women chapters typically formed between 1930 and 1950. Recent movements have included the "lists" of the 1990s (e.g., EMILY's List and various spin-offs such as Carol's and Lillian's Lists), many of whom donate to women candidates. Since the 2000s, leadership and candidate skill-based groups have flourished. Groups that have existed for years, such as state NOW chapters, have also added candidate training to their activities. We have observed an increase of over 60 groups since 2000. It is important to note, however, that Democratic groups far outnumber Republican ones during this time.

We can also conclude that groups at least acknowledge the importance of diversity among the types of women candidates they recruit, train, and fund. One problem is that many groups list diversity generally as a goal without being specific about who they mean or how they intend to fulfill this focus. When it is defined by a WCG, diversity includes many groups along racial/ethnic, sexuality, and economic lines. As Brown and Dowe highlight in Chapter 10, women of color are less likely to be supported as candidates by political parties. WCGs have real potential to fill this void and increase diversity among women candidates, but only if they employ an effective strategy to diversify their participant pool.

We might also consider the partisan diversity of women. Many groups recruit women on partisan and/or abortion opinion criteria. This reliance on an abortion litmus test limits opportunities for Republican women candidates, which somewhat mirrors the distribution of Republican and Democratic women in office. If groups wish simply to increase the number of women in office, increasing truly nonpartisan training groups might be a way to do so. Disproportionately, current groups wish to recruit specific kinds of partisan women to office with specific opinions on reproductive policy.

With our current data, we ultimately cannot assess the success of WCGs in the long run as a vehicle to increase women's representation in office. As Sanbonmatsu and Dittmar argue in Chapter 13, participants in candidate training programs find them to be positive experiences and places where they learn the skills associated with campaigning. Their individual data show that participants were more likely to say they might run for office after participating in the program. Schneider and Sweet-Cushman, in Chapter 14, do not find a direct link between program participation and the desire to run for office; however, they do find the training increases women's confidence and perceptions of holding elected office in general. It is tempting to conclude that these positive outcomes for individuals in specific training programs amalgamate to an overall increase in women's representation where candidates have access to programs. Our chapter here indicates that not all women may have access to the sorts of opportunities available in a training program. Furthermore, training programs engage in a variety of activities, some of which may be more effective than others for potential or current women candidates. Gazing at the network of WCGs from afar allows us to consider how we might continue to assess the success of the WCG network as a whole.

NOTES

1. Kelly Dittmar, "Encouragement Is Not Enough: Addressing Social and Structural Barriers to Female Recruitment," *Politics and Gender* 11, no. 4 (December 2015): 759–765.

2. See, for example, Melody Crowder-Meyer, "Gendered Recruitment without Trying: How Local Party Recruiters Affect Women's Representation," *Politics and Gender* 9 (2013): 390–413; Jennifer L. Lawless and Richard L. Fox, *It Still Takes a Candidate: Why Women Don't Run for Office* (Cambridge: Cambridge University Press, 2010); Kira San-

bonmatsu, "Do Parties Know That 'Women Win'? Party Leader Beliefs about Women's Electoral Chances," *Politics and Gender* 2 (2006): 431–450.

3. We do have significant data on national groups, so we include a few observations on them here. We did not systematically collect all of their information, however.

4. Elin Bjarnegård and Meryl Kenny, "Revealing the 'Secret Garden': The Informal Dimensions of Political Recruitment," *Politics and Gender* 11 (2015): 748–753.

5. Crowder-Meyer, "Gendered Recruitment without Trying"; Kira Sanbonmatsu, "Do Parties Know That 'Women Win'?"

6. More information is available at http://www.cawp.rutgers.edu/education_train ing/ready_to_run/overview.

13

Are You Ready to Run®?

Campaign Trainings and Women's Candidacies in New Jersey

KIRA SANBONMATSU AND
KELLY DITTMAR

What role do campaign trainings play in women's candidacy decisions? Women state legislators are more likely than their male colleagues to have attended a campaign training, raising questions about why trainings appear to be disproportionately important to women compared with men.[1]

We use data from an original eight-year panel study of participants in a state Ready to Run® campaign training program to investigate why women attend trainings and to what effect. Our main goals are to analyze the expectations that women have for the program and understand their experiences as participants. And of course, of central interest is whether women go on to seek elected office—as well as appointive office—in the years following the training. For reasons we describe below, it is difficult to pinpoint the causal effect of trainings. Because of these challenges, we analyze the extent to which the women who attend the program were already planning a bid for office and compare women's responses on this basis.

We also ask whether and how race/ethnicity situates women differently with respect to candidacy and campaign trainings, taking advantage of the Ready to Run® Diversity Initiative—a special preconference program that creates spaces specific to subgroups of minority women.[2]

One advantage of focusing on a single program over time is the ability to understand a specific political context in depth. In this case, we study the New Jersey Ready to Run® program, an annual bipartisan campaign training program. The pipeline of potential candidates that Ready to Run® has helped to build over the years has arguably contributed to an increase in women's presence in the New Jersey legislature.[3] Whereas New Jersey typically ranked in the bottom 10 of the 50 states for women's state legislative representation in the past, New Jersey today ranks 21st in the nation.

From 2010 to 2014, we asked first-time participants at Ready to Run® to complete a confidential paper-and-pencil survey prior to the start of the training. We call these survey data "the initial survey." For each year since then, we recontacted these women to learn about their evaluations of the program and their office-seeking experiences, if any. In this paper, we only analyze responses to the first follow-up survey that participants completed, which we call the "panel survey data." By capturing survey responses at two points in time, these data provide a unique window into the place of campaign trainings in electing women to office.

Why Do Women Attend Ready to Run®?

Our initial survey of first-time Ready to Run® participants provides useful insights into what motivated them to attend the program. Note that a total of 320 women completed the survey including 176 women of color and 134 nonhispanic White women. As Figure 13.1 shows, the most common response to why women were attending Ready to Run® was that they were interested in learning more about the political process; 71 percent of survey respondents chose this as one of the reasons they came to the campaign training, with more women of color than White women seeking this information ($p < 0.05$). A majority of attendees also said that they came to Ready to Run® to acquire or improve their skills (65.3 percent), for networking opportunities (61.6 percent), and to meet other women like them (56 percent).[4] While the differences between White women and women of color were minimal across these responses, women of color attending Ready to Run® for the first time were even more likely than their White counterparts to say that they came to the program to meet other women like them ($p < 0.01$).[5] We do not know the nature of the commonality among women that participants were seeking. However, this finding potentially points to both the need for and the appeal of the Ready to Run® Diversity Initiative, which provides women of color with the space to network and learn from other women within their racial and ethnic communities ahead of the main Ready to Run® conference.[6] Just over half (55.3 percent) of the first-time participants we surveyed told us that they came to Ready to Run® because they were planning to run for elected office, with no significant differences across race or ethnicity on this question.

When asked more specifically about their candidacy plans, 80 percent of attendees reported that they had at least *thought* about running for office before they came to the program. Of the women we surveyed, 15.6 percent had already run for office, 22.2 percent said they planned to run, and 42.2 percent said that they had thought about running. Just under one-fifth (19.1 per-

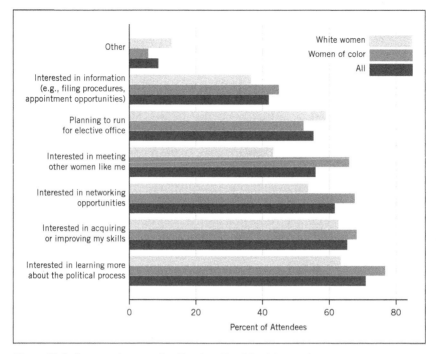

Figure 13.1. Reasons for attending Ready to Run® (initial survey).

cent) said they had never thought about running. This means that while most women in attendance (61.25 percent) had no plans to run, 37.8 percent were either running or had previously been candidates. These data confirm what could logically be expected: those women who seek out and attend a campaign training program like Ready to Run® are much more likely to view running for office as less of a question of "if" and more of a question of "when" and/or "how."

Some comparison to other populations provides useful context for these data. In Jennifer Lawless and Richard Fox's 2001 Citizen Political Ambition Study, just 10 percent of women surveyed as part of their likely candidate pool (with occupations in law, business, education, and politics) reported about running for office that they had "seriously considered it" and 33 percent said "it has crossed my mind."[7] We also find that Ready to Run® attendees are more likely to have been encouraged to seek elected office than women in other surveys. Nearly three-quarters (71.6 percent) of first-time Ready to Run® participants reported that someone had already suggested they run for office before they came to the program. White women attendees (76.9 percent) were slightly more likely than

women of color (67.6 percent) to tell us that they had been encouraged to run
($p < 0.10$).

Findings from Susan J. Carroll and Kira Sanbonmatsu's national survey
of state legislators demonstrate that encouragement like this matters more for
women than men in making the decision to run for office. They find that 44
percent of women state legislators surveyed in 2008 had not seriously thought
about running for office until someone else suggested it, while 47.9 percent of
male state legislators said it was entirely their idea to run.[8] Our data suggest
that most Ready to Run® participants come to the program with some level of
previous recruitment and that prior encouragement to run may have been
among the factors motivating them to attend the program. It is also possible
that encouragement to attend Ready to Run® coincided with encouragement
to seek office. For example, some past participants in the New Jersey program
have been sponsored by political groups like labor unions or county party organizations. While CAWP's marketing for the program appeals to broad audiences of women, these targeted efforts among political organizations might
contribute to our evidence of prior encouragement.

Unfortunately, discouragement is also a reality for many women considering a run for political office. About one-third of the women state legislators
surveyed by Carroll and Sanbonmatsu in 2008 said that they had encoun-
tered efforts to discourage their first candidacy, and—among Democrats—
women of color legislators were even more likely than White women to have
confronted discouragement in their paths to office.[9] In our survey of Ready
to Run® participants, just 17 percent of first-time attendees told us that someone had discouraged them from running for office. Unlike findings among
legislators, the cross-racial differences were insignificant and slightly fewer
women of color attendees reported being discouraged from running before
attending the training.

These findings suggest that the most important services of Ready to Run®
to attendees are educational, providing a setting in which women can learn
about the political process they must navigate and develop skills that they
will need to run and win. First-time women of color participants appear particularly motivated to meet women like them, also illuminating the importance of campaign trainings as a site for sharing experiences—both struggles
and successes—that will contribute to or even shape candidacies for women
attendees. Importantly, the majority of attendees come already encouraged
to run and with minimal discouragement in mind, and more than half of
attendees report planning to run for office before the training even begins.
These findings paint a picture of a primed population of potential candidates,
less weighted down by some of the typical inhibitors to women's political candidacy and more reliant on Ready to Run® to provide the information and skills
necessary to turn their plans for running into reality.

What Are the Benefits of Attending Ready to Run®?

The panel nature of our survey of Ready to Run® participants allows us to analyze the impact of the program on attendees in the years following their participation. Two caveats accompany our analyses of these panel data. First, not all respondents participated in the follow-up surveys that constitute the panel: about 40 percent of first-time participants answered at least one follow-up survey with a lower response rate among women of color compared with White women (33 percent compared with 51 percent, respectively). Other than race/ethnicity, the first-time participants who completed at least one follow-up survey were largely similar to those who did not participate in the panel.

Second, among those respondents who did participate in the panel, some women completed one annual follow-up survey while others completed more than one.[10] For these reasons, we have chosen to include in our analyses only the responses from the first time that respondents participated in a wave of the panel, regardless of whether that follow-up survey was completed one or several years after attending Ready to Run®.

Among the questions we posed in follow-up surveys of participants was one that asked whether the program fulfilled 9 different objectives, all listed in Figure 13.2. In their first post-participation reports to us, the outcome most commonly cited among women attendees (75.6 percent) was that Ready to Run® helped to improve their skills, consistent with one of the top motivations to attend the program among our first-time survey respondents. Similar proportions of attendees also told us that Ready to Run® helped them to acquire new skills (71.9 percent) and provided them with specific information (e.g., filing procedures, appointment opportunities) (71.1 percent). These findings are consistent with previous literature that finds greater doubt among women about their qualifications to run for or hold political office; if women arrive at the program with such doubts, their valuation of the skills and information for being an effective candidate gained at Ready to Run® will be greater. Seven in 10 panel respondents reported that attending Ready to Run® increased their interest in running for office, with that effect slightly more positive among women of color ($p = 0.10$). Importantly, less than 10 percent of attendees said that learning about the political process and hearing about women's experiences running for office at Ready to Run® *decreased* their interest in running. Nearly two-thirds reported that the training had expanded their network.

We also asked the women who participated in our panel study to reflect on which aspect of the training was most useful. The most popular aspect was the media training, noted by 42.7 percent of the panel survey respondents.[11] Campaign information was deemed useful by 21.4 percent, followed

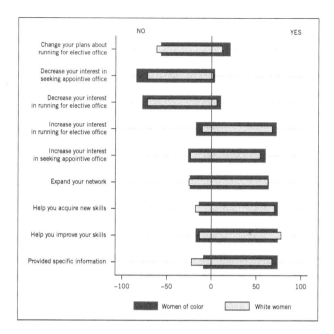

Figure 13.2. Ready to Run® outcomes (panel respondents).

by fundraising information (12.4 percent). Political party information (3.4 percent) was least commonly mentioned.

Another way to gauge the role of Ready to Run® is to analyze the appointive and elective office-seeking experiences of participants. These data arguably represent a conservative evaluation of Ready to Run®'s effects because they offer a snapshot of participants' experiences following the conference. The survey wording specified that we were seeking information about the women's experiences in the prior calendar year, and so we are evaluating a short time frame. Recall that we are analyzing only responses from the first follow-up survey.

Our analysis of these data from the follow-up surveys reveals a high frequency of experience with appointive and/or elected office seeking or plans to pursue these offices in the future.[12] These results are consistent with the paper-and-pencil versions of the surveys that we conducted in-person at the Ready to Run® training initially, given that over one-third of those first-time participants revealed that they had either run for elected office before or already had plans to run. Of all panel respondents in our analysis, about half were currently running for an elected office, had run in the past year, or were planning to run in the future (see Figure 13.3).[13]

The women who are perhaps of most interest to our study are those women who, at the time of the initial survey prior to experiencing Ready to Run®, either were not planning to run or had not thought about running. Because they enrolled in Ready to Run®, they are more politically active than most New

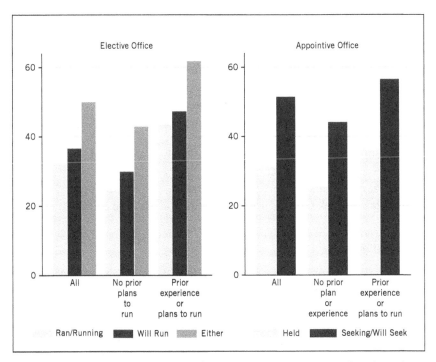

Figure 13.3. Elective office-seeking experiences (panel respondents) (*left*) and appointive office-seeking experiences (panel respondents) (*right*).

Jersey women. In other words, we do not claim that they are representative of the general population. But one way to evaluate the influence of the Ready to Run® program is to assess the subsequent political experiences of this group of women who were not planning a bid for elected office.

Figure 13.3 shows that, at the time of the panel study, nearly one-quarter were running or had run in the past year with about 30 percent planning to run in the future. Of course, these statistics do not take into account the election calendar or open seat opportunities; and planning to run is not the same outcome as having run. Nevertheless, these statistics are notable because this group did not have office-seeking plans at the time of Ready to Run® but most did subsequently.

Meanwhile, among the women who had prior campaign experience or concrete elected office-seeking plans prior to attending Ready to Run®, most—61.8 percent—reported currently running or running in the past year or having plans to run (see Figure 13.3).

Turning to experiences with appointive office, we find that nearly one-third of the panel respondents in our study had held appointive office and that a majority were seeking appointive office or had plans to do so in the future (see Figure 13.3, right side). If we compare these experiences with how women responded on the initial survey prior to attending Ready to Run®, we see that 44.1 percent of those respondents who initially voiced no experience or plans for appointive office were seeking or planning to seek those offices with 25.4 percent reporting appointive officeholding experience. Thus, one impact of attending Ready to Run® appears to be to introduce the idea of appointive office opportunities. This is consistent with Figure 13.2, which revealed that for most women, interest in appointive officeholding increased because of the training.

Among those who, prior to attending Ready to Run®, had appointive office experience or office-seeking plans, 36.2 percent had held appointive office in the prior year and a majority (56.5 percent) were seeking appointive office or had plans to seek such an office in the future at the time of our panel study.

Conclusion

Our initial and panel surveys of Ready to Run® New Jersey participants provide useful insights into the motivations of attendees, as well as their perceptions of benefits from completing the program. We find that respondents give overwhelmingly positive evaluations to the campaign training and that the short-term outcomes they report are consistent with the desires noted by first-time attendees. Specifically, participants both view and use the training program as a tool for education and skills development. We also find that the opportunity to build networks is sought by and valuable to program attendees, with women of color particularly motivated to meet other women like them. The inclusion of a networking reception, as well as the Ready to Run® Diversity Initiative, helps the program meet these expectations.

Finally, our data show that most Ready to Run® New Jersey attendees are already poised to run when they come to the program for the first time, benefiting from encouragement they have received prior to—and potentially motivating to—registration. And among those program participants without plans to seek elected or appointive office when they arrived at the training, our panel data show that completing the program seems to have had some positive effect on their plans for pursuing a political office. Ready to Run® also increased awareness of and interest in seeking appointive office.

What our survey data cannot conclusively provide is a measure of Ready to Run®'s direct effects on increasing the numbers of women in office in the state of New Jersey, a measure often sought by advocates, funders, and academics alike. Even our ability to determine how many attendees ultimately run for elected or seek appointive offices is constrained by who completes our panel surveys, the post-participation time period within which "effects" are measured, and the many other important factors not measured here that are likely to influence any potential candidate's plans to run and chances for election success. These other factors—such as the availability of open and/or competitive seats or a political climate friendly to political newcomers—are largely outside of the control of these training programs and their facilitators but can complicate gauging this type of program success.

We argue that it is necessary to rethink how success is measured for campaign training programs like Ready to Run®. Our findings show, for example, that the benefits that Ready to Run® New Jersey attendees identify after participation in the program are consistent with the outcomes they sought from the program before it began. More specifically, Ready to Run® is successful in educating participants about the political process and providing them with the skills and networks they seek in preparation for a possible bid for office. In doing so, the program has created a pool of credentialed women candidates that can exploit political opportunities as they arise. Hopefully, this preparation increases the likelihood that attendees will be elected or appointed when they do pursue these posts, but attributing political success or defeat solely to participation in a campaign training program neglects the complexities of the political system.

Additional research on candidate recruitment prior to attending a campaign training as well as the sites for and sources of campaign support after the training will better position studies like ours within the full timeline of any individual candidacy. Our findings indicate that campaign trainings are an added value to potential candidates, although we do not claim that they act alone in clearing the path to candidacy and officeholding for women.

NOTES

We are grateful to the campaign training participants who participated in this study and made this research possible. We thank Christabel Cruz, Tessa Ditonto, Hannah McVeigh, and Kathleen Rogers for assistance with the data collection and data entry. We also thank Jean Sinzdak and Debbie Walsh for their time and insights. Finally, we thank the editors and the other contributors for their helpful feedback on this chapter.

1. Susan J. Carroll and Kira Sanbonmatsu, *More Women Can Run: Gender and Pathways to the State Legislatures* (New York: Oxford University Press, 2013).

2. Kira Sanbonmatsu, "Electing Women of Color: The Role of Campaign Trainings," *Journal of Women, Politics, and Policy* 36, no. 2 (2015): 137–160.

3. Susan J. Carroll and Kelly Dittmar, "Preparedness Meets Opportunity: A Case Study of Women's Increased Representation in the New Jersey Legislature," in *Breaking Male Dominance in Old Democracies*, ed. Drude Dahlerup and Monique Leyenaar (New York: Oxford University Press, 2013).

4. Women of color were more likely than White women to seek networking opportunities ($p < 0.05$).

5. The women we surveyed reported their race/ethnic background. They could choose more than one racial/ethnic category. The largest group of minority respondents self-identified as Black or African American (28.75 percent), either alone or in combination with other racial categories; 17.2 percent identified as Hispanic or Latina; 7.8 percent as Asian, South Asian, or Pacific Islander; 1.9 percent as Native American; and 2.8 percent as Mixed Race.

6. Sanbonmatsu, "Electing Women of Color."

7. Jennifer Lawless and Richard L. Fox, *It Still Takes a Candidate: Why Women Don't Run for Office* (New York: Cambridge University Press, 2010), 52.

8. These statistics are for those legislators who ran for an office other than state legislature when they first sought elected office. See Carroll and Sanbonmatsu, *More Women Can Run*, 52.

9. Carroll and Sanbonmatsu, *More Women Can Run*, 107.

10. We sent the follow-up survey annually to each respondent for five years. Note, however, that we ended this study in 2017 in order to disseminate our results. Therefore, not all participants experienced the full five years of follow-up surveys: Participants in the 2013 and 2014 programs were sent follow-up surveys for four and three years, respectively, instead of five years.

11. These responses are for online survey respondents only ($N = 89$). As with all of the panel analyses in this paper, we report only the responses from the first time a woman completed a wave of the panel study. We conducted the panel surveys online using Survey Monkey and by mail. Although the survey instructed respondents to choose the most valuable aspect of the training, some respondents to the mail version of the survey checked more than one box.

12. We do not find racial/ethnic differences on these measures.

13. Most of this activity was directed at the local level.

14

Pieces of Women's Political Ambition Puzzle

Changing Perceptions of a Political Career with Campaign Training

Monica C. Schneider and Jennie Sweet-Cushman

When a woman decides to run for office, it is as though the final piece in a complicated puzzle has finally been put in the correct position. Of the many different pieces to this puzzle, some are part of our electoral system, including whether political insiders support her or if there is a vacancy in the office in which she is interested.[1] Other pieces are specific to the individual woman, such as her belief in her qualifications, her confidence that politics will solve the issues important to her, and acceptance of the costs of running for office.[2] In an effort to fill in another portion of the puzzle, a host of organizations invest time, money, and energy in sponsoring workshops and trainings for interested women. The training sponsors report that these experiences are very positive for the women who attend them, yet above and beyond these self-reports, the trainings' effects are not well understood. As Sanbonmatsu and Dittmar discuss in Chapter 13, in this volume, a causal link between trainings and candidacies is difficult to establish. To better grasp the way that these trainings might be part of the puzzle of women running for office, we studied participants in two Ready to Run® campaign trainings for women. We drew on a rich body of political science and psychological research to help illuminate the small ways a training might stir progress toward a run for office.

Consistent with Sanbonmatsu and Dittmar (also studying Ready to Run®), we find encouraging effects associated with attending a daylong campaign training for women. In our study, participation translated into the enhancement of women's attitudes on a number of factors that contribute to an inclination to run for office. The training increased participants' confidence and altered their perceptions about the goals of being a politician, affecting positive changes in their feelings toward a political career. The training did not, on average, increase women's stated interest in running for office, but, for a subset of women, their political ambition did improve. These analyses and conclusions help speak to the potential for campaign trainings to improve women's representation.

Ready to Run®: Overview of the Training

Ready to Run® is a daylong nonpartisan training created by academics at the Center for American Women and Politics (CAWP) at Rutgers University and is primarily delivered by scholars of women and politics around the country. While programs vary from location to location, many of the topics, formats, and types of speakers are quite similar. We studied trainings hosted by the Pennsylvania Center for Women and Politics in two cities—Philadelphia and Pittsburgh—in February 2017. Participants in this program frequently attend because gatekeepers, such as political party elites and leaders in the community, encouraged them to do so. Others were encouraged to participate by training alumnae, while some found the training on their own through advertisements or their own internet search. There is less formal recruitment (e.g., by political parties) for the Pennsylvania trainings than for the New Jersey trainings Sanbonmatsu and Dittmar study, and we suspect our participants may be earlier in the candidate emergence process than those in the New Jersey sample.

Attendees arrived at the training in the morning and, over the course of a nine-hour day, participated in a number of presentations and panel discussions designed to be informative, skill building, and inspirational. Though the speakers and trainers varied between the two locations, the themes of the panels offered to participants were the same. Professional practitioners conducted sessions on designing a campaign plan, fundraising, and managing the media. The other panels were composed of individuals—most of whom are or were elected officials themselves—with experience in the topical areas. Training organizers made purposeful attempts to offer a diverse set of presenters, ensuring that both major political parties, minorities, and women and men with varied backgrounds were represented.

A women of color breakfast panel began the day, followed by the start of the full program with a keynote address by a high-profile female political leader. After the keynote, attendees participated in one of two panels, either about getting started in their community or on how to write a campaign plan. Over lunch, everyone participated in a fundraising training. In the afternoon, attendees split between panels on navigating the state's political party and nomination system or running for judicial office.[3] The day ended with professional media training designed to help the potential candidates present themselves and their platforms more effectively.

We surveyed participants before and after they attended the Ready to Run® campaign training. By comparing the responses of the 56 women who completed the questionnaires after the training to their responses before the training began, we explore how the training influenced them. This approach complements the rich data on long-term results of the program from Sanbonmatsu and Dittmar's panel study of training participants by offering some ability to isolate training effects.

Before examining the results, we take a moment to note that we cannot provide an intersectional analysis with our sample, due to the small number (seven) of women of color in the sample. However, we can isolate just the White women. The results we present are the same whether we limit our analyses to White women only or if we utilize the full sample. Thus, we can say with some certainty that *White women* in particular respond to the trainings in the ways described throughout the paper. Women of color may be responding the same way, but without a larger sample we cannot know for sure.

Did the Training Matter?

What is a realistic outcome of a one-day campaign training? The academics and practitioners who deliver these trainings would certainly feel that the training was a success if most of the women left and immediately declared their candidacy for office. Of course, as Sanbonmatsu and Dittmar point out, this outcome may take years to achieve, making it hard to isolate the effects of the training itself since many other factors can be influential as well. In the interim, however, the daylong training might place a piece of the puzzle, even if the puzzle is not completed on that day. These pieces include women's perceptions that a career in politics fits their desired goals, assessment of their own likelihood of success, or a stated interest in running for office. Each of these outcomes has been shown separately to be a catalyst for a political run[4] and has the potential—as Piscopo suggests in Chapter 15, in this volume—to compensate for other structural barriers women face in the candidate emergence process.

Perceptions of Political Careers

Campaign trainings have the potential to change how women think about political careers. Current psychological research shows that many women prefer careers that are aligned with communal goals, such as helping or working with others, more than careers that give the opportunity to pursue power-related goals, such as status and recognition.[5] Not surprisingly, given the ways that politics is overly masculine, both men and women alike perceived the political career as conflictual and offering the opportunity pursue power and recognition at the expense of helping and working with others. These per-

ceptions were particularly demotivating for women, given their greater interest in helping and working with others. Interestingly, when a political career was described as a series of activities that involved helping others and
working on a team, women's perceptions of how enjoyable a political career
would be matched those of men, eliminating the gender gap.[6] Personal interviews with women revealed that they expect that elected office is not an effective means for solving issues of concern to them.[7] Instead, women tend to
be involved in nonprofit work, engaging in their to effect change instead of
pursuing elected office. In short, negative perceptions of the political career
as masculinized may be uniquely damaging to women's interest in running
for office or their generalized feelings toward holding political office.[8] A campaign training is an opportunity to enhance positivity toward political careers and change expectations about communal and power-related goals of
political careers; after all, politics is not only all about power and recognition
but also a means through which people can work together to help their fellow
citizens.

We find that the campaign training did indeed improve women's evaluations of the political career. Participants expressed more positivity toward
a political career after the training than before, going up nearly a half point
on a 7-point scale from a mean of 5.24 (SE = 0.17) to a mean of 5.71 (SE =
0.13) (see Figure 14.1, top, right side). This difference was statistically sig-

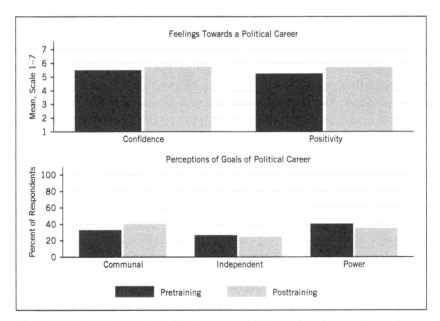

Figure 14.1. Positivity toward a political career and feelings of confidence (*top*) and
perceptions of the goals of a political career (*bottom*). (Source: Graphic created by Taylor
Gordon, based on data from the authors.)

nificant ($p < 0.01$). Positivity on the scale increased for 40 percent of respondents, and only 9 percent showed less positivity after the training.

Importantly, participating in the training seemed to change how women perceive the nature of what politicians do. We asked training participants what percent of time they thought politicians spent on power-related goals of status and recognition, communal goals of helping and working with others, and independent goals of working individually. Before the training, women reported their perception that politicians spend about 41 percent of their time on power goals of gaining status and recognition, but only 33 percent of their time on communal goals of helping others. By the end of the training, their views changed significantly, estimating that politicians spend less time on power goals (35 percent) and more time on communal ones (about 40 percent) (see Figure 14.1, bottom, right side).

This change in perceptions, if long lasting, could facilitate a run for office for the female participants. Our data show that, at the start of the training day, the women believed that politicians spend their time on the type of goals women tend to value least—power-related goals. Yet, after hearing the speakers and participating in the training, participants left with the impression that politicians spend their time on communal goals, those in which women show the most interest. Given that women in office actually do pursue more communal goals, it is possible that the female speakers changed perceptions of the career making it more appealing to female training participants.[9]

Improving Confidence

Women are aware of the significant obstacles awaiting them when entering a profession that is traditionally male dominated.[10] The "gendered psyche" of politics—the masculinity contained within—causes women to feel that they do not belong in politics.[11] Having few women in office further symbolizes that women are unwelcome.[12] Even women who have relevant skills and experience for political life tend to downgrade the significance of those skills, opting to assess themselves as unqualified until they have acquired the entire set of skills perceived to be necessary for success.[13] Women's confidence levels seem to stem from a view that politics will be difficult for them, perhaps even not relevant for them, and they need every resource at their disposal to succeed. In contrast, men's overconfidence in their abilities may help spur a run for office more readily than might occur for women, but it also may result in underqualified men charging toward a political run.[14] This is true even outside of politics, where men reported greater self-esteem and confidence in their ability and skills relative to women.[15]

Thus, women might benefit from feeling more confident in their political acumen; a campaign training that included a focus on skill development could certainly promote this confidence. Much like Sanbonmatsu and Dittmar find, the training did seem to help build participants' skills and provide valuable information as evidenced by the improvement of the women's scores on how successful they think they will be in a political career. Their confidence increased by about a quarter of a point on a seven-point scale (Pretraining Mean = 5.49, SE = 0.12, Posttraining Mean = 5.75, SE = 0.12, $p < 0.05$) (see Figure 14.1, top, left side). We also anticipated that the training might affect women's confidence in their ability to address power-related goals, communal goals, or independence goals; however, this was not the case. Although women's confidence in these specific areas did not change as a result of the training, they did report significantly more confidence in their ability to fulfill communal goals than their confidence in completing power-related goals, both before and after the training. This finding underscores the importance of changing women's beliefs about what politicians do; after the training, they were more likely to think that the political career involves helping others, the very goal with which they feel most confident.

Inclination to Run

Many of the institutional, contextual, relational, and psychological factors that influence a decision to run are impossible to alter over the course of a short training. Yet, programs like Ready to Run® might change women's stated intention to run, or what scholars refer to as their nascent political ambition. Many argue that political ambition, measured by whether a person states that they are likely to run or even just interested in running, precedes the decision to run for office.[16] As the editors and contributors of this volume detail, there is considerable debate over the concept of nascent political ambition, whether it exists in the same way for women as for men, and the extent to which it is malleable.[17] We utilize this construct to understand an additional route through which the training can affect female participants, noting that nascent political ambition may not be the most important outcome of the training when there are so many other puzzle pieces in play.

   Previous academic research has demonstrated that nascent ambition is sensitive to small interventions;[18] our data add credence to the idea that women's stated intentions about political office are neither static nor innate. While the training did not improve women's interest in running for office, on average, the training seemed to affect subgroups of women differently. Some women in our sample reported that they were more likely to run after the training, some reported that they were less likely to run, while the majority of women stayed the same. Even though the training did not have a uniformly positive effect on women's stated ambition, the increase shown by those few women could improve the likelihood that they run in the future.

   We asked several different questions about the participants' nascent political ambition and come to the same conclusion regardless. That is, there was

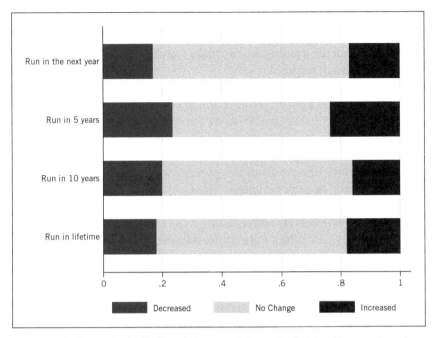

Figure 14.2. Change in the likelihood of a potential run after training. (Source: Graphic created by Taylor Gordon, based on data from the authors.)

no difference in the average likelihood of running for office in the next year, next 5 or 10 years, or even in the lifetime for women after the training compared to before it, though some women moved up and others moved down on these questions (see Figure 14.2). When we asked about their nascent political ambition in a slightly different way—how seriously they considered a run for office or how likely they would be to run in the future—just about three-quarters of respondents did not change their response. Of the small number of respondents who did change their response, they were equally likely to say they were more interested in running as they were to say they were less interested. To illustrate, of the women who said before the training that they might undertake running for office if the opportunity presented itself ($n = 31$), after the training only 1 reported having no interest in running, 8 indicated that they would definitely like to run in the future, and 22 expressed no change.

How the Puzzle Pieces Fit

Research demonstrates that women have less ambition for politics compared to men because they lack efficacy and feel more negativity toward the conflict, power, and recognition involved in political life.[19] Thus, positive changes in these factors should positively affect their nascent political ambition. While our data have limitations in the extent to which we can make causal statements about the training, we can make use of some analyses to examine how these pieces fit together.

Among those who participated in the survey, the improvement in positive feelings toward a political career and in confidence seem to relate to an increase in political ambition. First, we found that change in positivity toward a political career (the pretraining measure subtracted from the posttraining measure) was positively correlated with change in the likelihood of running for office (the pre-from-the-post average of likelihood of running for office in varying time periods; $r = 0.41$, $p < 0.01$). We also found that a change in respondents' assessment of how successful they would be in a political career was positively correlated with change in likelihood of running for office ($r = 0.43$, $p < 0.001$). Put another way, the greater the positive changes in feelings of success and positivity, the greater the positive increase in political ambition. This relationship is even more important when we consider that the ambition of most women in the study did not change at all.

We also examined those participants who, after the training, reported that the political career was less likely to promote power-related goals than they initially suspected. This group ($n = 24$) improved their positivity toward a political career by 0.75 points. This represents a marginally statistically significant change ($p < 0.10$) in positivity compared to participants who did not change their perceptions or who saw the political career as *more* likely to fulfill power-related goals after the training as compared to before ($n = 30$). These participants had an average change in positivity toward the political career of only 0.21 points. While we did not see statistical significance when examining the effect of changes in political career perceptions on a different political ambition measure, likelihood of running for office ($p = 0.11$), the pattern still held. Those respondents who now viewed the political career as less likely to involve power-related goals improved their ambition by 0.28 points, compared to the remainder of the respondents whose ambition *declined* by 0.03 points. Therefore, the training's ability to change participants' perceptions of a political career, such as viewing a political career as spending less time on power-related goals, seems related to improvements in women's ambition and positivity toward political careers.

Conclusion: Campaign Trainings as a Puzzle Piece

This chapter offers unique insights into an important tool in the effort to encourage more women to run for office: campaign trainings designed specifically for women. As this volume clearly details, practitioners and academics all over the world have invested critical resources in establishing a variety of campaign trainings for women, including Ready to Run®. This is especially true after the 2018 election where a historic number of women were elected to the U.S. House and Senate. These trainings are designed to give women the skills, and thus the confidence, needed to run for elected office.[20] However, as several authors in this volume note, it is both practically and method-ologically difficult to make the connection between a woman's participation in a campaign training and the likelihood she will emerge as a candidate. Our analysis measures the immediate effects of campaign trainings and, in doing so, offers insight into the positive role such trainings can play in the effort to increase women's political representation.

In our study, the training had promising effects on several factors that could be considered pieces of the political ambition puzzle. We found, for instance, that after the program, participants felt more positively toward po-litical careers. They were also more confident in their ability to succeed in a political career. The increases in positivity and confidence were related to im-provements in nascent political ambition. While these changes did not also manifest in participants' confidence or interest in various types of goals that a political career affords, participants did continue to value the communal goals they felt most efficacious in handling. This offers potentially valuable insight to training organizers, as it would be feasible to consciously tailor con-tent within the trainings to provide a stronger focus on communal goals. Doing so could have the potential to specifically encourage a growing confidence among the participants.

Interestingly, the training altered perceptions about the daily life of poli-ticians. After the training, our participants shifted their initial view that poli-ticians spend 40 percent of their time fulfilling power-related goals, such as status and recognition. After the training, participants reported that politi-cians likely spend 40 percent of their time on communal-related goals of helping and working with others. Given the finding from Sanbonmatsu and Dittmar that women attend the trainings in part to find people who are like them, we speculate that the camaraderie developed among the women in the training improved their sense of belonging in a political career, which may have been a catalyst for the shift in perceptions of communal goals. Future research could disentangle the reasons for this shift. Yet, we note that this finding rep-resents a substantial transformation in perceptions of political careers, par-ticularly when we consider that women *prefer* communal-oriented goals and careers that fulfill those goals. Those who came to view the political career as being more focused on communal goals were much more pleased with the idea of one.

Research in psychology shows that people choose or avoid roles depend-ing on whether the role will allow them the opportunity to pursue their preferred goals. The participants in Bernhard et al.'s study of Emerge partici-pants (Chapter 2, in this volume) identified *time* as the number one reason why women who had already demonstrated nascent political ambition did not run for office. We speculate that perceptions of the political career might underlie this response. Many of these women have other time-consuming commitments, yet they made time for the training, suggesting that they make time for things that they value. If they don't see the political career as an enterprise that will allow them to help and work with others but that instead requires the pursuit of power and recognition, "time" may be a proxy for lack of inclination to expend resources on the less-preferred objectives they perceive politics as affording.

We believe these findings delineate an important function for campaign trainings for women. Yet, understanding which part of the training produced this shift remains a mystery. Moreover, future research might try to understand if these perceptions are long lasting. After all, much of the media reports about politics focus on the conflictual nature of political life to the detriment of positive stories about helping others and working together to solve problems.[21] Women and men alike receive a lifetime of messages about the nature of political careers; the ability of a daylong training to change those perceptions could be momentous for women's interest in politics if the effect lasts beyond the training day.

We found that the training did not improve nascent political ambition for all of the women. While some participants did report a greater interest and higher likelihood in running for office at some point in the future, others' ambition was depressed following the trainings. This limited effect might be partially explained by ceiling effects: those that chose to attend a training for potential political candidates already had relatively high levels of political ambition, making further elevation unlikely. Moreover, our sample size was relatively small, making it hard to detect subtle changes in political ambition. That some women came away from the training with depressed levels of political ambition makes sense; a run for office and a political career remains a difficult prospect with many hurdles. However, given the argument that women's ambition is embedded in relationships, arising only just before they decide they will run, even these negative changes in nascent ambition might not prevent a future candidacy.[22]

Future research could try to disentangle which particular aspects of the training have positive or negative effects on women's feelings toward a political career, their confidence, and their nascent political ambition. An intersectional view could provide a richer perspective; follow-up analyses could reveal if there are patterns of characteristics among the women who were encouraged by the training versus the women who were not. Training coordinators could perhaps split participants by their responses on a pretraining questionnaire and tailor sessions accordingly.

Of course, no one would suspect that campaign trainings negatively affect their participants and, indeed, our findings more than confirm the potential for positive influence on participants—enhancing the ambition of some, the confidence of many, and the feelings and perceptions of political careers in ways demonstrated to be associated with improved ambition and positive feelings toward a political career. Because the questionnaires were given out immediately preceding and immediately following the training, we can be quite confident that our findings are not affected by other factors but rather can be attributed to something about the experience at the campaign training. Given the high bar to achieving *any* statistically significant results in a small sample—women are socialized to lack confidence and interest in careers that involve power and conflict; this socialization is powerful—we remain optimistic about the efficacy of such trainings. Our findings have the potential to inform training facilitators and practitioners in ways that may help bring these pieces of the puzzle all together for this pool of potential female candidates.

NOTES

Authors' Note: Special thanks to the Pennsylvania Center for Women and Politics for their support of this research and Taylor Gordon for creating the figures.

1. Pippa Norris and Joni Lovenduski, *Political Recruitment: Gender, Race, and Class in the British Parliament* (Cambridge: Cambridge University Press, 1995).

2. Shauna Shames, "Making the Political Personal: A Challenge for Young Women," *Politics and Gender* 10, no. 2 (2014): 287–292; Jennifer L. Lawless and Richard L. Fox, *It Takes a Candidate: Why Women Don't Run for Office* (Cambridge: Cambridge University Press, 2005); Jennifer L. Lawless and Richard L. Fox, *It Still Takes a Candidate: Why Women Don't Run for Office* (Cambridge: Cambridge University Press, 2010); Shauna L. Shames, *Out of the Running: Why Millennials Reject Political Careers and Why It Matters* (New York: New York University Press, 2017).

3. Judicial offices are elected in Pennsylvania, and there are unique considerations for a judicial candidacy.

4. Monica C. Schneider, Mirya R. Holman, Amanda B. Diekman, and Thomas McAndrew, "Power, Conflict, and Community: How Gendered Views of Political Power Influence Women's Political Ambition," *Political Psychology* 37, no. 4 (2016): 515–531; Lawless and Fox, *It Takes a Candidate*; Lawless and Fox, *It Still Takes a Candidate*; Shames, *Out of the Running*.

5. Schneider et al., "Power, Conflict, and Community," 515–531; Amanda B. Diekman, Elizabeth R. Brown, Amanda M. Johnston, and Emily K. Clark, "Seeking Congruity between Goals and Roles: A New Look at Why Women Opt Out of Science, Technology, Engineering, and Mathematics Careers," *Psychological Science* 21, no. 8 (2010): 1051–1057.

6. Schneider et al., "Power, Conflict, and Community," 515–531.

7. Shames, "Making the Political Personal."

8. Lawless and Fox, *It Takes a Candidate*; Lawless and Fox, *It Still Takes a Candidate*.

9. Schneider et al., "Power, Conflict, and Community," 515–531; Georgia Duerst-Lahti, "But Women Play the Game Too: Communication Control and Influence in Administrative Decision Making," *Administration and Society* 22, no. 2 (1990): 182–205; Lyn Kathlene, "Uncovering the Political Impacts of Gender: An Exploratory Study," *Western Political Quarterly* 42, no. 2 (1989): 397–421; Esther Lang-Takac and Zahava Osterweil, "Separateness and Connectedness: Differences between the Genders," *Sex*

Roles 27, nos. 5–6 (1992): 277–289; Louise A. Tilly and Patricia Gurin, eds. *Women, Politics and Change* (Russell Sage Foundation, New York 1990).

10. Hannah R. Bowles and Kathleen L. McGinn, "Claiming Authority: Negotiating Challenges for Women Leaders," in *The Psychology of Leadership: New Perspectives and Approaches*, ed. D. Messick and R. Kramer, 191–208 (Mahwah, NJ: Lawrence Erlbaum Associates, 2004).

11. Lawless and Fox, *It Still Takes a Candidate.*

12. Laurie L. Cohen and Janet K. Swim, "The Differential Impact of Gender Ratios on Women and Men: Tokenism, Self-confidence, and Expectations," *Personality and Social Psychology Bulletin* 21, no. 9 (1995): 876–884.

13. Lawless and Fox, *It Still Takes a Candidate.*

14. We frame women's confidence positively by considering that it may not be that most men have an appropriate level of confidence, as is traditionally assumed, but that women have a rational level of confidence and men are overconfident in their abilities.

15. Kristen C. Kling, Janet Shibley Hyde, Carolin J. Showers, and Brenda N. Buswell, "Gender Differences in Self-esteem: A Meta-analysis," *Psychological Bulletin* 125, no. 4 (1999): 470; Alan Feingold, "Gender Differences in Personality: A Meta-analysis," *Psychological Bulletin* 116, no. 3 (1994): 429; Judith A. Hall, *Nonverbal Sex Differences: Accuracy of Communication and Expressive Style* (Baltimore, MD: Johns Hopkins University Press, 1990).

16. Lawless and Fox, *It Takes a Candidate*; Lawless and Fox, *It Still Takes a Candidate.*

17. Susan J. Carroll and Kira Sanbonmatsu, *More Women Can Run: Gender and Pathways to the State Legislatures* (New York: Oxford University Press, 2013).

18. Schneider et al., "Power, Conflict, and Community," 515–531; Mirya R. Holman and Monica C. Schneider, "Gender, Race, and Political Ambition: How Intersectionality and Frames Influence Interest in Political Office," *Politics, Groups, and Identities* 6, no. 2 (2018): 264–280.

19. Lawless and Fox, *It Still Takes a Candidate*; Schneider et al., "Power, Conflict, and Community," 515–531.

20. Mark J. Rozell, "Helping Women Run and Win: Feminist Groups, Candidate Recruitment and Training," *Women and Politics* 21, no. 3 (2000): 101–116; Kira Sanbonmatsu, "Electing Women of Color: The Role of Campaign Trainings," *Journal of Women, Politics, and Policy* 36, no. 2 (2015): 137–160.

21. Diana C. Mutz, "Effects of Horse-Race Coverage on Campaign Coffers: Strategic Contributing in Presidential Primaries," *Journal of Politics* 57, no. 4 (1995): 1015–1042, available at https://doi.org/10.2307/2960400.

22. Carroll and Sanbonmatsu, *More Women Can Run.*

15

Women Running in the World

Candidate Training Programs in Comparative Perspective

JENNIFER M. PISCOPO

Much of the conventional wisdom on women's political ambition comes from the United States, where candidates self-nominate. The argument goes as follows: women doubt their qualifications and therefore express less ambition, and they may also fear competitive activity, so overcoming this ambition gap requires encouraging and recruiting women to run. Candidate training programs have emerged precisely to bolster women's enthusiasm, confidence, and preparedness for running for elected office. In this sense, women's candidate training programs match the individualistic nature of the U.S. political system, where candidacies are formally open to anyone willing to step forward. The popularity of candidate training in the United States— over four hundred active initiatives at the state or local level, as Kreitzer and Osborn document (Chapter 12, in this volume)—is therefore not surprising.

Candidate training programs' global popularity *is* surprising, however. The self-nomination feature of the U.S. political system is unique. In most other political systems, candidates cannot self-nominate. Political parties control ballot access, so the question for feminist activists and researchers outside the United States has not been why do women not step forward, but *why do parties not choose women.* Party leaders typically draw candidates from among their members, and globally, women comprise 40–50 percent of party members.[1] Scholars of global gender and politics long have argued that discrimination by party leaders—and not any crisis of confidence among women aspirants—explains women's underrepresentation in elected office. Yet despite the fact that women aspirants in most countries cannot self-nominate, there are scores of candidate training programs in every global region, from Botswana to Japan, Mexico to Nepal. Why are measures to boost women's individual preparedness and ambition so popular, when it is parties—not women themselves—who are the main barriers to women's political underrepresentation in other countries?

This chapter assesses the global popularity of training programs for women candidates, given contexts where political parties place significant limitations on women's political ambition. Candidate training intervenes at the individual level, but women's primary obstacles to political careers are at the system level. Even in the United States, deciding to run is not enough. Women who step forward in *any* country still face systemic bias from voters, donors, and the media. Women *especially* face bias from their copartisans and their party leaders. Candidate training helps women overcome this systemic bias. Training programs correct for the disadvantages women face in accessing the elite networks that impart political savviness, and women's completion of a training program signals their preparedness and qualifications to audiences otherwise skeptical that women are up to the job. But credentialing women in order to mitigate bias is not the same as undoing that bias in the first place. Moreover, the global programs follow their U.S. counterparts in emphasizing that women's presence in office improves democratic outputs, potentially creating unrealistic expectations about women's ability to transform unrepresentative or unresponsive systems.

The poor fit between the reasons women are underrepresented and the solution of candidate training programs cautions against overly relying on these programs to correct for women's disadvantage. This lesson also applies in the United States, where the focus on women's individual decision to run often masks how U.S. women face equally daunting systemic obstacles.

This chapter proceeds as follows. First, I review the academic literature explaining women's underrepresentation outside the United States, focusing on the role of political parties as gatekeepers to elected office. I highlight where the global literature's focus on system-level explanations coincides with the U.S.-based literature. Scholars working in the U.S. context also have emphasized that women's lesser political ambition is not biologically or even socially inherent, but a rational response to an uneven playing field. Said another way, no matter the country, the "game" of politics is biased in favor of men. I then provide an overview of candidate training models across the globe, focusing on two broad types: programs that are locally run but internationally funded (international programs) and programs that are locally run and locally funded (domestic programs). I discuss how these programs resemble their U.S. counterparts, especially in relation to their credentialing role and their emphasis on women's transformative potential. I conclude by reflecting on these programs' limitations, both abroad and in the United States. Making democratic politics more representative and more responsive is not just women's work, but the obligation of all political actors, men and women alike.

Political Parties as the Gatekeepers to Elected Office

Political parties in most countries control ballot access and therefore control candidate selection. Aspirants cannot become candidates unless formally affiliated with and nominated by a political party. This closed system of candidate selection contrasts with the open system in the United States, where anyone can step forward, declare themselves beneath a party label, and run for office. Candidates in the U.S. system may face other competitors in a party primary, but these competitors are also self-declared underneath that party label. But in most other political systems, candidate selection happens within the party, through processes determined or controlled by the party leadership. Primaries, when they happen, are organized by parties and involve candidates (often referred to as "precandidates") who are party members and whose entrance into the primary is permitted by the party. Once the candidates who will contest the general election are chosen, these candidates are formally registered with the election authorities *by the party*. Unlike in the United States, candidates cannot register themselves.[2]

Consequently, the phrase "when women run, women win" makes little sense outside the United States. In most countries, the first step to becoming a candidate is not deciding to run; the first step is joining a political party. And becoming a party member also differs. In the United States, voters affiliate with parties by checking a box on a form. In other countries, party membership is active, not passive: members pay dues, participate in events and rallies, and generally volunteer their time and money to support the party. Members sustain the party's organizational life. Those with office-seeking ambition will undertake these tasks and work their way up through the party, perhaps first attaining a local-level party office and hoping that party leaders will later reward their hard work with a nomination for elected office. Even political outsiders must first affiliate with parties to get on the ballot. When celebrities, activists, journalists, or business leaders decide to run, they first become party members, or they form and build parties of their own.

For these reasons, in most democratic or democratizing countries, feminist activists and scholars have framed the problem of women's political underrepresentation not in terms of an ambition gap but in terms of persistent discrimination. The issue is not persuading women to step forward, as women often comprise nearly half of party members. The issue is getting party leaders to choose *and support* women as candidates. Nomination itself remains insufficient, because parties control more than ballot access. They control ballot ranking (in systems where candidates are elected via lists) as well as district assignments (in many systems, district residency rules are lax or nonexistent). In many parts of the world, parties also receive public funding for campaigns, and parties and candidates are prohibited from receiving private donations. These rules mean that parties—who receive state resources and then redistribute these resources to candidates—determine which candidates get the money necessary to run high-profile campaigns. Candidates' access to television and radio advertisement may be among those resources that the state allocates to parties and that parties in turn allocate to candidates. Thus, even when parties nominate women, they can make other decisions that shape women's electoral fortunes: parties can assign women to losing districts, underresource their campaigns, and make men and men's leadership central to the party's public image.

Party Bias against Women

Party leaders pressed to improve gender equity often protest using the same reason frequently invoked in the United States: that women do not wish to run. However, scholars of global politics largely believe that women's reluctance to run stems not from an inherent lack of ambition but from a rational assessment that the playing field is not level. Researchers working in non-U.S. contexts have documented significant party biases against women. This problem also characterizes the U.S. context (see Part I, in this volume), where a focus on candidates' individual decision to run often obscures the unique obstacles that women face. The uneven playing field makes running unattractive, even for the ambitious.

To begin, the criteria party leaders use when nominating candidates are biased in favor of men. Party leaders recruit first from among their networks, which are homosocial groups that typically exclude women.[3] Members of these groups are thought to have the "right qualities"—which include having attended certain universities; having certain pastimes (e.g., golf) or being a member of certain clubs (e.g., sporting clubs or business associations); working in certain professions; and already holding office or a leadership position within the party. As scholars have shown, men and women politicians often hold equivalent qualifications, but these qualifications follow gendered patterns. For instance, women and men legislators are equally likely to have university degrees, but men's degrees are in finance while women's degrees are in education or the liberal arts. Women and men are equally likely to have prior political experience, but men have held party or local office while women have worked as activists or community organizers.[4] Women start off outside the "right" networks.

Women also face systemic bias in winning their races. In countries that use multimember districts and elect their representatives via list (a system known as proportional representation), parties use women to diversify their lists but place women in the unwinnable positions. Many countries do not require that candidates be from the district, or they have lax rules regarding district residency, which allows party leaders to place women candidates in losing districts. Party leaders marginalize women candidates in these ways even when voter bias does not exist and even when men's and women's résumés are comparable.[5] Commonly, women candidates are seen as taking opportunities that rightfully belong to men, and women and their families can be harassed, intimidated, and even assaulted by members of their own party. Researchers also have documented pervasive gender bias in party leaders' distribution of campaign funds.[6] And in countries where financing is not public, and candidates must finance their campaigns with personal funds or donor contributions, women are especially disadvantaged (as Johnson describes in Chapter 17, in this volume). Women often lack the networks from which to raise funds and asking for money—or spending their family's money on their careers—violates cultural norms, especially in more traditional societies.

Importantly, parties cannot defend their marginalization of women by claiming that women—as relative newcomers—are too unpredictable or too green for parliament. Women legislators are as loyal, if not more loyal, than men. On metrics from attendance to introducing legislation, women govern as effectively as men. In fact, women legislators often overperform, likely because they understand how double standards shape their political careers. Women often have to do better than men to succeed, and they face greater punishment than men when they fail. Following the 2009 expenses scandal in the United Kingdom, for instance, women and men Members of Parliament (MPs) were found equally likely to have abused their slush funds (though women spent more on childcare services and men on club memberships), but the women stood down from reelection more frequently than the men.[7]

The global gender and politics research thus explains women's underrepresentation by highlighting how political parties dominated by men block women's opportunities for advancement. Through ways both subtle and obvious, parties preserve most electoral chances for men. Indeed, the more competitive the election, the fewer the chances parties will run women.[8] Moreover, the very fact that politics is dominated by men can discourage women from stepping forward. Political climates where insults, hostility, aggression, and even physical violence are normalized as just-how-things-are-done can prove off-putting to women, who are socialized to behave differently and punished when they start behaving like men.

Minority women especially face constraints to manifesting and realizing ambition, as they confront party bias but also gender bias from within their own communities. In fact, minority women are dramatically underrepresented in the world's legislatures.[9] There are some circumstances that may cause parties to favor women candidates over men candidates: namely when voter dissatisfaction is high, and parties run women to signal renewal or change.[10] Minority women may benefit when parties use their presence to symbolize inclusion, secularism, and an adherence to Western values.[11] Overall, however,

minority women find themselves facing an uphill battle to obtain nominations (especially viable nominations) and to receive resources, support, and
encouragement from their party.

Though this unequal playing field is most pronounced in political systems where parties control ballot access, researchers have documented similar patterns in the United States. Party leaders in the United States cannot
keep candidates off the ballot, but they can choose whom to recruit, whom
to officially endorse, and whom to support financially. Research shows that
party elites in the United States are "old boys' clubs" that doubt women can
win. Women correctly anticipate that they will not receive local leaders' support.[12] Those women in the aspirant pool—those preparing for careers in public policy and law—perceive that men have an advantage in every aspect of
campaigning and winning, from receiving fair media coverage to raising money
and being forgiven for minor flaws.[13]

Women in the United States are also discouraged from running for office,
as Sanbonmatsu and Dittmar show in Chapter 13, in this volume. These hurdles are especially pronounced for women of color: for instance, Latina aspirants report being told by local political leaders to "wait their turn"—meaning
after the next man in line.[14] Even in 2018, women aspirants reported being told
to wait. From house races in Kentucky to California, local Democratic leaders
had already tapped men for the position and saw women aspirants as upstarts
and spoilers.[15] Like their counterparts internationally, U.S. women may have
considerable amounts of ambition, but ambition alone cannot overcome the
effects of hostile environments and systemic discrimination.

Reforms That Level the Playing Field—or Not

Women remain underrepresented in politics, but improvements have occurred in recent decades. In 1995, women held only 11.6 percent of seats in
the lower or single houses of the world's parliaments (including democracies,
semidemocracies, and nondemocracies).[16] As of March 2018, they held 23.4
percent of seats. This average contains significant variation, but many countries elect large proportions of women. One-quarter of the world's parliaments have over 30 percent women in the lower or single chamber. Countries
as diverse as Mexico, Namibia, Grenada, and Sweden elect over 40 percent
women. The regional average for lower or single chambers in Latin America
is 28 percent and in sub-Saharan Africa, 23.7 percent. For comparison, women
hold 19.4 percent of the seats in the U.S. House of Representatives, and 22
percent in the Senate—below the global average and below the averages of
regions thought far-less advanced in terms of gender equality.[17]

This global increase has been driven almost exclusively by the adoption
of gender quotas, the most popular electoral reform of the late twentieth and
early twenty-first centuries. Quota laws require that political parties nomi-

nate specified percentages of women for office (candidate quotas) or that countries set aside a certain percentage of districts or parliamentary seats for women (reserved seats). Candidate quotas are usually set at 30, 40, or 50 percent, whereas the percentage of reserved districts or seats is typically much lower. The predominance of candidate quotas in Western Europe, Latin America, and certain countries of sub-Saharan Africa explains why these regions excel at electing women to parliament. Thanks to gender quotas, Rwanda and Bolivia have the world's two majority-women legislatures. Overall, candidate quotas or reserved seats are found in over 80 countries worldwide, in every global region. An additional 30 countries have at least one political party applying a "voluntary" quota for women candidates.[18]

Party quotas are generally considered less effective, because political parties consistently violate their own rules, especially those regarding gender equality. However, party quotas can significantly boost women's political representation in one-party dominant regimes. Party quotas adopted by a hegemonic party explain women's high levels of representation in certain African countries, such as South Africa and Mozambique. Some countries also twin ethnic candidate quotas with gender candidate quotas. These quotas benefit minority women—but they do so because nominating a minority woman allows the party to fill both quotas with one person, thus preserving more seats for majority men.

The numerical success of candidate quotas, reserved seats, and party quotas indicates their ability to level the playing field, at least in terms of distributing nominations more equitably between men and women. Gender quotas are commonly supported by grassroots networks of women activists, politicians, professionals, and journalists, indicating that women clearly demand more electoral opportunities. Their adoption is grounded in global discourses about democracy and equality, namely that modern and democratic (or democratic-aspiring) states incorporate women. This discourse explains why quotas appear not just in democracies but also in semidemocracies or even authoritarian countries.

Their widespread use notwithstanding, gender quotas have provoked controversy in nearly every case. Indeed, most research on gender quotas has documented party leaders' resistance. Most commonly, parties fill quotas but continue placing women in unelectable list positions or unwinnable districts, unless the quota law expressly forbids these practices. In France, party leaders pay fines rather than nominate women.[19] In Mexico, one party nominated men posing as transgendered women; the party tried to count the men, who did not identify or live as women prior to the election, as filling the quota.[20] Thankfully, the Mexican court was not convinced, but these shenanigans demonstrate how political parties look to preserve most electoral opportunities for men.

Consequently, quotas force party leaders to recruit and nominate women— but they work only when political parties face sanctions for noncompliance and the sanctions are enforced. Success stories notwithstanding, quotas in many places fail to meet their numerical targets. Parties often mask their own responsibility for seeking women candidates or creating environments hospitable for women candidates, claiming that there simply "are not enough women." Campaigns such as "women, ready for the lists" in Uruguay and Bolivia demonstrate women's readiness to run. Similarly, the women's wings of parties in Spain and Germany prepare lists of qualified women. Partially to appease party leaders skeptical about women's credentials—and partially to help women aspirants looking to *prove* their credentials—candidate quota laws in eight Latin American countries currently require that political parties allocate specified percentages of their budgets (which usually come from the state) to candidate training for women.

The diffusion of gender quotas, coupled with party leaders' resistance, has fueled the global mania for women's candidate training. International and national organizations spent the 1990s and 2000s pushing for quotas, but with the measures now widely adopted, the focus has shifted to ensuring that the nominees are not tokens or proxies, but "real" candidates. This pressure exists even in nonquota countries because increasing women's presence in elected office remains an international priority and a key indicator of development and democratization. For women candidates, completing training helps them confront gender bias in party leaders' candidate selection processes. For the international and national organizations that fund, design, and implement women's candidate training, the initiatives support broader efforts to promote equality and improve democracy. Candidate training exists at the intersection where laws, norms, or both demand more women elected officials, but party leaders remain reluctant to change their practices and behaviors in ways that would meaningfully increase women's access to political power.

Candidate Training Programs Worldwide

My research assistant and I identified scores of women-only candidate training programs in every world region. There are probably dozens more examples, as we could only conduct research in English and Spanish and were limited to information available online or through personal communications and interviews with gender and politics scholars across the globe. Even with these limitations, we uncovered programs in diverse places. Interventions appeared in wealthy, advanced industrialized democracies, such as Canada, and in less developed, democratizing or semidemocratic countries, such as Myanmar and Liberia. In Azerbaijan, the U.S. Agency for International Development (USAID) funds candidate training that "promotes gender equality and empowers women to become confident and capable leaders."[21] In the United Kingdom, the nonpartisan Parliament Project has current and former politicians leading workshops on how to run for office.[22] Multiple initiatives often exist in the same country: the U.K., for instance, has other programs run by non-profits as well as by the major political parties.

All programs aim to boost the proportion of women in elected office, but they vary in their design and content. The modalities range from in-person seminars to online courses, to hybrid structures with both online and in-person components. Sessions take place over one day or one weekend or happen regularly over weeks or months. The content covers the nuts and bolts of becoming a candidate, such as understanding the electoral and legal system, as well as the strategic aspects of campaigning, such as developing and communicating a message, managing a team, networking with women and other politicians, navigating traditional and social media, and confronting bias. Programs also foment networks and nurture mentoring relationships: US-AID's initiatives in Azerbaijan, Kyrgyzstan, Tunisia, and Lebanon, among others, emphasize forming networks of women leaders; the Parliament Project has online "peer support circles" (hour-long webinars that create safe space for discussion); and the Caribbean Institute for Women's Leadership pairs former MPs with first-time candidates.[23] Some programs also train the trainers as well as offer specialized training. For example, the National Democratic Institute (NDI; the international organization associated with the U.S. Democratic Party) organized an online and in-person training course in Mexico that focused specifically on combating violence and harassment against women in politics.[24] Party-led programs, by contrast, focus on ensuring candidates understand and follow the party's ideological and programmatic commitments.[25]

Who benefits from candidate training also varies. Some programs enroll women who might someday consider running, while others enroll those already on the campaign trail. The vast majority aim to keep participants' costs low, charging either no fee or a nominal fee (usually less than US$50); have an application or screening process; and recruit participants through social media and direct contacts with those likely to know aspirants—university professors, business leaders, activists, and party leaders. Some programs focus specifically on young women and impose age cutoffs. Involving diverse participants remains important in the U.S.-based programs, as Kreitzer and Osborn and Sanbonmatsu and Dittmar show, but we could not assess the frequency with which programs outside the United States attended to diversity among women participants. The identities important for diversity vary across national contexts, and countries' unique histories and social norms shape how diversity is or is not considered by program planners.

Nonpartisan initiatives enroll all women, whereas partisan interventions select participants based on party membership or ideological litmus tests. However, unlike in the United States, where most candidate training programs do have ideological litmus tests (as Kreitzer and Osborn show), we found partisan programs less common internationally. Party-led initiatives notwithstanding, the vast majority of programs we examined were nonpartisan, most likely because programs in the Global South—meaning programs in lesser-developed and/or democratizing countries—rely on foreign donors to bankroll their work. For their part, foreign donors can support interventions that align with normative goals, such as promoting gender equality and democracy, but would risk their own reputations (and their own funding sources) if they gave the impression of favoring certain parties and thus certain electoral outcomes.

In fact, funding has enormous consequences for candidate training programs' sustainability. Party-led programs last as long as there is political will among the leadership or the legal requirement to expend money on candidate programs remains in place. Nonparty programs are initiated either by organizations whose sole purpose is to train women candidates, along the models of She Should Run and Emerge in the United States, or are nested within nongovernmental organizations (NGOs) that have broader objectives, such as pursuing gender equality, encouraging civic participation, or improving governance and democracy. Stand-alone organizations, such as Women for Election Ireland and Equal Voice Canada, have greater longevity, and, like their counterparts in the United States, often become brand names that help women graduates signal their credentials. Nested programs, by contrast, have more volatility: because candidate training is just one of the organization's many priorities, funding determines whether interventions are one-off events or regular offerings. All candidate training programs depend on funding availability, but those in the Global South are far less likely to be stand-alone operations and far more likely to be nested within other development or gender equity organizations.

Candidate training programs thus vary on two key dimensions: who funds them and who runs them. To capture both dimensions, we grouped candidate training programs according to whether they are international or domestic. "International" describes initiatives that take place in Global South countries and are funded entirely or almost entirely by foreign aid. Foreign donors usually do not administer programs directly but fund local NGOs and/or local consultants to carry out the intervention.[26] In this sense, international programs are *internationally supported but locally run*—and, therefore, are less institutionalized and less regularized, because donors themselves have shifting resources and priorities. International programs are found in Latin America and the Caribbean, Africa, Oceania and the Pacific (excluding Australia and New Zealand), Eastern Europe, Central Asia, and South Asia. Donors include international government organizations, such as the United Nations and the Commonwealth Secretariat; international NGOs, such as the U.S.-based National Democratic Institute or Germany's Friedrich Ebert Foundation; and wealthy nations, with the Scandinavian countries, Australia, Canada, Germany, the United Kingdom, and the United States emerging as major players. Donor nations will channel funds in multiple manners: for instance, some programs receive support from countries' overseas development agencies (i.e., USAID), others through the local embassy. The same initiative may receive funding from different donor countries or organizations.

"Domestic" describes programs that are *locally supported and locally run*. These programs do not rely on foreign aid, drawing most of their financial support from within their home country. They are more common in the Global North, where countries and governments are wealthier, citizens have the ability to contribute to philanthropic initiatives, and foreign aid is not received. Domestic programs predominate in the United States, Canada, the United Kingdom, Ireland, Australia, and Japan. Typically, these programs are nonpartisan and run by civil society organizations. Very frequently, programs are administered by stand-alone organizations, like the Parliament Project in the United Kingdom and Women for Election in Ireland. We did find a few nonpartisan programs run by subnational governments. For instance, the province of Alberta, Canada, offers "Ready for Her," online webinars that prepare women to run for municipal office. More commonly, though, governments financially contribute to civil society initiatives, as in the case of the Academy for Gender Parity in Tokyo. Feminist academics designed the academy, obtaining funds from a private foundation and the municipal government.[27]

Generally, domestic programs that train women candidates are nonpartisan and nonprofit. There are two exceptions. First, a handful of domestic programs, all in the Global North, do impose an ideological litmus test. Modeled after the U.S.-based EMILY's List, Emily-in-Italy, EMILY's List Australia, and EMILY's List U.K. work exclusively with progressive women candidates. Second, party-led programs appear both in the Global North and the Global South, with initiatives emerging in the latter region often because they are required by quota laws. When not required by law, different parties within the same country vary on whether they provide training, with both right and left parties offering training. Party-led initiatives are found in the British Labour Party and the British Conservative Party, for instance.

Enhancing Preparedness, Promoting Democracy

Global initiatives to train women candidates vary in their structure, scope, and relationship to donors but are united in their belief that training can overcome the dearth of women standing for office. Organizers are committed feminists and gender equality activists. They see candidate training as fulfilling important normative goals while also strategically intervening in parties' candidate selection processes. Candidate training responds directly to parties' claims that "there aren't enough women." No matter whether international or domestic, the programs' promotional material, course content, fundraising documents, and internal evaluations all mention the importance of developing women candidates' capacities and preparedness for office. Programs also emphasize the benefits to policy, representation, and democracy that accrue from women's presence in office.

Program organizers recognize that candidate training signals women's credentials. Japan's Academy for Gender Parity emerged because activists anticipated the passage of a legislative measure that would have required the principle of gender parity to govern candidate selection, albeit with no sanctions for compliance. The feminist academics who created the academy explained their motivation: "We had learned from other countries' experiences how crucial training would become to counter the myth of women's lack of interest or capacity."[28] Though the legislative measure did not pass at the time, the academy still took place.

Similarly, the Zinzin initiative in Benin was designed to "help women gain the confidence of party leaders."[29] Zinzin receives funding from private foundations in Germany as well as the foreign aid agencies or embassies of the United States, Switzerland, Germany, and Holland. In Botswana, the Letesma initiative began with an NDI-funded project to understand the status of women in political parties. What emerged from dialogues with party leaders, particularly leaders of the parties' women's wings, was the dearth of women ready for leadership: as one women wing's leader reflected, "The time for women is coming, what is needed is to put strategies in place."[30] The local consultant on the project then began organizing training for women in all the parties, obtaining financial support from German foundations, the British High Commission, the Westminster Foundation for Democracy, the All-Party Women's Caucus of the Botswana National Assembly, and local NGOs.[31]

Confidence boosting and empowerment are significant components of programs' promotional materials and objectives. Global North programs rely heavily on the U.S. message that "when women run, women win" (even though this line has less meaning when parties control ballot access). Alberta's premier, Rachel Notley, and the minister of the Status of Women, Stephanie McLean, used this line when promoting "Ready for Her" in the Canadian press. Elsewhere in Canada, the nonprofit AskHer—which looks to increase the number of women on the Calgary city council—says in a promotional video, "The only way something can be done about it [women's low presence on the city council] is if more women run. . . . So have that confidence, be confident, and go ahead and take that leap . . . just go for it."[32] These messages suggest to women aspirants that running itself overcomes (at least some of) the gendered barriers to election.

This reassurance also appears in Global South programs. In Tanzania, UN Women concluded that participants in its training program "increased their public speaking, leadership and campaigning skills, and were empowered to go through the political party nomination process."[33] In fact, the word *empowerment* features so heavily in Global South programs that recounting all the individual examples would take too much space.

Both international and domestic programs further link inspiring and empowering women to building stronger democracies. Global North and Global South programs rely heavily on a "why women" narrative that encourages women to run not merely to fulfill personal career ambitions but to improve democratic practices and outcomes. Like justifying candidate training in terms of women's empowerment, the "why women" narrative is omnipresent. From Emerge America in the United States to NDI's initiatives in Southeast Asia, programs underscore how women bring different perspectives and unique policy-making preferences to government.[34] In postconflict countries, such as Liberia, programs emphasize the connection between women's presence and sustainable peace.[35]

Importantly, these arguments go beyond justice-based reasons for women's political participation. In a justice-based argument, women's presence *indicates* social equality and therefore democracy. In an instrumental argument, women's presence matters for *transforming* political practices and outcomes. Instrumental arguments emphasize how women are more empathetic, inclusive, collaborative, and caring. Bringing women into politics, therefore, means that politics, policy processes, and political parties themselves will become less exclusionary, less combative, and more attentive to citizens' needs. Instrumental arguments do have an empirical basis. Due to their lived experiences and gender role socialization, women *do* perform politics differently.[36] Nonetheless, the "why women" narrative frequently overlooks that carrying out the representative and responsive features of democratic government is the responsibility of *all* political actors.

The Limitations of Candidate Training at Home and Abroad

Candidate training programs do play the inspirational and empowering roles that local organizers envision. Programs contribute to social and gender justice, as other chapters in this volume show. Dittmar and Sanbonmatsu as well as Schneider and Sweet-Cushman (Chapter 14, in this volume) find that Ready to Run® assuages women's doubts about running for office, increases their interest in doing so, and leads them to more positively evaluate political careers. And Johnson finds that women in Benin benefited from learning the skills that candidate training provided.

Persistent gender bias often keeps women outside the networks through which men accrue the knowledge and expertise of how politics is done. Women *do* need an introduction into the rules, practices, and norms of politics—not because they are inherently less capable but because persistent exclusion means they have enjoyed fewer opportunities to learn the rules of the game. Women know that one cost to entering this arena is having their qualifications and preparedness subject to heavy scrutiny, and having completed a candidate training program adds to their résumé and gives them more credibility. Training can boost women's confidence about entering an inhospitable arena dominated by men, especially in contexts where women face hostility and resistance.

At the same time, programs often focus on correcting women's shortcomings without challenging the systemic biases that fuel women's underrepresentation in the first place. For example, a party leader from Cameroon stated, in support of candidate training, "Men are reluctant to give to women. Some of the women are shy."[37] This statement recognized party leaders' discrimination against women but also blamed women for their own marginalization. Indeed, researchers analyzing women's candidate training in Canada and India concluded that modules presented systemic barriers as women's problems and that participants in turn internalized these barriers as individual deficiencies. For instance, women's absence from meetings and the media was attributed to women's lack of communication skills, rather than men's reluctance to include or invite women.[38] As Johnson details for Benin, women aspirants themselves doubt that training corrects party leaders' gender bias.

Candidate training also does not tackle women's unequal access to resources. In Papua New Guinea, Australian foreign aid funded multiple candidate training programs over several years, and a record number of women candidates entered the 2017 election. Yet *no* women were elected. The women candidates reported their top problem was political parties' refusal to give them campaign funds.[39] This refrain—that what women really need is money, not training—has been repeated from Benin (see Johnson) to Brazil.[40] In Colombia, one woman senator stated that training was a "waste of money" since training could not give women campaign funds.[41]

Program organizers believe their interventions will eventually undo these systemic barriers. Programs hope that, once elites and voters see that women are capable and qualified, they will change their attitudes and that discrimination will cease. For example, NDI's Ukraine program was described as "teach[ing] women the skills needed to make a serious run for office and to take on more meaningful roles in political parties [and] seek[ing] to change the cultural perception of women in politics."[42] In Papua New Guinea, the United Nations Development Programme hoped their Practice Parliament would "showcase the abilities of women to participate in the political life of this country. . . . Show the nation what they can do when they are given the chance." Yet recall that, in 2017, no women candidates in Papua New Guinea received the party support or resources necessary to mount a successful campaign. Little evidence suggests that calling party leaders' attention to talented and qualified women matters in any substantial way.

Using credentialing to mitigate gender bias and undo discriminatory prac-tices may well have no effect. Even worse, it may backfire. Women-only can-didate training implies that women need support and skills, while men are seen as naturally possessing the aptitude for the job. Credentialing also re-inforces the practice of holding women to higher standards—of women hav-ing to do more and know more to justify their place. Credentialing signals that mediocre women cannot succeed, even though mediocre men have been winning for generations. Further, if women who complete the training still find themselves denied viable candidacies and campaign resources, they may internalize the loss as their individual failure. The "why women" narrative further places an unfair burden on women politicians.

The presence of candidate training distracts policy-makers, practition-ers, and the public from party leaders' gatekeeping role. Candidate training does not hold the political parties accountable for ending discrimination against women. Party elites create the rules of the game, and when these rules create inhospitable climates for women candidates and actively work against women candidates' success, then, it is not women who must improve or change, it is the party elites. For this reason, those looking to truly solve the problem of women's political underrepresentation will find candidate training a poor fit.

These limitations do not mean policy-makers and activists should aban-don women's candidate training altogether. Recognizing programs' limita-tions simply means not relying on women's candidate training as a panacea for women's persistent underrepresentation in and exclusion from politics. Candidate training does not challenge systemic bias and may even perpetu-ate the double standards to which women politicians are held. Candidate training can also disproportionately burden women with saving democracy. Yet my overview of women's candidate training programs worldwide indi-cates that considerable hype surrounds these initiatives—as if they were the next silver bullet for correcting women's political underrepresentation. Gen-der quotas have met with party leaders' resistance and frequently fail to meet their numerical targets, but they are now widespread. The international com-munity continues to push for more and stronger quotas but also has landed on candidate training as the latest solution. Raising the supply of talented women candidates does matter, but the ultimate responsibility for making the spaces and practices of politics more equitable, inclusive, just, and fair lies not with individual women but with the political parties. Development specialists must not abandon the hard work of holding party leaders account-able for ending women's political exclusion.

NOTES

I am grateful for the outstanding research assistance provided by Amanda Lucia Burk-hardt. I also thank the editors of this volume and participants at the 2017 "Good Reasons to Run Conference" in Philadelphia for their comments on earlier drafts.

1. National Democratic Institute, "Empowering Women for Stronger Political Parties," Washington, DC, 2012, p. ii, available at https://www.ndi.org/sites/default/files /Empowering-Women-Full-Case-Study-ENG.pdf.

2. An important political reform in many countries has been to allow candidates to run independent of political parties. Where allowed, independent candidates can self-register, but they run without any party label.

3. Elin Bjarnegård, *Gender, Informal Institutions, and Political Recruitment: Explaining Male Dominance in Parliamentary Representation* (New York: Palgrave, 2013).

4. Susan Franceschet, Mona Lena Krook, and Jennifer M. Piscopo, eds., *The Impact of Gender Quotas* (New York: Oxford University Press, 2012).

5. Maarja Luhiste, "Party Gatekeepers' Support for Viable Female Candidacy in PR-List Systems," *Politics and Gender* 11, no. 1 (2015): 89–116; Michelle K. Ryan, S. Alexander Haslam, and Clara Kulich, "Politics and the Glass Cliff: Evidence that Women are Preferentially Selected to Contest Hard-to-Win Seats," *Psychology of Women Quarterly* 34, no. 1 (2010): 56–64; Braum Wauters, Karolien Weekers, and Bart Maddens, "Explaining the Number of Preferential Votes for Women in an Open-List PR System: An Investigation of the 2003 Federal Elections in Flanders (Belgium)," *Acta Politica* 45, no. 4 (2010): 468–490.

6. Kristin N. Wylie, *Party Institutionalization and Women's Representation in Democratic Brazil* (New York: Cambridge University Press, 2018).

7. Georgina Waylen and Ros Southern, "Gender, Informal Institutions, and Corruption: The UK Parliamentary Expenses Scandal," paper presented at the Gender and Corruption Workshop, University of Gothenburg, Sweden, May 23–24, 2016.

8. Kendall D. Funk, Magda Hinojosa, and Jennifer M. Piscopo, "Still Left Behind: Gender, Political Parties, and Latin America's Pink Tide," *Social Politics* 24, no. 4 (2017): 399–424.

9. Melanie Hughes, "Intersectionality, Quotas, and Minority Women's Political Representation Worldwide," *American Journal of Political Science* 105, no. 3 (2011): 604–620.

10. Funk, Hinojosa, Piscopo, "Still Left Behind."

11. Liza M. Mügge, "Intersectionality, Recruitment and Selection: Ethnic Minority Candidates in Dutch Parties," *Parliamentary Affairs* 69, no. 3 (2016): 512–530.

12. Kira Sanbonmatsu, "Do Parties Know That 'Women Win'? Party Leader Beliefs about Women's Electoral Chances," *Politics and Gender* 2, no. 4 (2006): 431–450; Melody Crowder-Meyer, "Gendered Recruitment without Trying: How Local Party Recruiters Affect Women's Representation," *Politics and Gender* 9, no. 4 (2013): 390–413; Sarah A. Fulton, "Running Backwards and in High Heels: The Gendered Quality Gap and Incumbent Electoral Success," *Political Research Quarterly* 65, no. 2 (2012): 303–314; Jennifer L. Lawless and Kathryn Pearson, "The Primary Reason for Women's Underrepresentation? Reevaluating the Conventional Wisdom," *Journal of Politics* 70, no. 1 (2008): 67–82.

13. Shauna L. Shames, *Out of the Running: Why Millennials Reject Political Careers and Why It Matters* (New York: New York University Press, 2017).

14. Lawless and Pearson, "Primary Reason for Women's Underrepresentation?"

15. "Women Candidates Challenged by History, Party, and Sexism," accessed February 27, 2019, available at https://www.cnn.com/2018/10/28/politics/midterms-women -candidates-lah/index.html.

16. "Women in National Parliaments: 50 Years of History at a Glance," accessed March 17, 2018, available at http://archive.ipu.org/wmn-e/history.htm.

17. "Women in National Parliaments," accessed March 17, 2018, available at http:// archive.ipu.org/wmn-e/classif.htm.

18. Drude Dahlerup and Pippa Norris, "On the Fast Track: An Integrated Theory for the Global Spread of Electoral Gender Quotas," paper presented at the Annual Meeting of the American Political Science Association, Washington, DC, August 28-31, 2014.

19. Katherine A. R. Opello, *Gender Quotas, Parity Reform, and Political Parties in France* (Lanham, MD: Lexington Books, 2006), 31-32.

20. More information, accessed August 20, 2018, available at https://www.theguardian .com/world/2018/jun/22/mexico-elections-fake-transgender-candidates-disqualified.

21. More information, accessed March 18, 2018, for Azerbaijan, available at https:// www.counterpart.org/projects/womens-participation-program/.

22. More information, accessed March 18, 2018, available at http://www.parlia mentproject.co.uk/.

23. Interview with Lisane Thirsk, ParlAmericas, New Brunswick, NJ, May 25, 2017.

24. See NDI's program call, accessed March 18, 2018, available at https://drive.google .com/file/d/1ZKPiCwONzhtoPAHWwcgBvOsaU-Y6bN2W/view.

25. Interview with party leader, Santiago, Chile, May 4, 2018.

26. One exception is the Organization of American States, which directly runs its candidate training programs in Latin America.

27. Interview with Ki-young Shin and Mari Miura, Seoul, South Korea, March 5, 2018.

28. Interview with Ki-young Shin and Mari Miura, Seoul, South Korea, March 5, 2018.

29. More information, accessed March 19, 2018, available at http://www.lapressedu jour.net/archives/38704.

30. Notes on "Meetings with Party Officials," March 14, 2014, document from NDI consultancy provided by Sethunya Mosime to Jennifer Piscopo.

31. Personal communication from Sethunya Mosime, October 24, 2017.

32. See the "Ask Her" video, accessed January 24, 2018, available at http://ask-her.org /about-ask-her/.

33. More information, accessed January 24, 2018, available at http://www.unwomen .org/en/news/stories/2015/10/women-claim-their-space-in-tanzania-elections.

34. More information, for Emerge, accessed October 16, 2017, available at https://emerge .ngpvanhost.com/about; for NDI, accessed November 10, 2019, available at https://www .ndi.org/sites/default/files/StrengthenWomen_Southeast%20Asia.pdf.

35. More information, for Liberia, accessed August 20, 2018, available at http://www .womenscampaigninternational.org/campaign-skills-liberia/.

36. Diana O'Brien and Jennifer M. Piscopo, "The Impact of Women in Parliament," In *The Palgrave Handbook of Women's Political Rights*, ed. Susan Franceschet, Mona Lena Krook, and Netina Tan (New York: Palgrave, 2019): 53-72.

37. Quoted in *The Guardian*, accessed January 24, 2018, https://www.theguardian .com/world/2013/sep/09/women-african-politics-vote-cameroon.

38. Darlene E. Clover, Catherine Mcgregor, Martha Farrell, and Mandakini Pant, "Women Learning Politics and the Politics of Learning: A Feminist Study of Canada and India," *Studies in the Education of Adults* 43, no. 1 (2011): 18-33.

39. Debrief by Kerryn Baker, accessed February 5, 2018, available at http://devpolicy .org/experiences-of-female-candidates-png-general-election-20180206/.

40. Wylie, *Party Institutionalization*.

41. Kevin Casas-Zamora and Elin Falguera, "Political Participation and the Equal Participation of Women in Colombia: A Situation Analysis," International IDEA, Stockholm (2016): 30. Accessed March 19, 2018, available at https://www.idea.int/sites/default /files/publications/political-finance-and-equal-participation-of-women-in-colombia.pdf.

42. More information, accessed March 19, 2018, available at https://www.ndi.org/ru /node/5074.

PART V

The Special Role of Money

This part provides an in-depth look into the ways that fundraising and campaign finances play a role in who runs for and wins office by examining women running in U.S. congressional elections, statewide contests, and in a case study of Benin campaign support organizations. Campaign finances play an important role in running for office in many places, but especially in the United States. Since *Citizens United v. the Federal Election Commission*, money and campaign finance has become—and will continue to be—a foundational component to running for office.[1]

Women running for office understand that campaign finance is an essential part of running for office; for example, they spend similar amounts on campaigns at the local, state, and national levels as men.[2] And yet, we know that the time needed to get that money differs for men and women. Men have fundraising advantages thanks to PACs and bundled money; they are also more likely to get funding from party organizations.[3] Despite these disadvantages, women often end up on equal footing in campaign fundraising dollars; this may be because they spend more of their time in active fundraising.[4]

Gender differences also emerge among campaign donors; men are far more likely to give money to political candidates and to see those donations as an important tool for shaping access to political leaders.[5] The consequences of women controlling fewer economic resources in society are many: women express less political interest, possess lower levels of political knowledge, and are less likely to run for office.[6] We can see gendered behavior directly in fundraising as well: it is clear that women, particularly Democratic women, are more likely to give their money when women are running.[7]

Women's campaign fundraising networks, like EMILY's List (which stands for "early money is like yeast") also provide an opportunity for women to overcome some of the hurdles they face in fundraising. These organizations can provide strategic gifts that allow women to be competitive in a political system that routinely calls for candidates to raise millions of dollars to compete.[8] Organizational support is often partisan, however, or focused on giving to pro-choice women, which limits the path forward for Republican or pro-life women candidates.[9]

In this part, three chapters examine the role of varying sources of campaign finance in the U.S. congressional and state-level elections as well as in elections in Benin. The three chapters focus on the ways that parties, gender, and money interact to shape women's pathways to political office. In these investigations, we come to see a more nuanced and robust view of how money shapes politics in gendered ways.

In Chapter 16, "Building a Campaign Donor Network: How Candidate Gender and Partisanship Impact the Campaign Money Chase," Swers and Thomsen note, "Between 1998 and 2016 the amount of money spent on congressional races rose from $1.6 million to $4.1 million," which has significantly raised the bar in terms of barriers of entry for candidates running for congressional office. Swers and Thomsen evaluate how gender, ideology, and partisanship all shape access to campaign finance decisions, with a focus on the types of candidates that can most easily build a fundraising network. The authors rely on an extensive campaign database to find that men and women pursue different donation strategies. As a result, "Among Democrats, the gender affinity effect we find among donors means that female Democrats can count on the support of female donors but these women candidates will have to work harder than similarly situated men to attract male donors."

Chapter 17, "Training Women to Run in an African Democracy: The Case of Benin," by Johnson, examines the role of campaign networks and fundraising in Benin, an African country with some of the lowest levels of women's representation on the continent. Using interviews with elected women and women who ran for office unsuccessfully, Johnson provides a clear view of the various obstacles that women face in seeking political office. She finds that training programs provide "an important role in motivating potential women candidates, increasing women's knowledge about the election process, and improving family support" (Johnson, this volume). In particular, these training programs provide women with access to important fundraising networks. Yet, campaign fundraising programs have not yet overcome gendered biases in the country, nor have they been able to shift political party treatment of women. She finds that one reason parties are unwilling to place women on the ballot is "because they want candidates who can finance both their own campaign and that of the party." In evaluating Benin, Johnson provides a clear view of the challenges that women face in seeking political office in an environment where resources are scarce and political parties pay roles as key gatekeepers.[10]

In the final chapter, Chapter 18, Kettler's work in "Paying It Forward: Candidate Contributions and Support for Diverse Candidates" investigates a unique view of campaign finance: when candidates give to other campaigns. She examines candidate-to-candidate donations in elections in six states: Colorado, Iowa, New Mexico, North Carolina, Oklahoma, and Pennsylvania. In doing so, Kettler finds that women contribute to other women, but there are large differences across her states of analysis. Like Swers and Thomsen, Kettler finds that these donations are concentrated among Democratic women, who are much more likely to donate money to another woman, particularly if she is running for an open seat.

Taken together, these pieces illustrate the continued challenges that women face when seeking political office in the United States and abroad. Yet, they also reveal the in-group advantages that women can capitalize on: all three chapters point to women supporting other women as a key component to the ability of women running for office to fundraise and compete financially. Building on work in the previous parts, these chapters also demonstrate the importance of understanding the differences *among* women, not just between women and men. As money plays such an important role in politics generally and campaigning in particular—and will continue to do so without policy interventions like public financing and other campaign finance reform— these chapters help us understand key obstacles and opportunities for women interested in political office.

NOTES

1. Raymond J. La Raja and Brian F. Schaffner, "The Effects of Campaign Finance Spending Bans on Electoral Outcomes: Evidence from the States about the Potential Impact of *Citizens United v. FEC*," *Electoral Studies* 33 (March 1, 2014): 102–114.

2. Robert E. Hogan, "The Effects of Candidate Gender on Campaign Spending in State Legislative Elections," *Social Science Quarterly* 88, no. 5 (2007): 1092–1105.

3. Michael Barber, Daniel M. Butler, and Jessica Preece, "Gender Inequalities in Campaign Finance," *Quarterly Journal of Political Science* 11, no. 2 (2016): 219–248; Hogan, "Effects of Candidate Gender"; Danielle M. Thomsen and Michele L. Swers, "Which Women Can Run? Gender, Partisanship, and Candidate Donor Networks," *Political Research Quarterly*, March 9, 2017; Michael H. Crespin and Janna L. Deitz, "If You Can't Join 'Em, Beat 'Em: The Gender Gap in Individual Donations to Congressional Candidates," *Political Research Quarterly* 63, no. 3 (September 1, 2010): 581–593.

4. Brian E. Adams and Ronnee Schreiber, "Gender, Campaign Finance, and Electoral Success in Municipal Elections," *Journal of Urban Affairs* 33, no. 1 (2011): 83–97.

5. Crespin and Deitz, "If You Can't Join 'Em, Beat 'Em."

6. Mirya R. Holman, "The Differential Effect of Resources on Political Participation across Gender and Racial Groups," in *Distinct Identities: Minority Women in U.S. Politics*, ed. Nadia E. Brown and Sarah A. Gershon (New York: Routledge, 2016); Jennie Sweet-Cushman, "Gender, Risk Assessment, and Political Ambition," *Politics and the Life Sciences*, January 2016, 1–17, available at https://doi.org/10.1017/pls.2016.13; Heather L. Ondercin

and Daniel Jones-White, "Gender Jeopardy: What Is the Impact of Gender Differences in Political Knowledge on Political Participation?" *Social Science Quarterly* 92, no. 3 (2011): 675–694; Nancy Burns, Kay Lehman Schlozman, and Sidney Verba, "The Public Consequences of Private Inequality: Family Life and Citizen Participation," *American Political Science Review* 91, no. 2 (1997): 373–389.

7. Crespin and Deitz, "If You Can't Join 'Em, Beat 'Em"; Thomsen and Swers, "Which Women Can Run?"

8. Christine L. Day and Charles D. Hadley, "Who Contributes? Similarities and Differences between Contributors to EMILY's List and WISH List," *Women and Politics* 24, no. 2 (2002): 53–67; Rebecca J. Hannagan, Jamie P. Pimlott, and Levente Littvay, "Does an EMILY's List Endorsement Predict Electoral Success, or Does EMILY Pick the Winners?" *PS: Political Science and Politics* 43, no. 3 (2010): 503–508; Marian Sawer, "EMILY's List and Angry White Men: Gender Wars in the Nineties," *Journal of Australian Studies* 23, no. 62 (1999): 1–9.

9. Rosalyn Cooperman and Melody Crowder-Meyer, "A Run for Their Money: Republican Women's Hard Road to Campaign Funding," in *The Right Women: Republican Party Activists, Candidates, and Legislators,* ed. Shauna L. Shames and Malliga Och (Santa Barbara, CA: Praeger, 2018); Melody Crowder-Meyer and Rosalyn Cooperman, "Can't Buy Them Love: How Party Culture among Donors Contributes to the Party Gap in Women's Representation," *Journal of Politics* 80, no. 4 (2018).

10. Melody Crowder-Meyer, "Gendered Recruitment without Trying: How Local Party Recruiters Affect Women's Representation." *Politics and Gender* 9, no. 4 (2013): 390–413.

16

Building a Campaign Donor Network

How Candidate Gender and Partisanship Impact the Campaign Money Chase

MICHELE L. SWERS AND
DANIELLE M. THOMSEN

To run a credible campaign, candidates need to raise money and a lot of it. In 2018, Democratic House candidates raised an average of almost $819,680 and Republican House candidates collected about $780,639. The most successful fundraisers are incumbents, and these sitting members of Congress brought in an average of $1.87 million to support their campaigns.[1] Even with a historic number of women elected to Congress in 2018, women still only constitute 23.6 percent of House and Senate incumbents.[2] Therefore, to increase women's representation, more female candidates will need to run as challengers and in open seat races where there is no incumbent on the ballot. Yet, nonincumbent candidates confront the highest hurdles in the campaign money chase. While high-profile races that could flip party control of the House or Senate will draw heavy spending from Republican and Democratic super PACs, most challengers will not run in a competitive district and will not benefit from super PAC spending. Furthermore, most PACs prefer to support incumbents who are known quantities and may sit on committees with jurisdiction over the group's interests.[3]

As a result, new candidates are especially reliant on individual donations to fuel their campaigns, working to secure both small donations and the large contributions of $200 or more that must be reported to the Federal Election Commission (FEC). The individual donors that new candidates must court are more ideologically extreme than the average voter. To reach these donors, candidates must stake out more clearly liberal or conservative positions.[4] In recent years, women's issues have become a focal point of partisan warfare with Democrats portraying themselves as the party of women's rights and excoriating Republicans as engaged in a war on women.[5] Meanwhile, Republicans are strongly aligned with social conservatives and the party culture rejects group identity-based politics.[6] These internal party dynamics likely impact the composition of partisan donors and the types of candidates that can raise money from the Republican and Democratic donor bases.

Building a donor network is no easy task. In this chapter, we examine what kind of candidates can attract the support of Republican and Democratic donors. Analyzing the large individual donations of $200 or more collected by candidates who ran in the 2010 and 2012 primary and general elections, we find that a candidate's ideological profile is incredibly important. Conservative Republican and liberal Democratic candidates are more likely to convince today's partisan donors to contribute to their campaigns. Moreover, we find important differences among the male and female donors that constitute the two parties' electoral coalitions. As a group, Democratic donors respond to candidate gender with female Democrats valuing the election of women and male Democrats more inclined to give to men. By contrast, neither male nor female Republican donors consider the gender of candidates in their donation decisions, preferring to prioritize the ideological profile of the candidate. Our findings have implications for the types of female candidates that can successfully raise the money needed to run in the current political climate. Our research also indicates that Republican groups devoted to raising money for female candidates will have a more difficult time attracting party donors than Democratic groups seeking to elect women.

The Fundraising Imperative: A Higher Hurdle for Women Candidates?

In contrast to many European democracies where candidates run as part of a party slate and the length and cost of campaigns are more limited, in the United States, congressional campaigns are candidate-centered and increasingly expensive.[7] Between 1998 and 2018 the amount of money spent on congressional races rose from $1.6 million to $5.7 million.[8] Candidates must raise enough money to sustain themselves through both a primary and a general election campaign. In the primary phase, candidates are especially reliant on their own networks of friends, business associates, and community contacts. The major parties are generally reluctant to endorse in primaries, and they examine candidates' fundraising records as a sign of their viability. A demonstrated ability to raise money sends a signal to party leaders and allied groups who may then be convinced to promote the candidate to their donor networks.[9]

While the fundraising imperative is grueling, years of academic research finds little evidence that women have more trouble raising money than men do. Seat status, rather than gender, is the most important factor in determining how much a candidate will raise. Female incumbents raise just as much money as male incumbents and both male and female challengers have difficulty raising the necessary funds.[10] Thus, the fact that so many women must run as challengers is a greater obstacle for women candidates than their gender. Yet recent research indicates that among Republican challengers, the quality female challengers, meaning those who have held previous office like state legislators, have more difficulty raising money in the primary stage than male quality challengers. This suggests that the most viable Republican women confront a more difficult fundraising landscape than their male counterparts.[11] Moreover, women may have to work harder to raise money, as women raise more of their funds from small donors.[12]

Despite the fact that the women who run are equally successful at raising money, many female officeholders believe that fundraising is more difficult for women than for men.[13] The belief that women are disadvantaged in the money chase is a frequently cited reason for why women are reluctant to run.[14] Surveying state legislators, Carroll and Sanbonmatsu find that both Democratic and Republican women believe that it is harder for women to raise money than for men.[15] Lack of access to donor networks was the most commonly cited reason for women's fundraising difficulties. The legislators believed that women are less likely to have the necessary business and social connections to large donors. Furthermore, a female candidate's social network likely includes more women than a male candidate's network. Yet, women are much less likely to donate to political campaigns than men and women also give smaller amounts, compelling a candidate who is more reliant on contributions from women to solicit even more donors to raise the necessary funds.[16] Indeed, in 2016, women constituted only 37.1 percent of donors and they contributed only 29.6 percent of the total money raised across the presidential and congressional campaigns even as Hillary Clinton raised a record proportion—52 percent of her large donations of $200 or more—from women.[17] Similarly, even as a record number of women won congressional seats in 2018, women donors made up only 37.7 percent of donors to congressional races and they donated 29.5 percent of the money raised by congressional candidates.[18]

Given both the perception among women candidates that they confront a more difficult fundraising landscape and the male-dominated pool of citizens that donate to campaigns, we take a closer look to evaluate how the combination of a candidate's gender, ideology, and partisanship impacts the composition of their donor networks. Do male Republican challengers draw more support from male donors that support Republican candidates than female Republican challengers? Do female Democratic incumbents receive more support from female donors than male Democratic incumbents or do all Democratic incumbents share similar donor profiles based on the value of incumbency? What types of candidates can most easily build a fundraising network in today's political climate?

Analyzing Candidate Donor Networks

To answer these questions, we track the total amount of itemized donations of $200 or more that candidates received from male and female donors in the 2010 and 2012 election cycles. Our dataset incorporates all candidates who competed in the primary and/or general election, including 1,409 primary and/or general election candidates in the 2010 midterm wave and 1,275 candidates in the more status quo 2012 presidential cycle.[19] Given the small number of women who run for office, by including candidates who lost their primary we capture more female candidates than the vast majority of studies that focus solely on general election candidates. Across the two cycles, there are 188 Republican women and 284 Democratic women. We obtained information on the amount of money a candidate raised from male and female donors from the Database on Ideology, Money in Politics, and Elections.[20] The database provides the aggregate amount that a candidate received from male and female donors across the election cycle.

Table 16.1 provides an overview of the amount of money that male and female Republicans and Democrats running as incumbents, challengers, and open seat candidates received from male and female donors. We look at the universe of primary and general election candidates and the subset of general election candidates that are traditionally examined in campaign finance analyses. Corroborating previous research, men donate far more to congressional campaigns than women do.[21] These patterns hold across all candidate types. Looking at incumbents, the candidates with the largest advantages, male donors give more than twice as much money to incumbent Democrats and three times as much money to incumbent Republicans as female donors. Clearly, the universe of individuals who donate to campaigns is highly skewed along gender lines.

Keeping in mind that male donors dominate the fundraising networks of all candidates, there are important differences in the giving patterns of male and female donors that are reflected in the networks of male and female candidates. In the full sample of primary and/or general election candidates, women as a group raise significantly more money from female donors than men as a group, and, within the category of women candidates, Democratic women receive a greater boost than their female Republican counterparts ($p < 0.01$). Female donors also give more to Democratic women as a group than to Democratic men ($p < 0.01$). (These figures are in boldface in Table 16.1.) Republican women actually receive less money overall from female donors than Republican men, but this is largely because so few Republican women are running as incumbents. Thus, Republican women are particularly disadvantaged because a disproportionate number of them are challengers who raise little money and are unlikely to win.[22]

TABLE 16.1. AVERAGE AMOUNT RAISED FROM MALE AND FEMALE DONORS, BY CANDIDATE GENDER, PARTY, AND SEAT TYPE (2010 AND 2012)

	Number	Male donors	Female donors
All candidates			
Democrat, challenger, male	405	156,501	62,876
Democrat, challenger, female	130	149,633	99,476
Democrat, open, male	151	281,583	111,669
Democrat, open, female	54	274,117	173,230
Democrat, incumbent, male	300	560,222	187,275
Democrat, incumbent, female	100	496,549	284,097
Republican, challenger, male	750	159,952	53,888
Republican, challenger, female	108	131,014	51,681
Republican, open, male	278	243,326	79,729
Republican, open, female	44	193,977	90,434
Republican, incumbent, male	328	765,958	212,397
Republican, incumbent, female	36	600,295	221,147
Democratic men, all	856	320,057	**115,081**
Democratic women, all	284	295,456	**178,507**
Republican men, all	1,356	323,631	97,527
Republican women, all	188	235,612	**93,202**
Men, all	2,212	322,248	**104,320**
Women, all	472	271,620	**144,530**
General election candidates			
Democrat, challenger, male	216	248,424	100,479
Democrat, challenger, female	75	203,521	138,280
Democrat, open, male	62	504,902	205,923
Democrat, open, female	24	467,129	297,158
Democrat, incumbent, male	293	561,189	187,671
Democrat, incumbent, female	98	503,205	288,468
Republican, challenger, male	286	337,074	112,441
Republican, challenger, female	43	274,167	108,554
Republican, open, male	79	584,644	193,188
Republican, open, female	8	614,506	281,199
Republican, incumbent, male	322	770,657	213,225
Republican, incumbent, female	34	612,303	226,615

(*continued*)

TABLE 16.1. AVERAGE AMOUNT RAISED FROM MALE AND FEMALE
DONORS, BY CANDIDATE GENDER, PARTY, AND SEAT TYPE
(2010 AND 2012) (CONTINUED)

	Number	Male donors	Female donors
Democratic men, all	571	436,764	**156,670**
Democratic women, all	197	384,717	**232,349**
Republican men, all	687	568,765	168,964
Republican women, all	85	441,453	**172,027**
Men, all	1,258	483,658	**158,775**
Women, all	282	401,716	**214,020**

Note: The figures in boldface correspond to gender and partisan disparities discussed in the text.

When we limit the sample to include only general election candidates, women candidates continue to raise more money from female donors than male candidates ($p < 0.01$). Across these various groups of candidates, female Democrats again garner more money from female donors than Republican women and Democratic men ($p < 0.10$ and $p < 0.01$, respectively). (These figures are also in boldface in Table 16.1.) Conversely, male donors give more money to male candidates than female candidates, but many of these within-party relationships do not reach conventional levels of statistical significance. Since men dominate the fundraising system, gendered patterns of giving may be detrimental to female candidates.

The patterns in Table 16.1 give an initial picture of how gender, partisanship, and incumbency status influence which candidates can raise money and who the money comes from. To more fully understand the impact of candidate and donor gender, we need to take into account other factors that might influence male and female party donors to give to specific candidates. We utilize ordinary least squares regression analysis to understand the influence of a candidate's gender on the amount of large itemized contributions he or she collected from male and female partisan donors in the 2010 and 2012 elections. Regression analysis helps us predict how much money a candidate with a given set of characteristics is likely to raise from Republican and Democratic male and female donors. In addition to gender, partisanship, and incumbency, the regression models incorporate information on a variety of factors that affect donors' contribution decisions.[23] These include measures such as the number of candidates in the primary, the competitiveness of the general election race, whether the candidate is running in an open seat rather than challenging an incumbent, and the partisan lean of the district to indicate how safe the district is for a candidate's party.[24] Since issue agreement is highly valued by donors, we include a measure for candidate ideology.[25] We also factor in candidate fundraising experience by identifying candidates who have held previous office, such as state legislators.[26] Finally, we identify candidates who received donations from EMILY's List to account for the influence of this highly successful Democratic-leaning PAC and to make sure that gender-related differences among male and female candidates and donors are not solely attributable to the importance of EMILY's list.

Which Candidates Can Attract Individual Donors?

Only certain candidates can raise the funds necessary to run a credible congressional campaign. Our regression analyses confirm previous research demonstrating that incumbency, running in a competitive district, and candidate ideology are all very important determinants of how much a candidate can raise.[27] With respect to ideology, today's individual donors care deeply about candidates' issue positions.[28] Democratic donors prefer liberal candidates and Republican donors want candidates with strong conservative credentials. As a result, a moderate Democrat who, for example, opposes abortion and supports gun rights will have more difficulty raising money from Democratic donors. Indeed, researching state legislators, Thomsen finds that moderate legislators are much less likely to run for Congress than more conservative legislators because the benefits are too low and the costs are too high for them to do so.[29]

When we look more closely at the experiences of male and female partisan candidates and donors, we find additional differences in the fundraising networks of Republican and Democratic men and women and the donation patterns of male and female partisan donors. Among Democrats, Democratic donors exhibit clear gender affinity effects in their donation patterns with female donors more inclined to give to female Democratic candidates and male donors more likely to give to male Democratic candidates. To understand the magnitude of this gender affinity effect, we calculated predicted values to measure how much money a candidate with specific characteristics is expected to collect from donors. Compared to a similarly situated male Democratic candidate, a female Democrat would see a 54 percent increase in donations collected from female donors, but she would also experience a 32 percent decrease in money raised from male donors.[30]

Given that women are less likely than men to donate to campaigns and women contribute smaller amounts, it makes sense that surveys find that Democratic women are the most likely to believe that it is harder for women to raise money. For example, in their survey of state legislators, Carroll and Sanbonmatsu found that 61.7 percent of female Democratic state representatives compared to only 13.5 percent of male Democratic representatives believed that "it is harder for female candidates to raise money than male candidates."[31]

By contrast, candidate gender has no impact on the contribution decisions of Republican donors. The irrelevance of candidate gender reflects the

Republican Party culture, which focuses on ideological purity and rejects group identity-based politics.[32] Indeed, in Sanbonmatsu and Carroll's survey of state legislators, Republican women were much more likely than Republican men to believe that women face more difficulty in fundraising. However, compared to the large majority of Democratic women, only 43.9 percent of Republican women felt women were disadvantaged in fundraising. Meanwhile, a majority of Republican women, 56.1 percent believed that fundraising is "equally hard" for both men and women.[33]

While Republicans focus narrowly on ideology, political party scholars characterize Democrats as group oriented, meaning the party is a conglomeration of groups such as civil rights organizations, women's groups, and environmental associations collaborating to pursue group interests.[34] As a result, the party is more responsive to calls for diversity. Indeed, the National Supporter Survey, a recent survey of party donors, indicates that almost 60 percent of Democratic donors to party committees reported that gender issues were very important to their candidate support decisions while only 9 percent of Republican donors prioritized gender issues.[35] Moreover, our models demonstrate that while Democratic women are more likely to donate to female candidates generally, Democratic men are more inclined to donate to the female candidates who garner contributions from EMILY's List. It is possible that female Democratic candidates are more likely to receive donations from women because they have more women in their social networks who are committed to seeing more women in office. Male Democratic donors, by contrast, may be less likely than female Democrats to have women in their social and business networks. However, because Democrats value diversity, they will direct donations to female candidates who have been endorsed by party-aligned groups such as EMILY's List.

What Do Male and Female Partisan Donors Want?

Additionally, our research shows that male and female partisan donors pursue different donation strategies. First, as a group, both Republican and Democratic female donors give to more ideologically extreme candidates than male donors. The graphs in Figure 16.1 illustrate these trends. In Figure 16.1, we graph the contributions (in logged values) that Democratic and Republican female donors give to incumbent and nonincumbent partisan candidates. The solid line represents giving to female candidates and the dashed line represents donations to male candidates. The light and dark gray shaded areas represent confidence intervals that show the upper and lower bounds of our predictions. We can see that across incumbent and nonincumbent candidates, Democratic women receive more money from women donors than Democratic men, while Republican women do not receive a similar boost in support from women donors. The point estimates in the figures let us compare

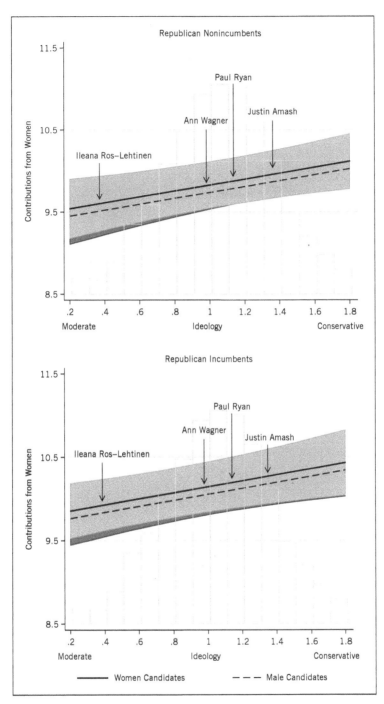

Figure 16.1a. Contributions from women donors, by candidate gender, ideology, and seat type. Note: The dependent variable is measured as logged contributions.

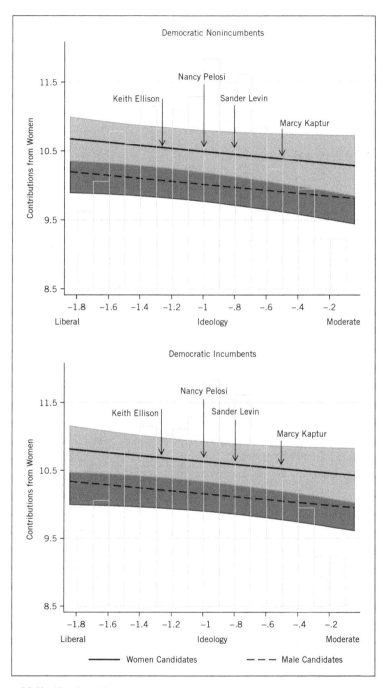

Figure 16.1b. (Continued)

the ideological leanings of candidates to specific members of Congress who are known to be more liberal and conservative so we can better imagine what kinds of candidates can get support from male and female party donors.

Looking at the bottom panel, among Democrats, Keith Ellison (D-MN) is the most liberal member pictured. Serving in Congress until 2019, Ellison was a leader of the Progressive Caucus and deputy chair of the Democratic National Committee (2017–2018). Ellison was also an early endorser of Bernie Sanders for president in the 2016 primary race against Hillary Clinton.[36] Moving to the right, the candidates get incrementally less liberal and Marcy Kaptur (D-OH), a pro-life, strong labor union–oriented Democrat from Ohio is the most moderate of these Democrats. Clearly, the figure demonstrates that Democratic women prefer to donate to more liberal candidates that resemble Keith Ellison (D-MN) or Speaker of the House Nancy Pelosi (D-CA) than more conservative candidates that align with Marcy Kaptur (D-OH).

Similarly, the top panel of Figure 16.1 tracks the donation patterns for Republican women. Like female Democratic donors, Republican women prefer to donate to more strongly ideological candidates. Thus, conservative women prefer firmly conservative candidates like former Speaker of the House Paul Ryan (R-WI) or Justin Amash (R-MI)[37] to more moderate Republicans like Ileana Ros-Lehtinen (R-FL), the first Hispanic woman elected to Congress who retired in 2018. Since women are much less likely than men to donate to political campaigns, only about a third of 2018 donors were women, but those who do contribute are likely to be highly committed partisans who care deeply about the candidates' positions on issues and want to contribute to candidates that share their ideological beliefs.[38]

By contrast, the panels in Figure 16.2 track the donation patterns of Democratic and Republican men. These graphs demonstrate that both Democratic and Republican men donate less to the most liberal and conservative candidates. This pattern may seem strange since we know that individual donors are more ideologically liberal or conservative than average voters and most donors are men.[39] However, the pool of candidates soliciting donations in these cycles is overwhelmingly composed of liberal Democrats and conservative Republicans. The gray bars indicate the ideological distribution of candidates and show where the bulk of the contributions are being directed. Thus, while male donors may be slightly more inclined to support less extreme candidates, the majority of candidates receiving money from men look more like former Speaker of the House Paul Ryan (R-WI) and Current Speaker Nancy Pelosi (D-CA) than Ileana Ros-Lehtinen (R-FL) and Marcy Kaptur (D-OH).

Finally, our research shows that female donors, particularly Democratic female donors, pursue unique donation strategies. Scholars note that to varying degrees, donors generally pursue two contribution strategies. Donors who want to influence policy will donate to competitive and open seat races in an effort to expand the number of seats controlled by the party.[40] Access-oriented

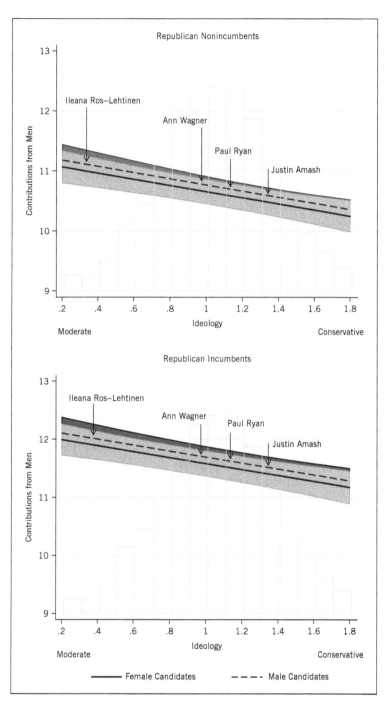

Figure 16.2. Contributions from male donors, by candidate gender, ideology, and seat type. Note: The dependent variable is measured as logged contributions.

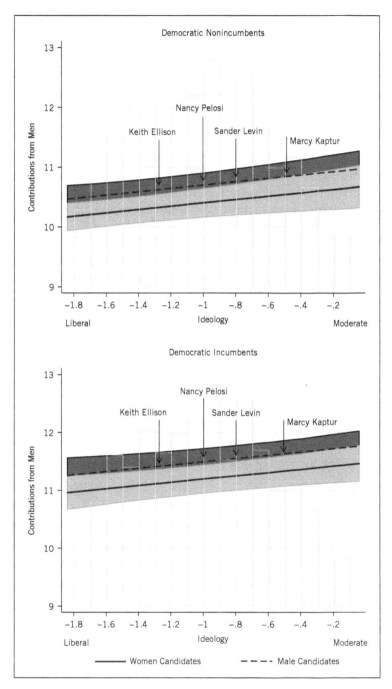

Figure 16.2b. (Continued)

donors seek to give to party and committee leaders and members with seats on influential committees.[41] Male Democrats and Republicans pursue both strategies, contributing to competitive races in an effort to expand the playing field for their party and giving donations to incumbents and members with important positions in the parties and committees to ensure access to powerful members. Republican women seem to reject access strategies in favor of policy influence, donating to ideologically like-minded candidates and in competitive races that will expand the Republican Party's seat share.

Democratic women, on the other hand, exhibit unique strategic considerations in their giving patterns. Female Democratic donors appear to value the election of women to office over other traditional predictors of campaign giving. Incumbents and open seat candidates did not receive more money from Democratic women donors. Instead, the focus of Democratic female donors on women candidates, liberals, quality candidates, and candidates who face a quality opponent is consistent with the idea that they prioritize backing female Democrats in primaries for safe seats so that a woman will emerge as the nominee and be elevated to Congress. The unique focus of female Democrats on electing women is consistent with the fact that liberal female activists prioritize women's rights initiatives such as equal pay and reproductive rights and they value the idea that expanding women's representation will lead lawmakers to devote more attention to these issues.[42] Moreover, women's organizations that are a key constituency of the Democratic Party and count many female donors as members press for the expansion of women's representation in government.[43]

Looking to the Future: Advice for Female Candidates and Party Leaders

In the campaign money chase, one size clearly does not fit all. Our research finds clear differences in the donor networks supporting male and female partisan candidates. For women thinking of running for office, to attract today's partisan donors, Democratic candidates must lean left and take liberal positions on the social and economic issues that motivate the party base. Similarly, women running as Republicans must stake out more strongly conservative positions to court Republican donors.

Among Democrats, the gender affinity effect we find among donors means that female Democrats can count on the support of female donors, but these women candidates will have to work harder than similarly situated men to attract male donors. Female Democratic women and their women's group allies should work aggressively to expand the number of female donors. Currently, the pool of campaign donors is heavily dominated by men. Yet, our finding that female Democratic donors are willing to prioritize the election of women over other factors that consistently predict contributions means that Democratic female candidates would be the primary beneficiaries of a growing set of female donors. Similarly, analyzing candidate-to-candidate donations in this volume, Kettler finds that only Democratic women candidates are strongly inclined to donate to fellow female Democrats. Confirming the preference of female Democratic donors for women candidates, in 2018, female donors gave the most money to Democratic female congressional candidates, and Senators Kirsten Gillibrand (D-NY), Elizabeth Warren (D-MA), and Tammy Baldwin (D-WI) each raised more than half their itemized individual donations from women.[44] Moreover, the fact that the Democratic coalition values diversity as a core principle of the party means that both male and female donors are responsive to calls for expanding the representation of women at the policy-making table.[45] Indeed, in the National Supporter Survey of party donors, Crowder-Meyer and Cooperman report that almost 60 percent of donors to Democratic Party committees consider gender issues very important to their candidate support decisions.[46]

By contrast, the mobilization of more Republican women donors likely will not provide the same boost to Republican women candidates. Neither male nor female Republican donors consider candidate gender. Republican Party culture eschews identity politics and our research indicates that donors focus largely on candidate ideology. Indeed, the Republican women who donate to campaigns are particularly focused on electing conservatives, making it even more difficult for a more moderate Republican woman to court these contributors.

While EMILY's List is among the most prolific fundraisers and is a prominent player in Democratic politics, Republican groups focused on electing women have more difficulty raising funds.[47] In their National Supporter Survey, Crowder-Meyer and Cooperman find only 9 percent of Republican donors prioritize gender issues. Furthermore, while 42 percent of donors to Democratic House and Senate congressional campaign committees reported also donating to EMILY's List, only 7 percent of donors to the Republican congressional campaign committees had donated to the most successful Republican women's PAC, Susan B. Anthony List. In fact, 80–90 percent of Republican Party donors have never heard of some of the groups that raise money for Republican women candidates including VIEW PAC, She PAC, and Maggie's List.[48]

Clearly, groups focused on electing Republican women confront steep hurdles as they must convince party donors who reject identity politics to focus on the need to elect women and they will need to mobilize a currently dormant set of female donors—more moderate Republican women who might be responsive to calls for diversity.

NOTES

1. Center for Responsive Politics, "Incumbent Advantage," 2018, accessed November 9, 2019, available at https://www.opensecrets.org/overview/incumbs.php.

2. Center for American Women and Politics, "Women in the U.S. Congress 2019," 2019, accessed November 9, 2019, available at https://www.cawp.rutgers.edu/women-us -congress-2019.

3. Paul S. Herrnson, *Congressional Elections: Campaigning at Home and in Washington*, 7th ed. (Washington DC: CQ Press, 2016).

4. Robert G. Boatright, *Getting Primaried: The Changing Politics of Congressional Primary Challenges* (Ann Arbor: University of Michigan Press, 2013); Michael J. Ensley, "Individual Campaign Contributions and Candidate Ideology," *Public Choice* 138 (2009): 221–238; Bertram Johnson, "Individual Contributions: A Fundraising Advantage for the Ideologically Extreme?" *American Politics Research* 38 (2010): 890–908.

5. Michele Swers, *Women in the Club: Gender and Policy Making in the Senate* (Chicago: University of Chicago Press, 2013).

6. Matt Grossmann and David A. Hopkins, "Ideological Republicans and Group Interest Democrats: The Asymmetry of American Party Politics," *Perspectives on Politics* 13 (2015): 119–139; Jo Freeman, "The Political Culture of the Democratic and Republican Parties," *Political Science Quarterly* 101 (1986): 327–356.

7. Paul Waldman, "How Our Campaign Finance System Compares to Other Countries," *American Prospect*, April 4, 2014, accessed October 2017, available at https://pros pect.org/power/campaign-finance-system-compares-countries/.

8. "Cost of Elections," Center for Responsive Politics, 2019, accessed November 9, 2019, available at https://www.opensecrets.org/overview/cost.php.

9. Gary C. Jacobson, *The Politics of Congressional Elections*, 8th ed. (Boston: Pearson, 2013); Raymond J. La Raja and Brian F. Schaffner, *Campaign Finance and Political Polarization: When Purists Prevail* (Ann Arbor: University of Michigan Press, 2015).

10. Michael Barber, Daniel Butler, and Jessica Preece, "Gender Inequalities in Campaign Finance," *Quarterly Journal of Political Science* 11 (2016): 219–248; Barbara Burrell, *A Woman's Place Is in the House: Campaigning for Congress in the Feminist Era* (Ann Arbor: University of Michigan Press, 1994); Barbara Burrell, *Gender in Campaigns for the US House of Representatives* (Ann Arbor: University of Michigan Press, 2014); Pamela Fiber and Richard L. Fox, "A Tougher Road for Women? Assessing the Role of Gender in Congressional Elections," in *Gender and American Politics: Women, Men, and the Political Process*, 2nd ed., ed. Sue Tolleson-Rinehart and Jyl J. Josephson (Armonk, NY: M. E. Sharpe, 2005); Joanne Connor Green, "The Times . . . Are They A-Changing? An Examination of the Impact of the Value of Campaign Resources for Women and Men Candidates for the U.S. House of Representatives," *Women and Politics* 25 (2003): 1–29; Robert E. Hogan, "The Effects of Candidate Gender on Campaign Spending in State Legislative Elections," *Social Science Quarterly* 88 (2007): 1092–1105.

11. Karin E. Kitchens and Michele L. Swers, "Why Aren't There More Republican Women in Congress: Gender, Partisanship, and Fundraising Support in the 2010 and 2012 Elections," *Politics and Gender* 12 (2016): 648–676.

12. Michael H. Crespin and Janna L. Dietz, "If You Can't Join 'Em, Beat 'Em: The Gender Gap in Individual Donations to Congressional Candidates," *Political Research Quarterly* 63 (2010): 581–593; Susan J. Carroll and Kira Sanbonmatsu, *More Women Can Run: Gender and Pathways to the State Legislatures* (New York: Oxford University Press, 2013).

13. Carroll and Sanbonmatsu, *More Women Can Run*; Shannon Jenkins, "A Woman's Work Is Never Done: Fundraising Perception and Effort among Female State Legislative Candidates," *Political Research Quarterly* 60 (2007): 230–239.

14. Jennifer L. Lawless and Richard Logan Fox, *It Still Takes a Candidate: Why Women Don't Run for Office* (New York: Cambridge University Press, 2010).

15. Carroll and Sanbonmatsu, *More Women Can Run*.

16. Burrell, *Gender in Campaigns*; Sarah Bryner and Doug Weber, "Sex, Money and Politics: A Center for Responsive Politics Report on Women as Donors and Candidates" (Washington, DC: Center for Responsive Politics, 2013); Nancy Burns, Kay Lehman Schlozman, and Sidney Verba, *The Private Roots of Public Action: Gender, Equality, and Political Participation* (Cambridge, MA: Harvard University Press, 2001).

17. Center for Responsive Politics, "Hillary Clinton (D): Donor Demographics, Federal Election Data Overview," 2019, accessed November 9, 2019, available at https://www.opensecrets.org/pres16/donordemcid?id=N00000019.

18. Center for Responsive Politics, "Donor Demographics," 2019, accessed November 9, 2019, available at https://www.opensecrets.org/overview/donordemographics.php?cycle=2018&filter=G.

19. To identify candidates, we examine the reports candidates filed with the FEC for the 2010 and 2012 elections and the FEC list of "Official Election Results for the U.S. House of Representatives." For example, the 2010 list of candidates is available at http://www.fec.gov/pubrec/fe2010/federalelections2010.shtml. We exclude 21 candidates who ran unopposed in both the primary and the general election, as these candidates do not face the same fundraising imperatives that most candidates confront. Similarly, in our models on general election candidates we exclude candidates who are unopposed. We also exclude 710 candidates who received no funds from either male or female donors, as we are unable to examine the gender composition of their donor networks. Finally, we exclude Michele Bachmann (R-MN) from the analysis. Gearing up for a 2012 presidential campaign, Bachmann far outraised her male and female counterparts across the partisan spectrum that year, raising $22 million compared to $1.6 million for the average incumbent. For more information on the sample and regression models, see Danielle M. Thomsen and Michele L. Swers, "Which Women Can Run? Gender, Partisanship, and Candidate Donor Networks," *Political Research Quarterly* 70 (2017): 449–463.

20. Adam Bonica, "Mapping the Ideological Marketplace," *American Journal of Political Science* 58 (2014): 367–386. The Database on Ideology, Money in Politics, and Elections is available at http://data.stanford.edu/dime/. When coding for gender there are two concerns, how to deal with gender ambiguous names and how to handle joint spousal contributions. The gender coding of names is based on an automated coding scheme that incorporates information on gender ratios of first names as reported by the Census and gender-specific titles such as Mr., Mrs., Jr., and Sr. If a donor with a gender ambiguous name at some point used a gender-specific title, all donations made by that individual were coded accordingly despite the ambiguous name. Using this coding scheme, very few donations are not gender coded. In 2010, for example, 98.3 percent of individual contributions are coded as male or female. With regard to spousal donations, the DIME data indicates a joint contribution anytime an "&" symbol appears for an individual contribution. If an individual made a joint donation and also made other donations on her own, then that individual was given credit for the joint donation. In cases where both spouses also made contributions on their own or the only donations made by the couple are joint donations, the donation is not included in the gender donor codes. In general, though, joint contributions constitute a very small proportion of individual donations. For instance, of the 13.4 million donor observations in 2010, only 0.6 percent included an "&" symbol and are considered joint contributions.

21. Bryner and Weber, "Sex, Money and Politics"; Burns, Schlozman, and Verba, *Private Roots of Public Action*.

22. The figures in Table 16.1 are average amounts raised from male and female donors for these various groups of candidates. Individual candidate numbers can be very different, so it is important to note that these are aggregate numbers for each of these various groups.

23. For more information on the regression models, see Thomsen and Swers, "Which Women Can Run?" The dependent variable is the log of the amount a candidate raised in itemized contributions over $200 from male and female donors in the 2010 and 2012 elections. Because of the skewed nature of contributions, we used the natural log of each contribution type as our dependent variable.

24. Cook Political Report ratings of races as toss up or leaning to one party indicate the competitiveness of the race. The district's presidential votes for Barack Obama in 2008 (for 2010 candidates) and 2012 (for 2012 candidates) are used to determine the partisan lean of the district. Additional district variables include the median household income, White population, and proportion of urban residents in the district. While incumbents always raise more money than other candidates, incumbents who hold important positions in the House have fundraising advantages. We include variables to capture members who are party leaders, committee chairs, ranking members, and members with seats on prestigious committees including Appropriations, Ways and Means, and Rules.

25. Bonica's DIME database includes Campaign Finance scores (CFscores) to measure candidate ideology. These scores are calculated based on the mix of donations candidates receive from PACs and individuals. Positive scores indicate more conservative candidates while negative values denote more liberal candidates. See Bonica, "Mapping the Ideological Marketplace," for more information on these scores.

26. Candidates who have held previous office and thus have previously run campaigns are considered quality candidates. In addition to these candidates, we include measures for whether a candidate is facing a quality opponent and whether a candidate has run for the seat in the past to incorporate frequent candidates who are less viable than other competitors.

27. Jacobson, *Politics of Congressional Elections*; Herrnson, *Congressional Elections*.

28. Peter L. Francia, John C. Green, Paul S. Herrnson, Lynda W. Powell, and Clyde Wilcox. *The Financiers of Congressional Elections* (New York: Columbia University Press, 2003); Peter L. Francia, John C. Green, Paul S. Herrnson, Lynda W. Powell, and Clyde Wilcox, "Limousine Liberals and Corporate Conservatives: The Financial Constituencies of the Democratic and Republican Parties," *Social Science Quarterly* 86 (2005): 761–778.

29. Danielle M. Thomsen, "Ideological Moderates Won't Run: How Party Fit Matters for Partisan Polarization in Congress," *Journal of Politics* 76 (2014): 786–797; Danielle M. Thomsen, *Opting Out of Congress: Partisan Polarization and the Decline of Moderate Candidates* (New York: Cambridge University Press, 2017).

30. See Thomsen and Swers, "Which Women Can Run?" for more information on how these predicted values are calculated.

31. Carroll and Sanbonmatsu, *More Women Can Run*.

32. Grossmann and Hopkins, "Ideological Republicans"; Freeman, "Political Culture."

33. Carroll and Sanbonmatsu, *More Women Can Run*.

34. Kathleen Bawn, Martin Cohen, David Karol, Seth Masket, Hans Noel, and John Zaller, "A Theory of Political Parties: Groups, Policy Demands, and Nominations in American Politics," *Perspectives on Politics* 10 (2012): 571–597; Grossmann and Hopkins, "Ideological Republicans."

35. Melody Crowder-Meyer and Rosalyn Cooperman, "Can't Buy Them Love: How Party Culture among Donors Contributes to the Party Gap in Women's Representation," *Journal of Politics*, 80 (2018): 1211–1224.

36. Sam Brodey, "Rep. Keith Ellison on Why He Is Backing Bernie Sanders for President," *Minnpost.com,* October 12, 2015.

37. In 2019 Justin Amash declared his support for impeaching President Trump and switched his party affiliation to independent. See Karen Zraick, "Justin Amash, A Trump Critic on the Right, Leaves the G.O.P." *New York Times,* July 4, 2019, accessed November 9, 2019, available at https://www.nytimes.com/2019/07/04/us/politics/justin-amash -trump.html?module=inline.

38. Center for Responsive Politics, "Donor Demographics," 2019, accessed November 9, 2019. available at https://www.opensecrets.org/overview/donordemographics.php ?cycle=2018&filter=G.

39. Boatright, *Getting Primaried*; Ensley, "Individual Campaign Contributions"; Johnson, "Individual Contributions"; La Raja and Schaffner, *Campaign Finance and Political Polarization.*

40. Michael J. Barber, "Ideological Donors, Contribution Limits, and the Polarization of State Legislatures," *Journal of Politics* 78 (2016): 296–310; Boatright, *Getting Primaried*; Francia et al., *Financiers of Congressional Elections*; Francia et al., "Limousine Liberals and Corporate Conservatives"; James G. Gimpel, Frances E. Lee, and Shanna Pearson-Merkowitz, "The Check Is in the Mail: Interdistrict Funding Flows in Congressional Elections," *American Journal of Political Science* 52 (2008): 373–394.

41. Barber, "Ideological Donors"; Francia et al., *Financiers of Congressional Elections.*

42. Swers, *Women in the Club.*

43. Burrell, *Gender in Campaigns.*

44. Grace Haley, "Democratic Women Outraise Men among Female Donors— Another Historic First," Center for Responsive Politics, October 30, 2018; Open Secrets, accessed November 9, 2019, available at https://www.opensecrets.org/news/2018/10/demo cratic-women-outraise-men-among-female-donors-another-record-breaking-first/; "Most Expensive Midterm Ever: Cost of 2018 Election Surpasses $5.7 Billion," Center for Responsive Politics, February 6, 2019, accessed November 9, 2019, available at https://www.open secrets.org/news/2019/02/cost-of-2018-election-5pnt7bil/.

45. Freeman, "Political Culture"; Grossmann and Hopkins, "Ideological Republicans."

46. Crowder-Meyer and Cooperman, "Can't Buy Them Love."

47. Burrell, *Gender in Campaigns*; Rosalyn Cooperman and Melody Crowder-Meyer, "A Run for Their Money: Republican Women's Hard Road to Campaign Funding," in *The Right Women: Republican Party Activists, Candidates, and Legislators,* ed. Malliga Och and Shauna L. Shames (Santa Barbara, CA: Praeger, 2018).

48. Crowder-Meyer and Cooperman, "Can't Buy Them Love."

17

Training Women to Run in an African Democracy

The Case of Benin

MARTHA C. JOHNSON

African countries today have some of the highest levels of legislative gender parity in the world. Unfortunately, this is not the case for Benin, a small African democracy located just to the west of Nigeria. In other African countries, quotas and reserved seats have produced dramatic increases in the proportion of women in national legislatures and, to a lesser extent, local governments and presidential cabinets. In Benin, where there are no formal provisions for ensuring women's political representation, there has been little improvement in women's representation since the first democratic elections in 1991. Women are dismally underrepresented in elected and appointed positions. In 2016, there were only six women in the National Assembly, just 7 percent of deputies. Sixty-four women served on communal councils, just 5 percent of total council membership. And only three women served in the president's cabinet, a mere 14 percent of ministers.

Benin's poor performance with regard to women's representation contrasts sharply with its democratic status in Africa, where it has long been a regional leader. It was one of the first countries on the continent to resurrect democracy in the 1990s, holding truly competitive elections in 1991 that produced turnovers in legislative and executive power. Since then, it has held regular, generally peaceful elections and seen numerous changes in presidential, legislative, and local leadership.[1] In addition, its courts are independent and assertive, and its press is free and active. Perhaps most remarkably, given the salience of ethnicity in Beninese politics and the high stakes of electoral competition, Benin has not experienced identity-based conflict even in hotly contested elections. Despite its democratic success, Benin has not adopted quotas or reserved seats to ensure women's representation in elected office, and women remain grossly underrepresented. As a result, Beninese activists, like their American counterparts, have had to use other strategies to bring women into politics, including candidate training programs.

This chapter describes these training programs and assesses their success and limitations in helping women access political office. The material presented here comes from semistructured interviews and focus groups with women politicians at the communal level in Benin. (I explain the levels of Beninese government in the next section.) From March to June 2017, I interviewed 59 elected women, unsuccessful women candidates, and women who aspired to be candidates but did not secure a spot on the ballot.[2] Our conversations covered many topics and were not initially aimed at assessing candidate training programs. However, as I spoke with women about their political experience, they repeatedly cited the confidence and skills gained through training programs. As a result, I expanded my research, gathering information on the nature of Beninese training programs and their benefits and limitations. This chapter presents my findings on the structure and impact of two organizations' candidate training programs: those of the Réseau pour l'Intégration des Femmes des Organisations Non-Gouvernementales et Associations Africaines—Benin (RIFONGA-Benin) and the Union des Femmes Conseillères Communales des Départements de l'Alibori, du Borgou, et des Collines (UFeC-ABC).[3] Although the U.S. Agency for International Development (USAID) and other foreign aid organizations support training programs in Africa, little research has been done on how training programs fare in non-Western contexts, particularly democracies where patronage and vote-buying are common like Benin's. This chapter helps fill this gap in the existing literature, offering a first take on the benefits and limitations of candidate training in developing country democracies. Benin offers a particularly interesting case precisely because its democratic strengths and international support have not produced international donors' hoped-for levels of women's representation.

I find that training programs play an important role in motivating potential women candidates, increasing women's knowledge about the election process, and improving family support. Unfortunately, as Jennifer Piscopo argues in Chapter 15, women trainees believe the programs do not and likely cannot counter gender biases among party leaders and inequalities in campaign resources, which they argue prevent women from getting on the ballot and winning elections. I conclude that training programs are important for expanding the pool of potential women candidates but need to pursue additional measures or be accompanied by financial and logistic support if more women are to be elected.

Understanding Politics in Benin

To make sense of candidate training programs' benefits and limitations in Benin, it is helpful to understand a few basics about how politics and elections operate. Benin has a unitary, rather than a federalist, system. There are no state-level governments, and most policy decisions are made by the president and National Assembly. (De facto power tends to lie with the president despite the National Assembly's formal powers.) In recent years, Benin has decentralized many state functions, turning them over to elected communal or municipal councils, of which there are 30 and 3, respectively. (I refer to them collectively as communal councils.) In this chapter, I focus on candidate training at the communal level rather than the national level because there are more elected seats at that level and thus potentially more women candidates. The councils receive national funding and levy their own local taxes to finance schools, health clinics, public record keeping, and other services. Perhaps most important, they determine (in negotiation with the central government) where infrastructure investments are made in their community. Over the years, both local and national politicians have come to see council seats as attractive political posts and competition has consequently increased. Because each council selects its own mayor and deputy mayors from within its ranks, powerful positions like mayor of the capital city, Cotonou, are secured through the communal election process.

In both legislative and communal elections, Benin uses a system of proportional representation (PR). For communal elections, each arrondissement (i.e., the administrative division just below the commune) is an electoral district. Depending on the population of the arrondissement, it elects between one and seven members to the communal council. Parties put forward ranked lists of candidates for all the seats in an arrondissement, and voters choose from these closed party lists. Parties, not voters, determine which politicians are first in line to get a seat on the communal council. One interesting twist in the system is that lists include both a main candidate and an alternate candidate who fills the main candidate's post if he or she is determined to be ineligible or steps down for any reason. Women are more likely to be found among the alternate than the main candidates. In a closed-list PR system like Benin's, a woman may be kept out of office because she is not placed on a party list, her party does not win any seats, she is too low on the party list to receive a seat, or she is an alternate and never has the chance to occupy her main candidate's seat.

Benin also differs from the United States in terms of candidate nomination procedures, which remain opaque. Unlike American political parties, parties in Benin tend to be weakly institutionalized. They are often regionally based and relatively small, and they move from coalition to coalition without a clear ideological core. Although they persist through several elections, they are often associated with one individual leader.[4]

One side effect of this weak institutionalization is that few parties have transparent or well-established procedures for selecting candidates. There are no formal primaries or regularly organized caucuses, and the internal workings of party-list formation remain unknown to most party members. Low transparency is common in countries with closed-list PR systems but seems to be particularly pronounced in Benin. Although the national electoral commission theoretically has clear rules and procedures for declaring party lists and candidacies, my interviewees argued these are not well enforced. They claim that party lists sometimes change at the last minute despite regulations to prevent this, and candidates are sometimes removed from lists despite meeting formal requirements. Some candidates reported that they did not see the official ballot until election day, and, thus, did not know for certain who was on the party list. This severe lack of transparency is problematic because party list placement is one of the most important factors determining whether one secures a seat on the communal council. Many arrondissements are not particularly competitive, and a party knows how many seats it will secure going into the election. As a result, winning a seat is a function of where one is placed on the ballot rather than voter preference. This party-controlled system is challenging for women who enjoy the support of their communities but lack strong party ties.

A final key difference between Benin and the United States is the nature of campaign financing. In Benin, candidates are largely self-financed. Parties rely on candidate contributions to finance their activities and provide little in the way of material or financial support to candidates. National Assembly deputies sometimes finance part of someone's communal campaign, but I found this among only one-third of the women I interviewed. Most had to self-finance, and contributions from businesses, PACs, individual donors, and the like are rare. (Interviewees could not believe it when I informed them that American voters gave money to candidates and not vice versa!)

Although inexpensive by American standards, campaigns in Benin are quite costly by local standards. Candidates reported spending at least 2 million CFA francs (roughly $3,500) on their communal campaigns in rural Benin, a country where per capita GDP is $1,040. In Cotonou, the capital, one councillor reported that someone at the top of his or her party list should expect to spend closer to 10 million CFA francs (roughly $17,500). Campaign costs include posters, T-shirts, transportation, and rallies, and voters expect candidates to provide food, drink, and the cost of transportation at rallies and events. Although illegal, vote-buying is also common, and door-to-door gift giving the night before the election has become the norm. Although parties sometimes help cover the costs of posters and rallies, they generally do not cover gifts and cash for voters, so this requires significant discretionary funds on the part of candidates. Almost all the candidates I interviewed cited vote-buying as a primary campaign expense and noted that it has become cost-lier as wealthier individuals have entered the political fray. Indeed, recent research suggests that self-financing of expensive campaigns has shifted who runs for and wins public office in Benin, with legislators increasingly drawn from the wealthiest segments of the population.[5] Given the high poverty rates among women in Benin and historic restrictions on their economic rights, they are rarely among the wealthiest in their communities.[6]

In sum, candidate training programs in Benin operate in a context where political parties hold significant sway over women's electoral prospects yet are weakly institutionalized. Candidate selection is not formalized or reli-able. And election campaigns are costly, competitive, and based on vote-buy-ing that is illegal but in high demand. I contend that all these factors limit what training programs can achieve.

The Organizations Providing Candidate Training in Benin

Before describing how training programs operate in Benin and assessing their impact, a note on the organizational context of training programs in Benin is needed. This chapter focuses on candidate training programs provided by RIFONGA and UfeC. RIFONGA is part of a regional network of nongov-ernmental organizations (NGOs) working to advance women's rights in Af-rica, while UFeC is an association led by elected women that seeks to expand women's political presence and make women more effective leaders.

Both organizations, as well as the majority of NGOs promoting women's political participation in Benin, are funded almost exclusively by internation-al development agencies. RIFONGA relies largely on USAID, and UfeC relies mainly on the Swiss Cooperation agency. Although RIFONGA and UFeC's leaders emphasize that they are locally driven, their reliance on external fund-ing means that they operate within the strict nonpartisan, nonpolitical guide-lines of foreign development agencies. Training must be completed before any campaign begins, and they cannot provide financial or material campaign support for any candidates. More generally, RIFONGA and UfeC must re-main attentive to foreign donors' funding priorities and preferred training models. For example, RIFONGA has recently shifted some of its focus to Be-nin's disabled population in response to changes in foreign agendas, and UfeC has joined a new mentoring-based program of candidate preparation spon-sored by foreign donors. Although American nonprofits are also responsive to their donors, RIFONGA and UfeC are extremely reliant on a small num-ber of international donors. As a result, they likely have less leeway in shaping their own priorities and programs than organizations working in the United States. As Jennifer Piscopo, in Chapter 15, argues of training programs in other developing countries, Beninese organizations' dependence on foreign fund-ing means they have an incentive to embrace training models shaped by Western assumptions about what it takes for women to compete in politics even if these may not be the best fit for Benin's very different political context.

How Candidate Training Programs Operate in Benin

There have been three rounds of candidate trainings at the communal level in Benin, corresponding to the 2002, 2008, and 2015 elections. In 2002, other NGOs played a more important role than RIFONGA and UFeC, but, since then, RIFONGA and UFeC have become the major players in the south and north of Benin, respectively. Their training programs last between one and two years and take place before candidates are selected for communal ballots. Trainings generally entail a series of workshops held monthly or quarterly that target a group of women aspirants and their spouses or extended family.[7] Participants generally receive a small per diem payment when they attend to help cover the cost of transportation and lost income. (Many women run small commercial businesses or farms, so taking a weekend off for training can be a burden.) The descriptions below are based primarily on documentation from and interviews with RIFONGA trainers.[8]

Recruitment

Training programs begin with the identification of possible participants. For the inaugural communal elections in 2002, trainers toured the country, seeking potential women candidates. According to interviewees, they asked local government officials and women's groups which women already stood out in their community for their leadership and activism. They were then invited to join the training. Later training programs have followed a similar pattern, with a somewhat greater emphasis on local women's associations as recruiting grounds in the case of RIFONGA. RIFONGA and UFeC also rely on the networks of previous women candidates and elected women to recruit participants. Finally, I met a few young women who applied directly to training programs because they wanted to run for office.

Regarding criteria for participation, training programs are relatively open to all interested women. The only restriction I could identify was party affiliation. In the first two communal elections, candidates could run as independents, and many women were encouraged to pursue that path; however, a new electoral law in 2013 eliminated that possibility. RIFONGA responded by adding party affiliation to its criteria for selecting trainees.

Structure and Content

The content of candidate training programs in Benin has evolved over time, although the basic structure remains the same: a series of workshops that involve lectures, role-play, and group study of booklets and worksheets. Women leaders from RIFONGA or UFeC generally lead the meetings. Some have run for or been elected to public office, others are simply longtime activists and community organizers. Women in elected office are often present even if they are not leading the trainings. The training workshops concentrate on three things, how to: become a candidate, run a campaign, and govern effectively once in office. Here, I focus on the first two.

Electoral law changes regularly in Benin and communal elections are relatively new. Consequently, training workshops devote significant time to the ins and outs of electoral law and the formal process of submitting one's candidacy. Potential candidates are taught how to fill out the application forms and secure the many legal documents required of candidates. Trainers also review national laws regulating campaign practices and spending.

People involved in candidate training programs admit that there is a disconnect between what programs advocate and what actually occurs in politics on the issue of campaign laws. The vice president of RIFONGA emphasized that they are trying to change how campaigns operate. They want women to win without relying on vote-buying or engaging in illegal activities. Yet, as noted earlier, vote-buying is a common practice and widely expected by voters. How women deal with the discrepancy between training and reality during the campaign is left up to them.

After covering the legal basics of candidate selection and campaigning, trainings turn to the tricky problem of getting on the ballot, which they refer to as the "pre-campaign." Women are taught to visit family, friends, and associates to express their interest in running and secure their support well before the election begins. They are also told to contact local civic and professional associations and customary authorities and religious leaders. The hope is to garner popular support for their candidacy before the party starts compiling its list, so that women can convince local or regional party leaders to place them on the ballot. To further help women get on the ballot, RIFONGA and UFeC representatives meet with local and regional party leaders and lobby for women's inclusion on the ballot. They share the names of women partisans from the training who would make attractive candidates, while underscoring the general advantages of having women candidates.

Trainings emphasize that the precampaign is not over until women are sure of their position on the ballot. Women are instructed to closely follow the progress of their application because it is common for party meetings and informal caucuses at the arrondissement level to produce one list of candidates and the actual ballot to include another. Many of the women I interviewed complained that, between the arrondissement meetings and the release of the final ballot, they were either removed from the party list or moved to a lower position. Party leaders have the legal right to make such changes, but it poses a significant challenge for women who are rarely present in the late-night, closed-door meetings in which party lists are finalized. One of the reasons that training programs emphasize the need for a perfect formal application is that party leaders can use the excuse of an incomplete or "lost" dossier to deny a woman's spot on the party list.

Unfortunately, insufficient enforcement of electoral laws means that even the most effective women candidates, who follow all the training guidelines about securing their spot on the ballot, can be pushed off. In one extreme example, I met a communal candidate who secured the top spot on her party's list and spent her life savings campaigning, only to find the night before the election that her party had pulled her from first position on the ballot. The next day the man who had replaced her on the ballot won what should have been her seat. RIFONGA and UFeC argue one of the best protections against being removed from a list is to have a perfect formal application that the electoral commission will not reject, but this case illustrates that a perfect dossier does not guarantee a woman's place on the ballot.

After teaching women about the precampaign, training programs turn to the actual election. They offer lessons in public speaking and persuasion, alliance building, and fundraising. Participants engage in simulations and fill out sample budget worksheets and timelines. They also create lists of individuals or groups who might offer financial support, like relatives or civil society groups in which they are active, and they identify potential volunteer campaign staff.

Finally, the group considers how to convince spouses, children, and extended family to support their campaigns. Interviewees report that, in these discussions, the emphasis is on how to reassure family that they will continue to fulfill wifely duties, like cooking and childcare, while running for or serving in public office. The discussions do not focus on how to change expectations about household or family duties. Women are taught to reassure their husbands and in-laws that they will remain dutiful spouses and emphasize that their election will bring the family prestige and opportunity.[9] This emphasis on family responsibilities and the relatively conservative gender roles in Benin may seem problematic for some readers, but it is important to note that women in American politics also express serious concerns about combining political and family responsibilities.[10]

Family Training

Recognizing the importance of family responsibilities to women's choices and the nature of gender hierarchies in Benin, RIFONGA and UFeC organize training sessions specifically for spouses. The husbands receive a small per diem payment to attend the daylong sessions, which are led by women leaders and try to include husbands of incumbent women councillors. The trainers first make the case that Benin needs more women councillors and discuss how women councillors benefit the community. They further emphasize the honor and prestige women's election can bring to their family, but they are realistic about the many critiques and verbal attacks women candidates face. Husbands are encouraged to be verbally supportive and enthusiastic about their wives' candidacies both in private and in public. Even more importantly, trainers emphasize that husbands need to defend their wives' choice before detractors in the family and community. Because women candidates invariably face disparaging rumors about their sexual promiscuity, husbands are warned to be prepared and ignore rumors. In addition, they are encouraged to accept that their wives hire a maid or invite other family members to take on household duties. Finally, they are told that offering their wife financial support, no matter how little, sends an important signal to their wife and family, and they are assured that their advice will be invaluable to their wives' campaign.

How Training Programs Help Aspiring Women Politicians in Benin

My interviews indicate that RIFONGA and UFeC trainings are achieving their direct goals of increasing women's desire to run for office, providing women with the practical skills needed to run, and improving family support. Women most commonly reported that training programs gave them the audacity and courage to run for public office. One focus group participant reported that she did not even realize women could be candidates for communal elections before receiving training.[11] Others noted that they were scared to run before completing the training programs.[12] According to these women, campaigning is risky: it can create tensions in the family, generate social ridicule and harmful rumors, and drain one's savings. They needed encouragement and support to face these risks, which training programs helped provide.

Women also appreciated the logistic information received in training programs. As one woman reported, her confidence to run came from the practical knowledge she gained in trainings.[13] Several women candidates noted that RIFONGA taught them the importance of attending all party meetings, even if they occurred late at night, and following the party list all the way to the national electoral agency. They also attributed their ability to get on the ballot to the lessons on putting together a complete dossier. In addition, when asked about how they ran their campaign, women candidates cited the budgeting procedures and "ground game" laid out in RIFONGA training. Several noted using budgeting worksheets and plans from the trainings. Others drew on communication tips and organizational strategies learned during workshops.

Finally, though somewhat less frequently cited by interviewees, women in two focus groups reported that RIFONGA trainings impacted their husbands' attitudes. One woman reported that her husband "gave her the order to run" after receiving the training. He convinced her in-laws to support her and helped her gain the local community's respect.[14] Another spoke of her husband accompanying her to late-night meetings and shuttling her around to ensure other men did not mistreat her and show the community he supported her work.[15] This particular husband eventually helped lead UFeC trainings for other spouses. A common theme in interviews was how much a husband's physical presence in rallies and meetings helped legitimize a woman's candidacy and prevent inappropriate behavior on the part of male partisans. As such, women were grateful that training programs targeted spouses.

Despite these three reported benefits of candidate training programs, their impact on women's actual election is less clear. Trainings have increased the pool of potential women candidates by giving women the audacity, practical tools, and sometimes family support to run, but their success rates leave something to be desired. It was not possible to get an exact number, but, in comparing a few lists of training participants with those of candidates and elected officials, it became clear that most women who received training do not run for office or win a seat on a communal council. For example, fewer than 5 percent of the trainees in one recent round of training were elected to office at the communal, or even the lower village, level in the 2015 election. The next section considers why, addressing the limitations of current training programs.

What Candidate Training Programs Have Not Overcome

Party Resistance

Although RIFONGA and UFeC trainers are fully aware of the need for political party buy-in to get women on the ballot, they have not been very successful in shifting political parties' treatment of women candidates. One trainer called herself a thorn in the side of regional party leaders. "They listen to me every election cycle, nod, and say the right thing, but when it comes time to form party lists, they ignore everything I said."[16] Across the board, the women I interviewed for this project believed that almost no political parties in Benin support women candidates, a general problem in many new democracies, as Jennifer Piscopo demonstrates in Chapter 15. In interview after interview, women cited party leaders as a major barrier to election. If they put women on the ballot at all, they do not put them in favorable positions.

Women interviewees did not agree on why parties resisted women candidates and were unresponsive to RIFONGA and UFeC's efforts. Some believed parties were responding to voter preference, while others believed voters would support women candidates if they were placed on the ballot. Those who saw voters as less likely to support women tended to believe that voting was largely a function of vote-buying, something women may struggle to finance. Those who believed voters would support women tended to see voters as more policy oriented. They blamed intraparty dynamics for the difficulties women faced in securing a spot on the ballot. Some women termed party discrimination misogyny, others simply called it gender bias; however, their basic argument was similar. Male party leaders at the local and national level are happy to have women campaign for them and mobilize voters, but they do not want women to occupy positions of political leadership. They do not believe women are meant for or capable of serving in public office.

Jealousy also figured among women's explanations. Because politics can be quite lucrative and bring high social status, male party members hold tenaciously to their own positions and fight women's candidacies. Even women who earned the support of a male patron in the party reported facing fierce resistance from other male party members at the communal level. Each ballot position given to a woman was perceived to come at the cost of a male candidate. When women and their patrons persisted and ensured women's position on the ballot, male party members sometimes defected to the opposition. As one councillor reported, several men left her party when she was put on the list, denouncing the "imposition" of a woman candidate.[17]

Finally, women emphasized that party leaders do not place them on the ballot because they want candidates who can finance both their own campaign and that of the party. As a result, party leaders push women off the list if a wealthier individual expresses the desire to run. Given gender inequities in Benin, wealthier individuals are far more likely to be men than women.

Research from other parts of the world indicates that having women in positions of party leadership can help ensure women are nominated, but few Beninese parties have women at the highest levels. As a result, there are rarely women present to defend other women's positions on the ballot. An influential woman politician in the north of Benin, who eventually joined the national government and rose to her party's central leadership, helps prove this point. Numerous candidates noted that they would not have made it onto the ballot without her activism.

Family Hierarchies

One of the more interesting barriers to women running for public office was an internal family hierarchy about who could run for office. Political activism is often a family affair, with men and women from the same family supporting the same party. When both a husband and a wife or brother and sister want to run for office, however, women's options may be limited. Several interviewees reported that their party would not allow candidates from the same family to run for office at the same level. As one reported, "My husband wanted to be a candidate as well, and the party would only accept one candidate."[18]

In her family, that candidate would clearly be her husband. For three of the women I interviewed, their unwillingness to accept this gendered hierarchy of political ambition resulted in marital strife and eventual separation.[19] Another former councillor stepped down from the list because her brother, who was the more influential politician, needed a spot for himself on the communal ballot after being ruled ineligible to run for parliament.[20] Trainings may generate support from some male kin, but it seems politically active husbands and brothers can, in fact, become competitors. In the face of husbands and brothers' political ambitions, family training is likely to be less effective.

Costs of Campaigning and the Need for Ongoing Support

As noted at the start of the chapter, elections in Benin are expensive by local standards. Many of the women I interviewed who had received candidate training but had not been placed on a party list were from seemingly humble backgrounds (judged subjectively by their home, mode of transportation, career, and clothing). Training programs do not limit participation according to financial means, but women without personal or family wealth have few other options for securing funding. Training programs are not complemented by the American-style PACs and parties that help finance women's candidacies in the United States (see Michele Swers and Danielle Thomsen's discussion of U.S. funding patterns in Chapter 16).

Women candidates sometimes criticized RIFONGA and UFeC for leaving them to their own devices during the campaign, but their withdrawal is a direct outgrowth of their effort to remain politically neutral and comply with the requirements of their international donors. In the United States, nonprofit training programs also aim to be politically neutral. However, many training programs, like Ready to Run® (see Chapter 13), provide women with considerable access to potential campaign donors, experts, consultants, and party officials during the training. In addition, explicitly partisan organizations, like Emerge America (see Chapter 2), offer ongoing consultation and support during campaigns, something Beninese women struggle to find. And American women candidates can tap PACs, parties, and women copartisans (see Chapter 18) for support. No such practical assistance is available to Beninese women once they declare their candidacy. As a result, women without significant personal wealth struggle to finance their campaign and keep up with the electoral "fight."[21]

Among the 35 current and former women councillors I interviewed, the majority had either influential male allies in the party or significant personal financial resources (or both). Many successful women candidates earned political parties' attention because they had used their career and personal wealth to build a local following. Some of these women were businesspeople, others civil servants. In either case, they were already among the wealthiest women in their community and seen as leaders. Not all successful women had their own money, but those with more limited means had already shown party leaders that they could consistently transform money into votes. One woman remembered being spotted by her party leader at a campaign rally where she worked the room, writing down names of attendees, organizing campaign teams, and the like. The party leader noted this and asked that "Madame Fastfood" (a nickname she earned because of the street-side eateries she owned) run his campaign. This set her on the path toward her own election in the next cycle.[22] More than training, women like Madame Fastfood had the financial resources and years of campaign experience parties want.

Conclusion: Where Should Training Programs Go from Here?

In speaking with leaders of RIFONGA, they clearly want women who are leaders in their community to step up and compete in communal elections. International development partners express the same desire. Yet, if party support and financial resources are a prerequisite to electoral success, then training programs' openness may be at odds with what it takes to be elected. Training programs may need to narrow their focus, concentrating on women who have already shown their skill in campaigning for male party colleagues or who have salaries, businesses, and families they can call on for financial support.

However, there may be alternatives to this restrictive approach. UFeC's new focus on mentoring young women by pairing them with elected women is designed to get women into professional and political pipelines early in life. This mentorship may help women build political party ties and status before trying to run for office. On the financial side, RIFONGA could work with donors to design innovative ways of funding women's campaigns. They likely cannot give women money directly, but they might be able to help with the chairs, tents, speakers, and facilities women need to campaign. Offering supplies to all women candidates regardless of party might provide a way around partisan concerns and fears of vote-buying.

Even if training organizations do not pursue these measures, it is important to emphasize that they are still increasing women's confidence, knowledge, and skills. As Jennifer Piscopo argues in Chapter 15, increasing the supply of potential women candidates does not guarantee women's election when there is little party demand for women candidates and structural barriers remain intact. However, women aspirants are a prerequisite for women's candidacies, and the interviews cited in this article suggest many eligible women did not see themselves as potential candidates before the trainings. In addition, when women become candidates, research from the United States suggests their candidacies positively impact girls' political ambition.[23] In other words, if current trainings manage to get women on the ballot, it may have ripple effects years later in Benin. Thanks to NGOs like RIFONGA and UFeC, it is highly unlikely any Beninese woman will again report that she did not even know women could run for office.

NOTES

1. The legislative elections in May 2019, which imposed strict new criteria on political parties and resulted in the disqualification of several parties, produced rare unrest and clashes between police and protestors.

2. The two organizations discussed in this chapter, RIFONGA and UFeC, helped arrange many of my interviews and provided information on their operations as well as access to several of their trainers. This was wonderful because it enabled me to speak with a wide array of women candidates and aspirants. However, contacting women via the NGOs that trained them may have led the women to overstate the effectiveness or impact of these NGOs and their training programs. I suspect this did occur; however, in the interviews I secured through different channels, women still complimented the work of training programs and highlighted similar positive impacts. In addition, all women were keen to discuss the limitations of NGO training programs.

3. In the chapter, I cite interviews when quoting women or offering examples from specific individuals. To conserve space, I do not provide citations for ideas and trends that emerged across multiple interviews. Fuller interview citations are available upon request.

4. Rachel B. Riedl and J. Tyler Dickovick, "Party Systems and Decentralization in Africa," *Studies in Comparative International Development* 49, no. 3 (2014): 321–342; L. Creevey, P. Ngomo, and R. Vengroff, "Party Politics and Different Paths to Democratic Transitions: A Comparison of Benin and Senegal," *Party Politics* 11, no. 4 (2005): 471–493.

5. Dominika Koter, "Costly Electoral Campaigns and the Changing Composition and Quality of Parliament: Evidence from Benin," *African Affairs* 116, no. 465 (2017): 573–596.

6. Benin is an extremely poor country. Its Human Development Index score is 0.485, placing it 167th out of 188 countries. Women struggle to receive adequate health, education, and workforce opportunities. According to United Nations Development Programme data, Beninese women receive less schooling than men, particularly at the secondary level (15 percent versus 30 percent), and occupy only 25 percent of paid employment outside of the agricultural sector. Moreover, until 2004, women were subject to coverture laws that limited their economic rights vis-à-vis husbands, fathers, and brothers.

7. It was difficult to collect specific information on the frequency of trainings, and there appeared to be variation over time, place, and organization. They appear to occur monthly or quarterly depending on funding, logistic, and other considerations.

8. The general plan of training programs is available in short training booklets prepared by RIFONGA. Electronic copies are available from the author upon request.

9. This is in stark contrast to my interviews with older women who participated in politics during the socialist regime of the 1970s. They emphasized the need to free women from domestic servitude.

10. Denise L. Baer and Heidi I. Hartmann, "Building Women's Political Careers: Strengthening the Pipeline to Higher Office," Washington, DC: Institute for Women's Policy Research, 2014.

11. Former communal candidate and alternative candidate for the National Assembly, Department of Zou, May 26, 2017.

12. Focus group, Department of Collines, May 17, 2017.

13. Former candidate for village council, Department of Zou, May 26, 2017.

14. Former communal candidate, participant in focus group, Department of Collines, May 26, 2017.

15. Former communal councillor, Department of Collines, May 20, 2017.

16. Trainer and former communal candidate, participant in focus group, Department of Collines, May 22, 2017.

17. Communal councillor, participant in focus group, Department of Ouémé, June 7, 2017.

18. Participant in focus group, Department of Ouémé, June 7, 2017.

19. As per their requests, I am not including specific references to these interviewees in publications.

20. Former communal councillor, Department of Borgou, May 16, 2017.

21. Focus group, Department of Ouémé, June 7, 2017.

22. Communal councillor, Department of Borgou, May 10, 2017.

23. David E. Campbell and Christina Wolbrecht, "See Jane Run: Women Politicians as Role Models for Adolescents," *Journal of Politics* 68, no. 2 (2006): 233–247.

18

Paying It Forward

Candidate Contributions and Support for Diverse Candidates

Jaclyn J. Kettler

I will help you run.

—U.S. SENATOR KIRSTEN GILLIBRAND to women thinking about running
for office (Traister, "Kirsten Gillibrand")

In 2011, U.S. senator Kirsten Gillibrand[1] created a PAC with the goal of re-cruiting more women to run for Congress. Her Off the Sidelines PAC supported eight women candidates for the U.S. Senate in 2016 and has fund-raised almost $6 million for other women candidates.[2] In addition to giving key financial resources to candidates, support from the PAC can provide can-didates with a psychological lift.[3] For women running for office for the first time, this type of emotional support may be significant. Moreover, the en-dorsement and financial support of party elites, like Senator Gillibrand, may send a signal about the candidate's quality to other key party actors and donors, thereby mobilizing more campaign contributions for the candidate.[4]

While scholars find that women candidates are as likely to win their races as men, we still have a significant problem with fewer women running for po-litical office than men. This continued to be true in the 2018 election, even with a record-breaking number of (Democratic) women running for office.[5] Repub-lican women are especially underrepresented as candidates. Campaigns are expensive, and women often report concerns about fundraising as the reason they do not run for office.[6] If not connected to traditional recruitment and es-tablished fundraising networks (like business associations), it can be difficult to acquire the necessary support.[7] One response to this concern has been the creation of women's PACs. These PACs, like EMILY's List, help fund women candidates.[8] However, these women's groups largely benefit Democratic women candidates and usually fund a select small group of candidates.[9]

We rarely think about candidates making contributions to other candi-dates, but could candidate transfers like Senator Gillibrand's to other women be a useful tool for helping more diverse candidates run and succeed?[10] Candidate contributions refer to the ability of candidates to redistribute their own resources to help other candidates' campaigns. By transferring their funds this way, candidates can signal the quality of other candidates. Additionally, they can provide financial support for diverse candidates who may have less access to traditional campaign fundraising paths. Finally, candidate contributions may help connect candidates, fostering close relationships and a feeling of belonging. As an added bonus, by donating to other candidates and party committees, candidates contribute to their party's success and facilitate connections in the party. These connections help candidates gain influence in their party.[11]

The opportunity to help other candidates' campaigns and advance their own career may motivate candidates to contribute to fellow candidates. If women are the beneficiaries of candidate contributions, this mechanism has great potential to at least remove a reason for not running. It may also offer an additional path for supporting women candidates' campaigns, helping offset the additional fundraising challenges they experience (especially Republican women). Do candidates, particularly women candidates, use the redistribution of funds to help other women candidates succeed? Moreover, are there party differences in the use of candidate contributions to support women candidates? I address these questions in this research with the goal of contributing to a better understanding of candidate-to-candidate contributions and the usefulness of these contributions as a tool for helping a more diverse set of candidates run for office.

Candidate Contributions as a Tool of Support

Similar to the male-dominated recruiting networks that largely recruit men to run for office,[12] traditional fundraising networks tend to favor men and overlook potential women candidates. Women state legislative candidates report that men's professional networks provide men with a fundraising advantage.[13] Moreover, men still contribute a majority of individual donations to candidates, and research finds that men donate more to men, especially in the Democratic Party.[14] As discussed by Malliga Och in Chapter 3, Republican women particularly struggle to access donors and funding in primaries, hindering their electoral success and contributing to the significant underrepresentation of Republican women in office. As a result, women interested in running for office may hesitate over concerns that funding will not be available or accessible.

When candidates have limited access to established fundraising networks, they often look to political party committees for campaign support. Indeed, more than men, women state legislative candidates rank state party and state legislative campaign committees as more important to their fundraising.[15] However, party committees tend to direct campaign resources to the races in which they will have the greatest impact, usually limiting their financial support to a small number of competitive districts.[16] While this strategy may help the party win or maintain majority status, it does not ensure broad fundraising support for the party's women candidates. Additionally, party committees are reluctant to fund primary candidates. As a result, women candidates may struggle to receive money from the party unless they are in a competitive race in the general election.

As mentioned previously, women's PACs help provide women candidates with funding, but they also tend to focus their resources on select candidates. For example, EMILY's List endorses and fundraises for pro-choice Democratic women. Furthermore, women donor networks largely benefit Democratic women candidates.[17] Although political parties and women's PACs help fund some women candidates, there is still a need for additional tools to provide fundraising support for women, especially for Republican women.

As mentioned above, another potential source of resources for candidates (or potential candidates) is other candidates and officeholders. Perhaps due to concerns about winning reelection, some incumbents raise more money than they spend in elections.[18] These war chests can be helpful in future elections, but they also allow members to redistribute funds to other party actors. When members transfer their campaign funds to other party actors, including party committees, they can help the party win races. Member contributions to party committees and candidates have grown immensely in the past several decades.[19] In Congress, members more active in redistributing funds to the party and other candidates are often rewarded with leadership positions.[20]

In this way, candidates can also use their own resources to encourage diverse candidates to run for office by investing in their campaigns. Campaign resources are valuable and limited, so the transfer of campaign funds to another party actor is a purposive and meaningful action. Candidate-to-candidate donations can provide key resources and seed money to candidates, helping the recipient establish or maintain their campaign.[21]

Additionally, donations from candidates and other political elites can signal a candidate's quality to potential donors and other political elites.[22] Many scholars now conceive of political parties as an extended party network, which includes party committees and allied interest groups working together to support candidates favorable to the party's agenda.[23] In the extended party network, donations from party actors (including candidates) work as endorsements and signals of support. This encourages other actors in the extended party network to also direct resources to the preferred candidate.[24] Therefore, receiving a donation from another candidate may help the recipient gain access to major contributors, resulting in a major fundraising boost for a candidate.

As discussed earlier, it is likely that women candidates have limited access to the extended party network and other traditional fundraising networks. Women candidates often report concerns about accessing donors.[25] This can make it difficult for diverse candidates to foster support for their campaign. Receiving transfers from other candidates may help women candidates develop their own funding network or gain access to the donor's fundraising network.

The transfer of campaign funds also has an "expressive benefit" that can reinforce social connections.[26] Candidates can develop or strengthen friendly relationships with other candidates by contributing to their campaign. Candidates can also demonstrate support for another candidate's campaign through a donation, providing the recipient with an emotional boost. For example, U.S. representative Cheri Bustos experienced a psychological lift after receiving support from Senator Kirsten Gillibrand—"I guess unless you've run for office at some point and especially if you're running for the first time, I can't say enough about how much it means when someone like Senator Gillibrand comes in and offers help."[27] For first-time candidates, this encouragement and financial support from other candidates can provide the necessary resources and motivation to run. Therefore, candidate-to-candidate contributions can help their campaign in several possible ways, providing a potential path for increasing candidate diversity.

Due to a desire to increase their gender's representation in elected offices, women candidates may focus on assisting the campaigns of other women with their contributions.[28] There is some evidence that women legislators prioritize supporting other women candidates with their donations. One study finds that women legislators in Minnesota and Oregon worked to improve the representation of women by giving larger donations to other women candidates, although women legislators in Washington did not.[29] Research on congressional leadership PACs suggests the relationship between candidate donations and the gender of the recipient is complicated and depends on the proportion of women present in the chamber.[30] Underrepresented groups, including women, face increasing resistance and declining support as the size of the minority group increases. As the proportion of women increases in the chamber, women with leadership PACs increase their financial support of men in their party, resulting in continued resource disparities.

Despite some previous research on the topic, there is much we do not yet know about the use of candidate contributions to support women candidates. In particular, we do not fully understand candidate contributions at the state level. State legislatures operate as pipelines to Congress and statewide offices,[31] so supporting women running for state legislative seats is important. Fostering the candidacies of women at the state level may help increase their presence in both state policy-making and races for higher offices. With the growth in fundraising both at the state level and with leadership PACs, the state research needs updating. It is likely that more state-level candidates are transferring their resources to other candidates now. Moreover, the political context may result in candidates adopting different strategies when distributing donations. Variations in states' political context allows for more evaluation of these potential different allocation patterns.

Process for Evaluating Candidate Contributions

In an attempt to increase our understanding of candidate contributions at the state level and examine their usage to support women candidates, I analyze candidate contributions in the 2010 and 2012 elections in six states: Colorado, Iowa, New Mexico, North Carolina, Oklahoma, and Pennsylvania. I selected states that varied in the percentage of women in the legislature,[32] the average two-party competition in state legislative elections,[33] and state legislative professionalism.[34] Additionally, Colorado and Oklahoma have term limits. While this is a limited sample, it allows me to examine the beneficiaries of candidate-to-candidate contributions and to determine if this is an avenue of support for women candidates. The diversity across the states also helps me evaluate whether the trends hold across institutional and political differences.

Candidate contributions include both direct donations and in-kind contributions. Direct donations are contributions of money, while in-kind contributions include the giving of goods or services (e.g., advertising, mailing lists, office equipment). This analysis does not include independent expenditures. Independent expenditures often involve spending against candidates, making them a fundamentally different type of financial support. Therefore, I focus on candidate-to-candidate contributions in state gubernatorial and legislative elections in the aforementioned six states.

Candidates can donate to other candidates from their personal campaign account or a leadership PAC. Candidates can also donate as an individual to other candidates. While leadership PACs are very common in Congress, they are less common in some states. This makes it important to evaluate all possible types of candidate contributions at the state level. As a result, this data required extensive cleaning to link up all the donations of a candidate, including fixing misspellings or variations in candidates' committee names. Thus, although the state sample size is small, it is a very complete set of candidate contributions for the states included.

I compiled campaign contribution data from the National Institute on Money in State Politics (NIMSP) and the Colorado secretary of state.[35] Through NIMSP's followthemoney.org website, I assembled candidate and election information, such as incumbency status and the race outcome. I collected additional data on candidate characteristics, including candidate gender and race, from state legislative websites.

In these six states, around 20 percent of the state legislative candidates were women (including incumbents not up for election) in the 2010 and 2012 elections. The percentage of women candidates varies across states with Colorado having the highest percentage of women candidates (34 percent in 2010 and 30 percent in 2012). The proportion of women running for state legislative office was considerably smaller in Oklahoma (14 percent in both elections combined) and Pennsylvania (17 percent in both elections combined). Only 3 percent of the candidates were women of color in the aggregate for all six states, with slighter higher percentages in New Mexico and North Carolina.

General Trends in Candidate Contributions

Do candidates redistribute resources to other candidates? Yes, but the proportion of candidates contributing to other candidates varies across states and elections. In the aggregate, state legislative and gubernatorial candidates contributed 30,306 donations to candidates in the 2010 and 2012 elections. Of these donations, 38 percent of them were self-donations.[36] Self-financing does not tell us much about candidates' support of other candidates, so I dropped them from the analysis. After removing self-financing and some local candidates, the data set includes 14,383 state legislative and gubernatorial candidate transfers to other candidates. Figure 18.1 plots key trends in these candidate transfers by state, aggregated for both elections. Table A18.1 in the online appendix includes the full descriptive statistics for candidate-to-candidate donations separated by election year.[37]

A majority of candidates contributed to other candidates in Colorado and New Mexico, with smaller percentages of candidates transferring resources to candidates in the other four states. Colorado and New Mexico both had competitive legislative chambers in these elections. This competition increases the incentives for candidates to redistribute their resources to others. We see much lower participation by candidates in Oklahoma, which had large Republican majorities in the state legislature during this time. This suggests that an opportunity to gain a majority in the chamber will motivate some candidates to contribute to other candidates, perhaps in an effort to help the party win more seats.

The presence of a competitive gubernatorial election also seems to increase the percentage of candidates donating to others. The proportion of candidates making donations is higher in Colorado, Iowa, New Mexico, Oklahoma, and Pennsylvania in 2010, when there was a competitive governor's race in those states. The percentage of candidates donating to other candidates in these states then drops in the 2012 election. Consequently, the higher number of candidates making contributions in the 2010 election pulls up the averages presented in Figure 18.1.

There are a sizable number of candidate-to-candidate contributions in these state elections, even if most are smaller donations. The average amount

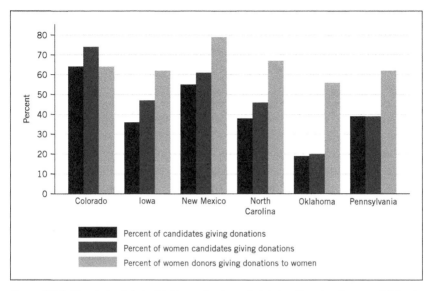

Figure 18.1. Trends in state legislative and gubernatorial donations to other candidates in 2010 and 2012 elections.

of a candidate transfer is $682. The average is driven higher by the value of candidate transfers in North Carolina ($876) and Pennsylvania ($1,447). Regardless of their size, Figure 18.1 indicates that candidate-to-candidate contributions are common in state elections. Additionally, a higher percentage of women candidates than men redistribute resources to other candidates in most state elections, suggesting they may be using this as a tool to increase candidate diversity.

Candidate Contributions to Women

As noted above, a higher percentage of women than men give donations to other candidates in most elections. Does this benefit women candidates? In the aggregate, women candidates receive around 29 percent of all candidate-to-candidate donations. This is a little higher than the percentage of candidates that are women (around 20 percent of candidates), suggesting that women candidates may have a slight advantage in receiving candidate donations relative to men. Moreover, women candidates are very involved in making these contributions to women. In all six states, over 50 percent of women candidates making donations give resources to other women candidates. In New Mexico and North Carolina, over 65 percent of women donors contribute to women candidates. This is noteworthy since women comprise a small share of the candidate pool. It appears that when women candidates make donations, they seek to support other women in their candidate-to-candidate contributions.

Additionally, almost 42 percent of all women candidates' donations went to other women in the aggregate, while only 25 percent of men's donations went to women candidates.[38] Furthermore, women candidates received a majority of transfers by women candidates in several state elections. Therefore, women making candidate-to-candidate contributions give a higher proportion of their donations to women candidates than do men.

Women of color run for state office in much lower numbers than White women. They also receive fewer transfers from other candidates. Only 3 percent of women candidates' donations went to women of color in the 2010 election; this percentage rose slightly to 5 percent in 2012. In these elections, men candidates gave about 3 percent of their donations to women of color in both elections. But, while only a small proportion of their donations went to women of color, women candidates did contribute 42 percent of the transfers to women of color in 2012. This suggests that even though women of color candidates are not major beneficiaries of candidate transfers, some women candidates are active in donating to women of color candidates.

There are some interesting state differences in terms of women candidates redistributing resources to other women. In Colorado, women give more donations to women challengers, women in open seat races, and women of color than men do. This is impressive since only 31 percent of candidates in the elections were women. There is a higher percentage of women candidates and officeholders in Colorado, so there are more women to support other women candidates than in the other states. Colorado also has more women in legislative leadership positions, which may help them fundraise and encourage them to donate to other candidates.

To further evaluate whether women are more likely to redistribute funds to other women candidates, I estimated a probit model to predict the probability of donating to a woman candidate in the general election. Candidate transfers are aggregated for both elections and all six states in this model. The key independent variable of interest is the gender of the donor. Additional independent variables included in the model are the candidate's incumbency status, whether the race is for an open seat, and the candidate's percentage of the vote received in the general election. All of these may affect the likelihood of a candidate making a donation to another candidate. I estimated separate probit models for Democratic and Republican candidate donations. The results provide some interesting evidence regarding the connection between candidate gender and candidate-to-candidate donations. Figure 18.2 plots the predicted effects of these models for nonincumbent recipients.

In Figure 18.2, we see that women candidates are generally more likely than men candidates to donate to women candidates. This is especially true

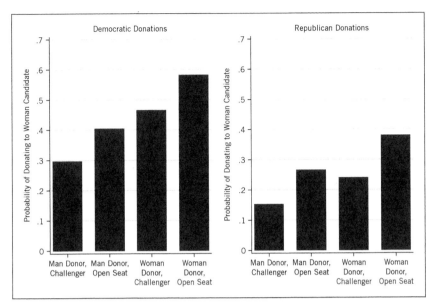

Figure 18.2. Probability of donating to a woman candidate by donor gender and candidate incumbency status.

for women candidates running for an open seat. For Democratic recipients, women candidates are almost 20 percent more likely than men to donate to women running in open seat races. While a smaller margin, women donors are about 10 percent more likely to contribute to Republican women in open races than are men. Furthermore, men candidates are much less likely than women candidates to transfer resources to women challengers. Therefore, women candidates are more likely than men to support women candidates. This support may be especially important for women challengers struggling to fundraise.

There are also some interesting party differences in Figure 18.2. Democratic women are more likely than Democratic men to redistribute funds to women candidates regardless of the race type. Republican women, on the other hand, are more likely than men to contribute to women candidates only when comparing within candidate type. Moreover, the predicted probability that Democratic women will donate to another woman candidate is higher than for Republican women. This suggests that the shared gender identity with women candidates motivates Democratic women's donations more than it does Republican women's donations. This result reflects previous findings that women Democratic donors value the election of women candidates and seek to financially support them, while Republicans are more motivated by candidates' ideology.[39]

Party Differences in Candidate Contributions

The preceding analysis uncovered some interesting party differences in the probability of donating to women candidates. Do other party differences exist? To evaluate that possibility, I examine descriptive statistics for candidate donations broken down by party in Figure 18.3.

Figure 18.3 identifies some interesting differences across the parties. Although the margin is diminished in the 2012 election, a higher percentage of Democratic women give donations to other candidates than Republican women. Additionally, a larger proportion of Democratic women donors redistribute resources to other women candidates. This party difference in giving donations to other candidates is also present for men. Proportionally more Democratic men redistribute funds to other candidates, including women candidates, than Republican men.

As noted above, these party differences are interesting in light of recent research on the variation in donor motivations for Democratic and Republican donors.[40] Similar to Swers and Thomsen's findings for individual donors in Chapter 16, it seems as though Democratic candidates are more motivated by gender identity in their donations than Republicans. It is impressive that slightly over 70 percent of Democratic women donors contribute to other women candidates. This suggests that Democratic women making donations actively seek to help the electoral efforts of other women candidates. Like

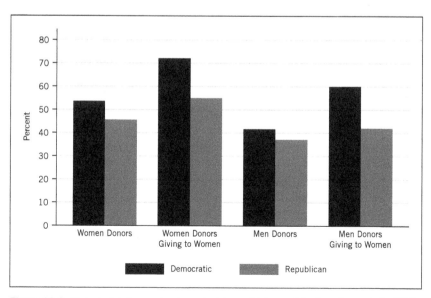

Figure 18.3. State legislative and gubernatorial candidate contributions by party in 2010 and 2012 elections.

individual Republican donors, it is possible that Republican candidates are more driven by ideology in their donation strategies. Even though Republican women candidates are more likely to donate to other women candidates than Republican men (and a majority of Republican women donors contribute to other women), fewer Republican women candidates seem motivated by a shared gender identity to donate to other women. As a result, Republican candidates are not currently using their resources to help make up for the additional fundraising challenges faced by Republican women candidates. Therefore, there is room for Republican candidates to offset fundraising challenges faced by Republican women candidates by contributing to them.

Benefits to Donors

In addition to helping the electoral efforts of women candidates, being active in redistributing resources to other candidates can also benefit the donor. These donations act as connections, helping the donor increase influence in the party. By giving campaign contributions to other candidates, the donor creates connections with the recipients of their transfers. Moreover, the transfer of campaign funds has an "expressive benefit" that demonstrates affection or a valuing of the relationship, developing or reinforcing a social connection or tie.[41] These connections (i.e., donations) allow candidates to develop relationships with other candidates, helping them grow both their formal and informal influence in the party.

We know that the members of Congress most likely to become leaders are those active in redistributing resources to party committees and other members.[42] In addition to supporting the candidacies of women, women candidates may be able to ensure their influence in the party through redistributing their campaign funds. In my research, I find that state legislative candidates are able to increase their influence by making contributions to other candidates. Candidates that are especially well connected through their redistribution activities are more likely to become legislative leaders than other candidates.[43]

For example, Colorado representative Dickey Lee Hullinghorst donated to several candidates in her first race in 2008. She increased her transfers to other candidates in subsequent elections, making over 40 transfers to other candidates in 2010 and almost 80 contributions in the 2012 election (including 22 to other women). By being active in redistributing funds, she was able to move up in the party. In the 2011 session, Representative Hullinghorst received a seat on the Appropriations Committee and was the deputy majority whip. She became the House majority leader in the 2013 session and the Speaker of the House in 2015.

Candidates may also be able to acquire support for their legislative proposals by making connections to other candidates through donations. Through her PAC's donations and other activities, Senator Gillibrand has garnered support for her policy agenda, including with other legislators.[44] These connections may have also helped motivate her ultimately unsuccessful 2020 presidential bid. In sum, in addition to helping other women's candidacies by donating to them, women can also increase their own influence in the party through this redistribution of resources to other party actors.

Keep Paying It Forward

This chapter argues that candidate-to-candidate contributions are an important tool for getting more diverse candidates to run for office. By donating to them, candidates can help other candidates launch their campaign. Candidate donations can also signal the recipient's quality to other key donors, helping them gain access to fundraising networks. Additionally, candidate donations are a symbol of support for the candidate, which may provide the recipient with a sense of belonging and a psychological lift. Furthermore, candidates active in redistributing resources to other candidates can grow their influence in their political party.

By examining candidate contributions in six states, I find that candidates are active in making contributions to other candidates. Moreover, many women candidates are supporting other women candidates with donations. Women provide a higher percentage of their donations to other women candidates and are more likely than men to donate to a woman candidate. However, there are plenty of candidates not contributing to other candidates, leaving room for this tool to be utilized more.

There are substantial barriers facing women candidates interested in donating more to other women candidates. Recent research suggests that women candidates do struggle more than men to fundraise,[45] and candidates need enough money to fund their own campaigns. For the contributing candidates in this sample, Democratic and Republican women raised tens of thousands of dollars less than men. As a result, women candidates may struggle to have enough money to redistribute to other candidates. Therefore, utilizing candidate contributions as a tool to increase the number of women running for office may require more fundraising by women candidates and incumbents. This may be difficult to achieve, but there is a growing base of women donors for women candidates to seek out.

By providing key resources for women running for office (especially for first-time candidates), candidate contributions have the potential to remove one reason why interested women do not run—concerns about fundraising. Even with a small donation, candidates can encourage financial support for the recipient from other actors. Moreover, women candidates active in redistributing their resources increase their influence in the party, aiding in their success in office. As a result, women candidates should consider fundraising extra (if possible) to contribute to other candidates, especially women and other underrepresented candidates that may struggle with fundraising.

NOTES

I am grateful to Lori Hausegger, Cook Jones, participants at the Good Reasons to Run conference, the Boise State School of Public Service Research Workshop, and the editors for helpful feedback on this chapter. This research was supported by the Carrie Chapman Catt Prize for Research on Women and Politics and the Rice University Social Science Research Institute.

1. Rebecca Traister, "Kirsten Gillibrand Is an Enthusiastic No," April 4, 2017, *New York*, accessed September 20, 2017, available at http://nymag.com/daily/intelligencer/2017 /04/kirsten-gillibrand-progressive-champion-2020-run.html.

2. Sarah Mimms, "Kirsten Gillibrand's Army," November 20, 2015, *The Atlantic*, accessed September 20, 2017, available at https://www.theatlantic.com/politics/archive/2015 /11/kirsten-gillibrands-army/450450/; Rebecca Traister, "Kirsten Gillibrand Is an Enthusiastic No."

3. Mimms, "Kirsten Gillibrand's Army."

4. Damon M. Cann, *Sharing the Wealth: Member Contributions and the Exchange Theory of Party Influence in the U.S. House of Representatives* (Albany: State University of New York Press, 2008); Bruce A. Desmarais, Raymond J. La Raja, and Michael S. Kowal, "The Fates of Challengers in U.S. House Elections: The Role of Extended Party Networks in Supporting Candidates and Shaping Electoral Outcomes," *American Journal of Political Science* 59, no. 1 (2015): 194–211.

5. Richard A. Seltzer, Jody Newman, and Melissa Voorhees Leighton, *Sex as a Political Variable: Women as Candidates and Voters in U.S. Elections* (Boulder, CO: Lynne Rienner, 1997); Susan J. Carroll and Kira Sanbonmatsu, *More Women Can Run: Gender and Pathways to the State Legislatures* (New York: Oxford University Press, 2013).

6. Shannon Jenkins, "A Woman's Work Is Never Done? Fund-Raising Perception and Effort among Female State Legislative Candidates," *Political Research Quarterly* 60, no. 2 (2007): 230–239.

7. Melody Crowder-Meyer, "Gendered Recruitment without Trying: How Local Party Recruiters Affect Women's Representation," *Politics and Gender* 9, no. 4 (2013): 390–413; Political Parity, "Shifting Gears: How Women Navigate the Road to Higher Office," 2014, accessed October 2, 2017, available at https://www.politicalparity.org/research/shifting -gears/.

8. Peter L. Francia, "Early Fundraising by Nonincumbent Female Congressional Candidates," *Women and Politics* 23, no. 1 (2001): 7–20.

9. Michael H. Crespin and Janna L. Deitz, "If You Can't Join 'Em, Beat 'Em: The Gender Gap in Individual Donations to Congressional Candidates," *Political Research Quarterly* 63, no. 3 (2010): 581–593.

10. "Diverse candidates" refers to individuals in underrepresented groups in politics running for political office. Diverse candidates include women, people of color, LGBT individuals, the working class, and others. I focus on women candidates in this chapter.

11. Jaclyn J. Kettler, "The Right to Party (Resources): Political Party Networks and Candidate Success," doctoral dissertation, Rice University (2014), accessed October 17, 2017, available at http://hdl.handle.net/1911/88359.

12. Melody Crowder-Meyer, "Gendered Recruitment without Trying"; David Niven, "Party Elites and Women Candidates: The Shape of Bias," *Women and Politics* 19, no. 2 (1998): 57–80.

13. Carroll and Sanbonmatsu, *More Women Can Run*.

14. Michael Barber, Daniel M. Butler, and Jessica Preece, "Gender Inequalities in Campaign Finance," *Quarterly Journal of Political Science* 11, no. 2 (2016): 219–248; Danielle M. Thomsen and Michele L. Swers, "Which Women Can Run? Gender, Partisanship, and Candidate Donor Networks," *Political Research Quarterly* 70, no. 2 (2017): 449–463; Michele L. Swers and Danielle M. Thomsen, Chapter 16, in this volume.

15. Shannon Jenkins, "A Woman's Work Is Never Done?"

16. David L. Schecter and David M. Hedge, "Dancing with the One Who Brought You: The Allocation and Impact of Party Giving to State Legislators," *Legislative Studies Quarterly* 26, no. 3 (2001): 437–456.

17. Crespin and Deitz, "If You Can't Join 'Em, Beat 'Em"; Thomsen and Swers, "Which Women Can Run?"

18. Stephen Ansolabehere and James M. Snyder Jr., "Campaign War Chests in Congressional Elections," *Business and Politics* 2, no. 1 (2000): 9–33.

19. Eric S. Heberlig and Bruce A. Larson, *Congressional Parties, Institutional Ambition, and the Financing of Majority Control* (Ann Arbor: University of Michigan Press, 2012).

20. Cann, *Sharing the Wealth*; Marian Currinder, *Money in the House: Campaign Funds and Congressional Party Politics* (Boulder, CO: Westview, 2009); Heberlig and Larson, *Congressional Parties*; Kristin Kanthak, "Crystal Elephants and Committee Chairs: Campaign Contributions and Leadership Races in the U.S. House of Representatives," *American Politics Research* 35, no. 3 (2007): 389–406.

21. Anne Bedlington and Michael J. Malbin, "The Party as Extended Network: Members of Congress Giving to Each Other and to Their Parties," in *Life after Reform: When the Bipartisan Campaign Reform Act Meets Politics*, ed. Michael J. Malbin (Boulder, CO: Rowman and Littlefield, 2003).

22. Cann, *Sharing the Wealth*; Garrett Glasgow, "The Efficiency of Congressional Campaign Committee Contributions in House Elections," *Party Politics* 8, no. 6 (2002): 657–672.

23. Gregory Koger, Seth Masket, and Hans Noel, "Partisan Webs: Information Exchange and Party Networks," *British Journal of Political Science* 39, no. 3 (2009): 633–653.

24. Desmarais, La Raja, and Kowal, "Fates of Challengers in U.S. House Elections."

25. Carroll and Sanbonmatsu, *More Women Can Run*.

26. Kristin Kanthak and George A. Krause, *The Diversity Paradox: Political Parties, Legislatures, and the Organizational Foundations of Representation in America* (Oxford: Oxford University Press, 2012).

27. Mimms, "Kirsten Gillibrand's Army."

28. Anthony Gierzynski and Paulette Budreck, "Women Legislative Caucus and Leadership Campaign Committees," *Women and Politics* 15, no. 2 (1995): 23–36.

29. Gierzynski and Budreck, "Women Legislative Caucus and Leadership Campaign Committees."

30. Kanthak and Krause, *Diversity Paradox*.

31. Carroll and Sanbonmatsu, *More Women Can Run*.

32. National Conference of State Legislatures, "Women in State Legislatures: 2011," 2011, accessed August 21, 2017, available at http://www.ncsl.org/legislators-staff/legislators /womens-legislative-network/women-in-state-legislatures-2011.aspx.

33. Keith E. Hamm and Gary E. Moncrief, "Legislative Politics in the States," in *Politics in the American States: A Comparative Analysis*, ed. Virginia Gray, Russell L. Hanson, and Thad Kousser (Los Angeles: CQ Press, 2008), 163–207.

34. Peverill Squire, "Measuring State Legislative Professionalism: The Squire Index Revisited," *State Politics and Policy Quarterly* 7, no. 2 (2007): 211–227.

35. National Institute on Money in State Politics, Follow the Money, 2017, accessed August 25, 2017, available at https://www.followthemoney.org/; Colorado Secretary of State, TRACER, 2017, accessed August 25, 2017, available at http://tracer.sos.colorado.gov /PublicSite/homepage.aspx#.

36. Around 40 percent of both men and women candidates' donations were self-funding.

37. The online appendix can be found through the Harvard Dataverse, available at https://doi.org/10.7910/DVN/BJTB1W.

38. A two-sample test of proportions confirms that this is a statistically significant difference, $p = 0.0000$.

39. Thomsen and Swers, "Which Women Can Run?"; Michele L. Swers and Danielle M. Thomsen, Chapter 16, in this volume.

40. Thomsen and Swers, "Which Women Can Run?"; Melody Crowder-Meyer and Rosalyn Cooperman, "Can't Buy Them Love: How Party Culture among Donors Contributes to the Party Gap in Women's Representation," *Journal of Politics* 80, no. 4 (2018).

41. Kanthak and Krause, *Diversity Paradox*.

42. Heberlig and Larson, *Congressional Parties*.

43. Kettler, "Right to Party (Resources)."

44. Mimms, "Kirsten Gillibrand's Army."

45. Barber, Butler, and Preece, "Gender Inequalities in Campaign Finance"; Karin E. Kitchens and Michele L. Swers, "Why Aren't There More Republican Women in Congress? Gender, Partisanship, and Fundraising Support in the 2010 and 2012 Elections," *Politics and Gender* 12, no. 4 (2016): 648–676.

Conclusion

A Reason and a Season to Run

Sometimes events in the real world leap ahead of our research-based understandings of them, and scholars have to race to catch up. Such is the case with women and politics in the first two decades of the twenty-first century. We have seen rapid growth in nongovernmental and nonpartisan programs specifically designed to recruit and train women as political candidates. And, particularly since the 2016 U.S. presidential election, the huge cohort of women that stepped forward to run for office has changed the landscape of candidates and representation. The early decades of this century have also produced changes in the types of women who run, with women candidates and elected officials in the Democratic Party far outnumbering Republican women. Indeed, the 2018 election featured the most women (including the most women of color) of any election to date, and the 2020 Democratic primary alone featured more women candidates for the presidency than all parties together fielded in any prior U.S. presidential contest.[1] And although in the past women of color have faced heightened discrimination based on both race and gender, the post-2016 landscape has also seen a record number of women of color run—and succeed. The election of 2020 looks likely to continue these trends, with a record six Democratic women who participated in the presidential primary race—marking the first time in U.S. history that more than two women have competed in the same party's presidential primary.[2]

Women's status was not static elsewhere in the world. Saudi Arabia gave women the right to vote in 2015, while Ecuador gave trans individuals the right to vote with their preferred gender in 2017. More than 130 countries have implemented legal gender quotas of some form, half of which occurred during the past decade.[3] In the past two decades alone, 75 percent of all female prime ministers and presidents ever elected took office.[4] Yet women's political participation around the world remains low, and the proportion of women in parliaments has remained nearly static over the past two years.[5] In many places, women running for office face violence, harassment, and sometimes even death.[6] Recent years saw particular outbursts of violence and harassment against women candidates in Zimbabwe; three murders of female candidates in Mexico and one in Brazil in 2018; death threats against female candidates in the United States; and sexual harassment of women members of Parliament in Britain and India.[7] Indeed, the problem is so persistent and widespread that in 2016 the National Democratic Institute began a new campaign called #NotTheCost to document violence against women running for office.[8] Even in postindustrial countries like the United States, where outright violence against candidates is fairly rare, women seeking political positions face gendered harassment, sometimes assault, and a number of psychological, emotional, financial, and other burdens. No wonder so many women find themselves lukewarm or downright cold at the prospect of entering politics.[9]

Faced with the persistent problem of women's underrepresentation, in countries around the world, programs meant to convince women to face the odds have proliferated (see Chapter 15 by Piscopo and Chapter 12 by Kreitzer and Osborn, in this volume). These organizations, whether formally affiliated with a party, ideologically sympathetic, or genuinely nonpartisan, bear the heavy load of identifying and recruiting women to run for office. While many of the earliest organizations of this kind began in the United States,[10] in recent years the demand to address women's underrepresentation has been so great that many other countries have simply exported approaches like weekend "candidate bootcamps" with little regard for whether the approach is likely to work in their specific political context. Given the difficulties of implementing systemic policy changes like campaign finance reform that might encourage more women to run,[11] it is easy to appreciate why the quick fix of telling women to "lean in" is so popular.

Nonetheless, the massive surge in American women's candidacies starting in 2017 asks us to question existing accounts of women's political ambitions, and, by extension, the role these nonprofits play in increasing women's ambitions (see Chapter 14 by Schneider and Sweet-Cushman, Chapter 2 by Bernhard et al., and Chapter 13 by Sanbonmatsu and Dittmar, in this volume). Some research on political ambition characterizes it as innate (or, at the very least, internal)—that is, largely fixed within individuals.[12] The second wave characterized ambition as the product of socialization,[13] institutional structures, and gender role imbalances like uneven caretaking burdens.[14] In these accounts, extant gender inequalities depress women's ambition and ability to run, generating an inevitable downward slope that can only be countered through heavy recruitment and support by elites, peers, and family members.[15] Nonprofits have largely accepted the mantle of making "asks" and training potential female candidates. Yet, the sudden dramatic change in the number of women running post-2016 throws a wrench into theories that women's ambition is innate (static) or sociostructural (a downward slope that can be "fixed" via extra recruitment).[16] As many women began expressing interest in running only days after Hillary Clinton's 2016 loss—Emerge America, a national women's candidate training organization, received a nearly 200 percent increase in program applications in the two weeks after the election[17]— one cannot reasonably imagine that nonprofit recruitment is responsible or that these socialized and structural responsibilities like caretaking suddenly disappeared.

Instead, women's behavior since 2016 better fits an account of ambition that is contextual and can be dramatically overhauled by major political upheavals. This suggests that what was a near steady state (and arguably suboptimal from the perspective of representation) can be thrust into a new equilibrium rather suddenly. Scholars have long thought that women engage in a rational calculation of the costs and benefits of running based on a host of considerations,[18] many of which fluctuate (like childcare responsibilities or geographic location; see Chapter 2 by Bernhard et al. and Chapter 8 by Ondercin, in this volume) throughout their lifetimes.[19] But now we have to reckon with the idea that the functional bases on which these calculations are made may have taken a new form. While we expect that women's ambition will still be guided by "relational" considerations, we surmise that the weight given to other considerations (such as duty, anger, or inspiration) may rise.[20] Thus, whereas the contextual and constantly evolving type of political ambition has been difficult for women's advocacy groups and political parties to address, the major setbacks for women in the U.S. public sphere after the 2016 election also suggest that ambition can be stimulated in the face of obstacles.[21]

In this volume, we sought to improve both scholars' and advocates' understanding of what ambition looks like and how it varies across women; to unpack the factors that motivate women to run and understand what discourages them; to probe the role that institutions and nonprofits play in shaping women's ambitions; and to outline best practices for the recruitment of women. In Part I, we described who runs, with a focus on individual-level characteristics (like income and race) that shape women's political ambitions. The midterm election in 2018 offers important lessons here, as women from a wide set of backgrounds—young, working class, veterans, bisexual, immigrant—ran for and won national office, although mostly in the Democratic Party. In Part II, we learned about a number of individual-level interventions, like participation in voluntary organizations and rebranding politics as a collaborative domain, that stimulated women's ambition—supplying answers to the question of "Why run?" The 2018 electoral landscape shows the success of these programs: in Nevada, for example, where women gained a majority of seats in the legislature for the first time ever,[22] key victories were won by alumnae of candidate training organizations.[23] Part III explored the larger structural and institutional factors, like unfavorable geography and lack of party sponsorship, that can suppress women's ambition. Looking forward to 2020 (and beyond), lessons from this part of the book may prove particularly useful for understanding where women are (still) not running and why. Part IV examined the role of nonprofits in women's paths toward candidacy. As many candidate training organizations move into their second (and third) decades of existence, the research in Part IV helps us understand how recent elections have been shaped by these organizations and how they might impact future contests and candidacies. Finally, Part V took a deep dive into the role of money, showcasing how and to what extent interventions can counter the structural difficulties women face in fundraising. While the gender gap in campaign donations continued into the congressional elections of 2018, female donors are giving more to female candidates. If this pattern continues into future elections, the research presented here suggests that donations from women to women will provide a key advantage to women running for office.[24]

In short, we believe that women need both a "reason" (higher intrinsic and extrinsic benefits) and a "season" (lower contextual costs) to run. We attempt to supply recommendations for both in this volume, drawing from the most cutting-edge research and most effective advocacy programs. Of particular note, what moves these levers will differ for subgroups of women: what works to get women of color running will differ from what convinces women in conservative states to run, from what convinces young women to run, and so on.[25] As such, we anticipate that programs aimed at increasing women's representation will have to employ a variety of approaches, either within a single organization (as in the case of party-affiliated programs) or across multiple specialist organizations that together can generate a deep and diverse pool of women candidates.

The findings contained here suggest that while nonprofit efforts to recruit women are vast and varied, they are unlikely to fully rectify women's underrepresentation in politics without attendant support from institutions (e.g., by supplying childcare funding to candidates[26]), parties (especially in cases where nominations are controlled by parties rather than candidates[27]), and major political changes. The United States' straggling progress in increasing women's numbers in office is surely influenced by how heavy the burden of recruitment is for nonprofits, which often operate with large missions but shoestring budgets and staffs. For the massive jolt in the number of female candidates to translate into different representational outcomes, we need the support of policy-makers and party leaders alike.

As extensive as this volume is, it still leaves many questions unanswered. While we have begun a dialogue between academics and nonprofits and candidates that we believe is essential to increasing the number of women in office, even 18 chapters are insufficient to explore the massive diversity of the women now running and the growing numbers of organizations attempting to give them a leg up. We hope that future research continues this collaboration and explores a number of contextual factors at which this volume has only begun to hint. How should these programs be adapted to countries outside the United States or to specific communities within the United States? What sorts of interventions are most effective at reducing the sexual harassment of women running for office? Are the motivations for Republican women different than for Democratic women? Does progressive ambition (the desire to move up to a higher office) vary by women's race or socioeconomic class? How does class and gender interact to shape political ambition? What might be the lessons for immigrant women, LGBTQ+ candidates, women who have served in the armed forces or come from working-class backgrounds, or disabled women?

Despite the bittersweet victories and defeats of the past few years for women's political representation, we remain hopeful that progress toward women's equality can and will be made. Our hope is due in no small part to the many advocates and women candidates whom we have had the opportunity to observe and learn from during the making of this volume. This optimism, in turn, is grounded in the knowledge that women have secured impressive victories—in attaining suffrage,[28] for instance—against greater odds. Finally, we hope the many hands that contributed to this volume, both named and unnamed, scholar and advocate alike, will make lighter the work of realizing women's equal representation in the twenty-first century.

NOTES

1. CAWP, "Current Numbers | CAWP" (New Brunswick, NJ: Center for American Women and Politics, Eagleton Institute of Politics, Rutgers University, 2018), available at http://www.cawp.rutgers.edu/current-numbers.

2. CAWP, "Women Presidential and Vice Presidential Candidates: A Selected List," June 30, 2015, available at https://cawp.rutgers.edu/levels_of_office/women-presidential-and-vice-presidential-candidates-selected-list.

3. Melanie M. Hughes, Pamela Paxton, Amanda B. Clayton, and Pär Zetterberg, "Global Gender Quota Adoption, Implementation, and Reform," *Comparative Politics* 51, no. 2 (January 2019): 219–238; Melanie M. Hughes, Mona Lena Krook, and Pamela Paxton, "Transnational Women's Activism and the Global Diffusion of Gender Quotas," *International Studies Quarterly* 59, no. 2 (June 1, 2015): 357–372.

4. Farida Jalalzai, "Shattered Not Cracked: The Effect of Women's Executive Leadership," *Journal of Women, Politics, and Policy* 37, no. 4 (October 1, 2016): 439–463.

5. IPU, "Women in National Parliaments" (Grand-Saconnex, Switzerland: Interparliamentary Union, 2015), accessed November 21, 2019, available at http://www.ipu.org/wmn-e/world.htm.

6. Mona Lena Krook, "Violence against Women in Politics: A Rising Global Trend," *Politics and Gender* 14, no. 4 (2018): 673–675.

7. Krook, "Violence against Women in Politics"; Mona Lena Krook, "Westminster Too: On Sexual Harassment in British Politics," *Political Quarterly* 89, no. 1 (2018): 65–72;

Maggie Astor, "For Female Candidates, Harassment and Threats Come Every Day," *New York Times*, August 26, 2018, sec. U.S., accessed November 21, 2019, available at https://www.nytimes.com/2018/08/24/us/politics/women-harassment-elections.html.

8. Accessed November 21, 2019, available at https://www.ndi.org/not-the-cost.

9. Julia Restrepo and Mona Krook, "Physical Violence and Psychological Abuse against Female and Male Mayors in the United States," working paper, 2019.

10. Rebecca J. Kreitzer and Tracy Osborn, "The Emergence and Activities of Women's Recruiting Groups in the U.S.," *Politics, Groups, and Identities* (November 19, 2018): 1–11.

11. Rachel Bernhard, Shauna L. Shames, Rachel Silbermann, and Dawn Langan Teele, "To Emerge or Not To Emerge?: Breadwinning and Income in Women's Decisions to Run," Paper prepared for presentation at the Annual Meeting of the Midwest Political Science Association (Chicago, IL: April 2018).

12. Gordon S. Black, "A Theory of Political Ambition: Career Choices and the Role of Structural Incentives," *American Political Science Review* 66, no. 1 (March 1972): 144–159, available at https://doi.org/10.2307/1959283; Joseph A. Schlesinger, *Ambition and Politics: Political Careers in the United States* (New York: Rand McNally, 1966).

13. Richard L. Fox and Jennifer L. Lawless, "Entering the Arena? Gender and the Decision to Run for Office," *American Journal of Political Science* 48, no. 2 (2004): 264–280; Jo Freeman, *A Room at a Time: How Women Entered Party Politics* (Rowman and Littlefield, 2002).

14. Jill Greenlee, *The Political Consequences of Motherhood* (University of Michigan Press, 2014); Ronald D. Hedlund, Patricia K. Freeman, Keith E. Hamm, and Robert M. Stein "The Electability of Women Candidates: The Effects of Sex Role Stereotypes," *Journal of Politics* 41 (1994): 513–524.

15. Jennifer L. Lawless and Richard Logan Fox, *It Takes a Candidate: Why Women Don't Run for Office* (Cambridge University Press, 2005).

16. Mirya R. Holman and Monica C. Schneider, "Gender, Race, and Political Ambition," *Politics, Groups, and Identities* 6, no. 2 (April 3, 2018): 264–280.

17. Rachel Bernhard, "Gendering Political Campaigns," The European Conference for Politics and Gender, Amsterdam, July 4–6, 2019.

18. Jessica Robinson Preece and Olga Bogach Stoddard, "Why Women Don't Run: Experimental Evidence on Gender Differences in Political Competition Aversion," *Journal of Economic Behavior and Organization* 117 (2015): 296–308.

19. Melody Crowder-Meyer, "Baker, Bus Driver, Babysitter, Candidate? Revealing the Gendered Development of Political Ambition among Ordinary Americans," *Political Behavior* (September 11, 2018).

20. Susan J. Carroll and Kira Sanbonmatsu, *More Women Can Run: Gender and Pathways to the State Legislatures* (New York: Oxford University Press, 2013).

21. Holman and Schneider, "Gender, Race, and Political Ambition"; Monica C. Schneider, Mirya R. Holman, Amanda B. Diekman, and Thomas McAndrew, "Power, Conflict, and Community: How Gendered Views of Political Power Influence Women's Political Ambition," *Political Psychology* 37, no. 4 (2016): 515–531; see also Shauna L. Shames, *Out of the Running: Why Millennials Reject Political Careers and Why It Matters* (New York: New York University Press, 2017).

22. Leila Fadel, "A First: Women Take the Majority in Nevada Legislature and Colorado House," NPR, February 4, 2019, Washington, DC, accessed November 21, 2019, available at https://www.npr.org/2019/02/04/691198416/a-first-women-take-the-majority-in-nevada-legislature-and-colorado-house.

23. "Nevada Could Elect First-Ever Female-Majority Statehouse," Emerge Nevada, July 24, 2018, accessed November 21, 2019, available at https://nv.emergeamerica.org/nevada -could-elect-first-ever-female-majority-statehouse/.

24. Sarah Bryner and Grace Haley, "Race, Gender, and Money in Politics: Campaign Finance and Federal Candidates in the 2018 Midterms" (Washington, DC: Center for Responsive Politics, 2019).

25. Andrea Silva and Carrie Skulley, "Always Running: Candidate Emergence among Women of Color over Time," *Political Research Quarterly*, July 28, 2018.

26. Wallis Watkins, "Ethics Board Backpedals Child Care Decision for Political Candidates in Louisiana," February 19, 2019, accessed November 21, 2019, available at https:// www.wwno.org/post/ethics-board-backpedals-child-care-decision-political-candidates -louisiana; Danielle Kurtzleben, "FEC Says That Candidates Can Use Campaign Funds for Child Care," NPR, May 10, 2018, Washington, DC, accessed November 21, 2019, available at https://www.npr.org/2018/05/10/610099506/fec-says-that-candidates-can-use -campaign-funds-for-child-care.

27. See Melody Crowder-Meyer, "Gendered Recruitment without Trying: How Local Party Recruiters Affect Women's Representation," *Politics and Gender* 9, no. 4 (2013): 390–413.

28. Dawn Langan Teele, *Forging the Franchise: The Political Origins of the Women's Vote* (Princeton, NJ: Princeton University Press, 2018).

Bibliography

Aaldering, Loes, and Daphne Joanna Van Der Pas. "Political Leadership in the Media: Gender Bias in Leader Stereotypes during Campaign and Routine Times." *British Journal of Political Science* (March 2018): 1–21.

Adams, Brian E., and Ronnee Schreiber. "Gender, Campaign Finance, and Electoral Success in Municipal Elections." *Journal of Urban Affairs* 33, no. 1 (2011): 83–97.

Atkeson, Lonna Rae. "Not All Cues Are Created Equal: The Conditional Impact of Female Candidates on Political Engagement." *Journal of Politics* 65, no. 4 (2003): 1040–1061.

Bade, Rachael. "'Congress Wasn't Built for Members Like Me.'" *Politico.* November 26, 2018. Available at https://politi.co/2r5VyUh.

Baitinger, Gail. "Meet the Press or Meet the Men? Examining Women's Presence in American News Media." *Political Research Quarterly* (2015).

Barber, Michael, Daniel M. Butler, and Jessica Preece. "Gender Inequalities in Campaign Finance." *Quarterly Journal of Political Science* 11, no. 2 (2016): 219–248.

Barnes, Tiffany D. *Gendering Legislative Behavior: Institutional Constraints and Collaboration in Argentina.* New York: Cambridge University Press, 2016.

Barnes, Tiffany D., and Mirya R. Holman. "Gender Quotas, Women's Representation, and Legislative Diversity." *Journal of Politics* Forthcoming (2020).

———. "Taking Diverse Backgrounds into Account in Studies of Political Ambition and Representation." *Politics, Groups, and Identities* (published online November 8, 2018): 1–13.

Bauer, Nichole M. "Rethinking Stereotype Reliance." *Politics and the Life Sciences* 32, no. 1 (Spring 2013): 22–42.

———. "Running Local: Gender Stereotyping and Female Candidates in Local Elections." *Urban Affairs Review*, April 30, 2018.

Bauer, Nichole M., Laurel Harbridge Yong, and Yanna Krupnikov. "Who Is Punished? Conditions Affecting Voter Evaluations of Legislators Who Do Not Compromise." *Political Behavior* 39, no. 2 (2017): 279–300.

Beaman, Lori, Esther Duflo, Rohini Pande, and Petia Topalova. "Female Leadership Raises Aspirations and Educational Attainment for Girls: A Policy Experiment in India." *Science* 335, no. 6068 (2012): 582–586.

Benjamin, Andrea. "Coethnic Endorsements, Out-Group Candidate Preferences, and Perceptions in Local Elections." *Urban Affairs Review* 53, no. 4 (July 1, 2017): 631–657.

Berinsky, Adam J., Gregory A. Huber, and Gabriel S. Lenz. "Evaluating Online Labor Markets for Experimental Research: Amazon.com's Mechanical Turk." *Political Analysis* 20, no. 3 (2012): 351–368.

Bernhard, Rachel. "Gendering Political Campaigns." The European Conference for Politics and Gender, Amsterdam, July 4–6, 2019.

Bernhard, Rachel, Dawn Langan Teele, and Shauna L. Shames. "Breadwinner Moms: The Critical Role of Resources in Women's Political Ambition." Working paper (2018).

Brown, Nadia E. *Sisters in the Statehouse: Black Women and Legislative Decision Making*. New York: Oxford University Press, 2014.

Browning, Rufus P., Dale Rogers Marshall, and David H. Tabb. "Protest Is Not Enough: A Theory of Political Incorporation." *PS* 19, no. 3 (1986): 576–581.

Burns, Nancy, Kay Lehman Schlozman, and Sidney Verba. *The Private Roots of Public Action*. Cambridge, MA: Harvard University Press, 2001.

———. "The Public Consequences of Private Inequality: Family Life and Citizen Participation." *American Political Science Review* 91, no. 2 (1997): 373–389.

Burns, Peter F. *Electoral Politics Is Not Enough: Racial and Ethnic Minorities and Urban Politics*. New York: State University of New York Press, 2006.

Campbell, David E., and Christina Wolbrecht. "See Jane Run: Women Politicians as Role Models for Adolescents." *Journal of Politics* 68, no. 2 (2006): 233–247.

Carnes, Nicholas. *The Cash Ceiling: Why Only the Rich Run for Office—and What We Can Do about It*. Princeton, NJ: Princeton University Press, 2018.

———. *White-Collar Government: The Hidden Role of Class in Economic Policy Making*. Chicago: University of Chicago Press, 2013.

Carroll, Susan J., and Kira Sanbonmatsu. "Entering the Mayor's Office: Women's Decisions to Run for Municipal Positions." In *Women and Executive Office: Pathways and Performance*, edited by Melody Rose. Boulder, CO: Lynne Rienner, 2013.

———. *More Women Can Run: Gender and Pathways to the State Legislatures*. New York: Oxford University Press, 2013.

CAWP. "Current Numbers | CAWP." Rutgers, NJ: Center for American Women and Politics, Eagleton Institute of Politics, Rutgers University, 2018. Available at http://www.cawp.rutgers.edu/current-numbers.

Coffé, Hilde, and Catherine Bolzendahl. "Same Game, Different Rules? Gender Differences in Political Participation." *Sex Roles* 62, no. 5 (2010): 318–333.

Cooperman, Rosalyn, and Melody Crowder-Meyer. "A Run for Their Money: Republican Women's Hard Road to Campaign Funding." In *The Right Women: Republican Party Activists, Candidates, and Legislators*, edited by Shauna L. Shames and Malliga Och. Santa Barbara, CA: Praeger, 2018.

Costantini, Edmond. "Political Women and Political Ambition: Closing the Gender Gap." *American Journal of Political Science* 34, no. 3 (August 1990): 741–770.

Covert, Bryce. "Teaching Matters: Why It May Put More Women into Public Office." *Forbes*, July 2012. Available at https://www.forbes.com/sites/brycecovert/2012/07/26/could-teachers-be-a-secret-weapon-in-closing-congresss-gender-gap/#1acbe5265d7e.

Crespin, Michael H., and Janna L. Deitz. "If You Can't Join 'Em, Beat 'Em: The Gender Gap in Individual Donations to Congressional Candidates." *Political Research Quarterly* 63, no. 3 (September 1, 2010): 581–593.

Crowder-Meyer, Melody. "Baker, Bus Driver, Babysitter, Candidate? Revealing the Gendered Development of Political Ambition among Ordinary Americans." *Political Behavior* (September 11, 2018).
———. "Gendered Recruitment without Trying: How Local Party Recruiters Affect Women's Representation." *Politics and Gender* 9, no. 4 (2013): 390–413.
Crowder-Meyer, Melody, and Rosalyn Cooperman. "Can't Buy Them Love: How Party Culture among Donors Contributes to the Party Gap in Women's Representation." *Journal of Politics* 80, no. 4: 1211–1224.
Crowder-Meyer, Melody, Shana Kushner Gadarian, and Jessica Trounstine. "Electoral Institutions, Gender Stereotypes, and Women's Local Representation." *Politics, Groups, and Identities* 3, no. 2 (2015): 318–334.
Dahl, Robert. *Who Governs? Democracy and Power in an American City.* New Haven, CT: Yale University Press, 1961.
Day, Christine L., and Charles D. Hadley. "Who Contributes? Similarities and Differences Between Contributors to EMILY's List and WISH List." *Women and Politics* 24, no. 2 (2002): 53–67.
Deckman, Melissa Marie. "School Board Candidates and Gender: Ideology, Party, and Policy Concerns." *Journal of Women, Politics, and Policy* 28, no. 1 (2007): 87–117.
De Toqueville, Alexis. "Democracy in America." New York: G. Dearborn & Co., 1838.
Dittmar, Kelly. "By the Numbers: Women Congressional Candidates in 2018." CAWP, September 12, 2018. Available at https://cawp.rutgers.edu/potential-candidate-summary-2018.
———. "Encouragement Is Not Enough: Addressing Social and Structural Barriers to Female Recruitment." *Politics and Gender* 11, no. 4 (December 2015): 759–765.
———. *Navigating Gendered Terrain: Stereotypes and Strategy in Political Campaigns.* Philadelphia: Temple University Press, 2015.
Dittmar, Kelly, Kira Sanbonmatsu, Susan J. Carroll, Debbie Walsh, and Catherine Wineinger. "Representation Matters: Women in the U.S. Congress." New Brunswick, NJ: Center for American Women and Politics, Eagleton Institute of Politics, Rutgers University, 2017.
Eagly, Alice H. "Female Leadership Advantage and Disadvantage: Resolving the Contradictions." *Psychology of Women Quarterly* 31, no. 1 (2007): 1–12.
Einstein, Katherine Levine, David M. Glick, Maxwell Palmer, and Robert J. Pressel. "Do Mayors Run for Higher Office? New Evidence on Progressive Ambition." *American Politics Research*, January 25, 2018.
Farris, Emily M., and Mirya R. Holman. "Social Capital and Solving the Puzzle of Black Women's Political Participation." *Politics, Groups, and Identities* 2, no. 3 (July 3, 2014): 331–349.
Fowler, Linda L., and Robert D. McClure. *Political Ambition: Who Decides to Run for Congress.* New Haven, CT: Yale University Press, 1990.
Fox, Richard L., and Jennifer L. Lawless. "Entering the Arena? Gender and the Decision to Run for Office." *American Journal of Political Science* 48, no. 2 (2004): 264–280.
———. "Gaining and Losing Interest in Running for Public Office: The Concept of Dynamic Political Ambition." *Journal of Politics* 73, no. 2 (2011): 443–462.
———. "If Only They'd Ask: Gender, Recruitment, and Political Ambition." *Journal of Politics* 72, no. 2 (2010): 310–326.
———. "Reconciling Family Roles with Political Ambition: The New Normal for Women in Twenty-First Century US Politics." *Journal of Politics* 76, no. 2 (2014): 398–414.
———. "To Run or Not to Run for Office: Explaining Nascent Political Ambition." *American Journal of Political Science* 49, no. 3 (2005): 642–659.

Fox, Richard L., and Zoe M. Oxley. "Gender Stereotyping State Executive Elections: Candidate Selection and Success." *Journal of Politics* 65, no. 3 (2003): 833–850.

Freeman, Jo. *A Room at a Time: How Women Entered Party Politics.* Lanham, MD: Rowman and Littlefield, 2002.

Fridkin, Kim L., and Patrick J. Kenney. *The Changing Face of Representation.* Ann Arbor: University of Michigan Press, 2014.

Fulton, Sarah A., Cherie D Maestas, L. Sandy Maisel, and Walter J. Stone. "The Sense of a Woman: Gender, Ambition, and the Decision to Run for Congress." *Political Research Quarterly* 59, no. 2 (2006): 235–248.

Gidengil, Elisabeth, Janine Giles, and Melanee Thomas. "The Gender Gap in Self-Perceived Understanding of Politics in Canada and the United States." *Politics and Gender* 4, no. 4 (December 2008): 535–561.

Gilardi, Fabrizio. "The Temporary Importance of Role Models for Women's Political Representation." *American Journal of Political Science* 59, no. 4 (2015): 957–970.

Greene, Zachary, and Diana Z. O'Brien. "Diverse Parties, Diverse Agendas? Female Politicians and the Parliamentary Party's Role in Platform Formation." *European Journal of Political Research* 55 (2016): 435–453.

Greenlee, Jill S., Mirya R. Holman, and Rachel VanSickle-Ward. "Making It Personal: Assessing the Impact of In-Class Exercises on Closing the Gender Gap in Political Ambition." *Journal of Political Science Education* 10, no. 1 (2014): 48–61.

Guo, Chao, and Juliet A. Musso. "Representation in Nonprofit and Voluntary Organizations: A Conceptual Framework." *Nonprofit and Voluntary Sector Quarterly* 36, no. 2 (2007): 308–326.

Hannagan, Rebecca J., Jamie P. Pimlott, and Levente Littvay. "Does an EMILY's List Endorsement Predict Electoral Success, or Does EMILY Pick the Winners?" *PS: Political Science and Politics* 43, no. 3 (2010): 503–508.

Hansen, Susan. "Talking about Politics: Gender and Contextual Effects on Political Proselytizing." *Journal of Politics* 59, no. 2 (1997): 73–103.

Hogan, Robert E. "The Effects of Candidate Gender on Campaign Spending in State Legislative Elections." *Social Science Quarterly* 88, no. 5 (2007): 1092–1105.

Holman, Mirya R. "The Differential Effect of Resources on Political Participation across Gender and Racial Groups." In *Distinct Identities: Minority Women in U.S. Politics,* edited by Nadia E. Brown and Sarah A. Gershon. New York: Routledge, 2016.

———. "Sex and the City: Female Leaders and Spending on Social Welfare Programs in U.S. Municipalities." *Journal of Urban Affairs* 36, no. 4 (2014): 701–715.

———. "Women in Local Government: What We Know and Where We Go from Here." *State and Local Government Review* 49, no. 4 (September 25, 2017): 285–296.

———. *Women in Politics in the American City.* Philadelphia: Temple University Press, 2015.

Holman, Mirya R., and Monica C. Schneider. "Gender, Race, and Political Ambition." *Politics, Groups, and Identities* 6, no. 2 (April 3, 2018): 264–280.

———. "Gender, Race, and Political Ambition: How Stereotype Threat and Perceptions of Discrimination Influence Interest in Political Office." *Politics, Groups, and Identities* Online First (2016).

Hughes, Melanie M. "Intersectionality, Quotas, and Minority Women's Political Representation Worldwide." *American Political Science Review* 105, no. 3 (2011): 604–620.

Kalla, Joshua, Frances Rosenbluth, and Dawn Langan Teele. "Are You My Mentor? A Field Experiment on Gender, Ethnicity, and Political Self-Starters." *Journal of Politics* 80, no. 1 (October 17, 2017): 337–341.

Kanthak, Kristin, and George A. Krause. *The Diversity Paradox: Political Parties, Legislatures, and the Organizational Foundations of Representation in America*. New York: Oxford University Press, 2012.

Kanthak, Kristin, and Jonathan Woon. "Women Don't Run? Election Aversion and Candidate Entry." *American Journal of Political Science* 59, no. 3 (November 1, 2014): 595–612.

Karp, Jeffrey A., and Susan A. Banducci. "When Politics Is Not Just a Man's Game: Women's Representation and Political Engagement." *Electoral Studies* 27 (2008): 105–115.

Karpowitz, Christopher F., J. Quin Monson, and Jessica Robinson Preece. "How to Elect More Women: Gender and Candidate Success in a Field Experiment." *American Journal of Political Science* (March 1, 2017).

Keeter, Scott, Cliff Zukin, Molly Andolina, and Krista Jenkins. "The Civic and Political Health of the Nation: A Generational Portrait." The Center for Information and Research on Civic Learning and Engagement, 2019. Available at http://pollcats.net /downloads/civichealth.pdf.

Keith, Tamara. "Best Way to Get Women to Run for Office? Ask Repeatedly." NPR, March 4, 2014. Available at https://www.npr.org/2014/05/05/309832898/best-way-to -get-women-to-run-for-office-ask-repeatedly.

Kerevel, Yann P. "(Sub)National Principals, Legislative Agents: Patronage and Political Careers in Mexico." *Comparative Political Studies* 48, no. 8 (July 1, 2015): 1020–1050.

Koenig, Anne M., Alice H. Eagly, Abigail A. Mitchell, and Tiina Ristikari. "Are Leader Stereotypes Masculine? A Meta-Analysis of Three Research Paradigms." *Psychological Bulletin* 137, no. 4 (2011): 616–642.

La Raja, Raymond J., and Brian F. Schaffner. "The Effects of Campaign Finance Spending Bans on Electoral Outcomes: Evidence from the States about the Potential Impact of *Citizens United v. FEC*." *Electoral Studies* 33 (March 1, 2014): 102–114.

Lawless, Jennifer L., and Richard L. Fox. "Girls Just Wanna Not Run the Gender Gap in Young Americans' Political Ambition." Washington, DC: American University, March 2013.

———. *It Still Takes a Candidate: Why Women Don't Run for Office*. Cambridge University Press, 2010.

——— *It Takes a Candidate: Why Women Don't Run for Office*. Cambridge: Cambridge University Press, 2005.

LeRoux, Kelly. "Paternalistic or Participatory Governance? Examining Opportunities for Client Participation in Nonprofit Social Service Organizations." *Public Administration Review* 69, no. 3 (2009): 504–517.

Mahoney, Anna Mitchell. *Women Take Their Place in State Legislatures: The Creation of Women's Caucuses*. Philadelphia: Temple University Press, 2018.

Mansbridge, Jane. "Rethinking Representation." *American Political Science Review* 97, no. 4 (2003): 515–528.

McAdam, Doug. *Freedom Summer*. New York: Oxford University Press, 1990.

———. "Gender as a Mediator of the Activist Experience: The Case of Freedom Summer." *American Journal of Sociology* 97, no. 5 (March 1, 1992): 1211–1240.

McAdam, Doug, and Cynthia Brandt. "Assessing the Effects of Voluntary Youth Service: The Case of Teach for America." *Social Forces* 88, no. 2 (December 1, 2009): 945–969.

Mo, Cecilia Hyunjung, and Katharine M. Conn. "When Do the Advantaged See the Disadvantages of Others? A Quasi-Experimental Study of National Service." *American Political Science Review* 112, no. 4 (November 2018): 721–741.

Moncrief, Gary, Peverill Squire, and Malcolm Jewell. *Who Runs for the Legislature?* Upper Saddle River: Prentice Hall, 2001. Available at https://scholarworks.boisestate .edu/fac_books/257.

Ness, Molly. *Lessons to Learn: Voices from the Front Lines of Teach for America.* New York: Routledge, 2013.

Norris, Pippa, and Joni Lovenduski. "Women Candidates for Parliament: Transforming the Agenda?" *British Journal of Political Science* 19, no. 1 (1989): 106–115.

Och, Malliga, and Shauna L. Shames, eds. *The Right Women: Republican Party Activists, Candidates, and Legislators.* Santa Barbara, CA: Praeger, 2018.

Ondercin, Heather L., and Daniel Jones-White. "Gender Jeopardy: What Is the Impact of Gender Differences in Political Knowledge on Political Participation?" *Social Science Quarterly* 92, no. 3 (2011): 675–694.

Osborn, Tracy. *How Women Represent Women: Political Parties, Gender and Representation in the State Legislatures.* New York: Oxford University Press, 2012.

Preece, Jessica Robinson, Olga Bogach Stoddard, and Rachel Fisher. "Run, Jane, Run! Gendered Responses to Political Party Recruitment." *Political Behavior* 38, no. 3 (2016): 561–577.

Quintelier, Ellen. "Who Is Politically Active: The Athlete, the Scout Member or the Environmental Activist? Young People, Voluntary Engagement and Political Participation." *Acta Sociologica* 51, no. 4 (December 1, 2008): 355–370.

Rombough, Shirley, and Diane C. Keithly. "Women in Politics: An Analysis of Personal Characteristics Leading to Success in Gaining Local Elective Office." *Race, Gender, and Class* 17, nos. 3–4 (2010): 173–188.

Rosenstone, Steven J. "Economic Adversity and Voter Turnout." *American Journal of Political Science* 26, no. 1 (1982): 25–46.

Sanbonmatsu, Kira. *Where Women Run: Gender and Party in the American States.* Ann Arbor: University of Michigan Press, 2006.

Sanbonmatsu, Kira, and Susan J. Carroll. "Poised to Run: Women's Pathways to the State Legislatures." Rutgers, NJ: Center for American Women and Politics, Eagleton Institute of Politics, Rutgers University, 2009.

Sawer, Marian. "EMILY's List and Angry White Men: Gender Wars in the Nineties." *Journal of Australian Studies* 23, no. 62 (1999): 1–9.

Schlesinger, Joseph A. *Ambition and Politics: Political Careers in the United States.* New York: Rand McNally, 1966.

Schneider, Monica C., and Angela L. Bos. "Measuring Stereotypes of Female Politicians." *Political Psychology* 35, no. 2 (2014): 245–266.

Schneider, Monica C., Mirya R. Holman, Amanda B. Diekman, and Thomas McAndrew. "Power, Conflict, and Community: How Gendered Views of Political Power Influence Women's Political Ambition." *Political Psychology* 37, no. 4 (2016): 515–531.

Serfaty, Susan. "Babies Now Allowed on Senate Floor after Rare Rule Change—CNNPolitics." CNN. April 18, 2018. Available at https://www.cnn.com/2018/04/18/politics /tammy-duckworth-senate-baby-rules/index.html.

Shames, Shauna L. "American Women of Color and Rational Non-Candidacy: When Silent Citizenship Makes Politics Look Like Old White Men Shouting." *Citizenship Studies* 19, no. 5 (July 4, 2015): 553–569.

———. *Out of the Running: Why Millennials Reject Political Careers and Why It Matters.* New York: New York University Press, 2017.

Silbermann, Rachel. "Gender Roles, Work-Life Balance, and Running for Office." *Quarterly Journal of Political Science* 10, no. 2 (2015): 123–153.

Sweet-Cushman, Jennie. "Gender, Risk Assessment, and Political Ambition." *Politics and the Life Sciences* (January 2016): 1–17.

———. "Where Does the Pipeline Get Leaky? The Progressive Ambition of School Board Members and Personal and Political Network Recruitment." *Politics, Groups, and Identities* (2018). Available at https://doi.org/10.1080/21565503.2018.1541417.

Swers, Michele. "Are Congresswomen More Likely to Vote for Women's Issue Bills Than Their Male Colleagues?" *Legislative Studies Quarterly* 23, no. 4 (1998): 435–448.

Teele, Dawn Langan. *Forging the Franchise: The Political Origins of the Women's Vote.* Princeton, NJ: Princeton University Press, 2018.

———. "How the West Was Won: Competition, Mobilization, and Women's Enfranchisement in the United States." *Journal of Politics* 80, no. 2 (April 2018): 442–461.

Teele, Dawn Langan, Joshua Kalla, and Frances Rosenbluth. "The Ties That Double Bind: Social Roles and Women's Underrepresentation in Politics." *American Political Science Review* 112, no. 3 (August 2018): 525–541.

Teorell, Jan. "Linking Social Capital to Political Participation: Voluntary Associations and Networks of Recruitment in Sweden." *Scandinavian Political Studies* 26, no. 1 (2003): 49–66.

Thomsen, Danielle M., and Michele L. Swers. "Which Women Can Run? Gender, Partisanship, and Candidate Donor Networks." *Political Research Quarterly* (March 9, 2017).

Traister, Rebecca. "Kirsten Gillibrand Is an Enthusiastic No." New York, April 4, 2017, Available at http://nymag.com/daily/intelligencer/2017/04/kirsten-gillibrand-progressive-champion-2020-run.html.

Trost, Christine, and Matt Grossman. *Win the Right Way: How to Run Effective Local Campaigns in California.* Berkeley: Berkeley Public Policy Press, 2005.

Valian, Virginia. "Beyond Gender Schemas: Improving the Advancement of Women in Academia." *NWSA Journal* 16, no. 1 (2004): 207–220.

Verba, Sidney, Kay Lehman Schlozman, and Henry E. Brady. *Voice and Equality: Civic Voluntarism in American Politics.* Cambridge, MA: Harvard University Press, 1995.

Weikart, Lynne A., Greg Chen, Daniel W. Williams, and Haris Hromic. "The Democratic Sex: Gender Differences and the Exercise of Power." *Journal of Women, Politics, and Policy* 28, no. 1 (2007): 119–140.

Windett, Jason. "Differing Paths to the Top: Gender, Ambition, and Running for Governor." *Journal of Women, Politics, and Policy* 35, no. 4 (October 2, 2014): 287–314.

Wolbrecht, Christina, and David E. Campbell. "Leading by Example." *American Journal of Political Science* 51, no. 4 (2007): 921–939.

Contributors

Alejandra Gimenez Aldridge is a political science Ph.D. candidate at Stanford University with research interests in American politics. She is a graduate of Brigham Young University's political science program.

Georgia Anderson-Nilsson is a Ph.D. candidate at Vanderbilt University who works on comparative and American politics.

Rachel I. Bernhard is assistant professor of political science at the University of California, Davis. Her work sits at the intersection of political psychology and group identity, particularly gender. In particular, she examines how American voters evaluate female candidates for office, particularly in local and state elections, how candidate appearance influences voting behavior, the political economy of gender, and the political effects of information complexity.

Chris W. Bonneau, professor of political science at the University of Pittsburgh, is also coeditor of *State Politics and Policy Quarterly*. His work primarily focuses on judicial selection. He has coauthored three books, edited two others, and published numerous scholarly articles.

Nadia E. Brown is associate professor of political science and African American Studies chair, Political Science Graduate Recruitment and Admissions Committee at Purdue University. Her book *Sisters in the Statehouse* (Oxford University Press, 2014) analyzes black women's representation and legislative successes in the United States.

Rebecca E. Deen, an associate professor and chair of the Department of Political Science at the University of Texas at Arlington, conducts research on women in the political process, civic engagement, effective pedagogy, and the U.S. presidency. Her work has appeared in journals such as *Women and Politics, State and Local Government Review, Congress and the Presidency* and *Judicature*. She is also the recipient of a number of teaching awards, including the UT Board of Regents Outstanding Teaching Award.

Kesicia Dickinson is a graduate student at Michigan State University and a 2018 APSA Minority Fellowship Program Fellow. Her research focuses on race and politics—specifically representation, women of color, and elections. Before joining the Political Science Department at Michigan State University, she worked for a Mississippi-based civic engagement organization where she led numerous campaigns to increase statewide voter participation and create economic development in rural communities. She also created and conducted youth seminars about civil liberties and community organizing in this capacity.

Kelly Dittmar is assistant professor of political science at Rutgers University–Camden and scholar at the Center for American Women and Politics at the Eagleton Institute of Politics. She is author of *Navigating Gendered Terrain: Stereotypes and Strategy in Political Campaigns* (Temple University Press, 2015) as well as multiple book chapters on gender and American politics. Most recently, she managed Presidential Gender Watch, a project tracking gender dynamics in the 2016 presidential election, and authored the project's final report, *Finding Gender in 2016: Lessons from Presidential Gender Watch.*

Pearl K. Dowe is acting professor of political science and African American Studies with a joint appointment between the university's Oxford College and Emory College of Arts and Sciences. She has published numerous articles and book chapters on African American political behavior that have appeared in journals such as the *Journal of African American Studies, Political Psychology, Presidential Studies Quarterly,* and *Social Science Quarterly.* Her most recent book, coauthored with the late Hanes Walton Jr. and Josephine Allen, *Remaking the Democratic Party: Lyndon B. Johnson as a Native-Son Presidential Candidate* was published in the fall of 2016 from University of Michigan Press.

Mirya R. Holman is associate professor of political science at Tulane University. She conducts research on women in politics, urban politics, and religion and politics. Her book, *Women in Politics in the American City* (Temple University Press, 2015) is a comprehensive evaluation of the effect of electing women to local office in the United States.

Martha C. Johnson is associate professor of political science at Mills College, a liberal arts college for women in Oakland, California. She received her Ph.D. in political science from the University of California, Berkeley, and has conducted fieldwork in Senegal, Burkina Faso, and Benin. She was recently a Fulbright Scholar in Benin where she studied women's political representation, interviewing women politicians and activists around the country.

Kristin Kanthak is associate professor of political science at the University of Pittsburgh, her research focuses on the effects on political representation of exogenous constraints such as political institutions in order to understand political systems' pathologies of representation.

Christopher F. Karpowitz is codirector of the Center for the Study of Elections and Democracy and professor of political science at Brigham Young University. His coauthored book with Tali Mendelberg, *The Silent Sex: Gender, Deliberation, and Institutions* (Princeton University Press, 2014), received the Robert E. Lane Award for the best book in political psychology (APSA), the David O. Sears Award for the best book in mass politics (ISPP), and the APSA Experimental Research Section Best Book Award.

Jaclyn J. Kettler is assistant professor of political science at Boise State University in Idaho. She received her BA from Baker University in political science and her MA and

Ph.D. from Rice University in political science. Her research focuses on state politics, political parties and interest groups, campaign finance, and women in politics. Dr. Kettler has published research in *Political Research Quarterly, Journal of Elections, Public Opinion and Parties,* and *The Forum: A Journal of Applied Research in Contemporary Politics.*

Rebecca Kreitzer is assistant professor of public policy at the University of North Carolina at Chapel Hill. She is the author of several articles on women's representation and influence on public policy.

Cecilia Hyunjung Mo is associate professor of political science, University of California, Berkeley. Her research interests include a broad array of issues in political behavior, public policy, and the political economy of development.

J. Quin Monson is associate professor of political science at Brigham Young University. He received his Ph.D. from Ohio State University in 2004. He does research in public opinion, campaigns and elections, survey research methods, and religion and politics. He is the coauthor of *Seeking the Promised Land: Mormons and American Politics* (Cambridge University Press, 2014) and his work has also appeared in the *American Journal of Political Science, Political Analysis, Public Opinion Quarterly,* and *Political Behavior,* among others.

Malliga Och is assistant professor of global studies at Idaho State University, Pocatello, Idaho. Previously, she was the research director of Political Parity, a program of Hunt Alternatives in Cambridge, Massachusetts. She received her Ph.D. from the University of Denver. She has recently joined the inaugural advisory editorial board of the *European Journal of Politics and Gender* and has published in the Women's Studies International Forum, the *Huffington Post,* the Conversation, and the Duck of Minerva. An expert on conservative women in politics, she is the coeditor of *The Right Women: Republican Party Activists, Candidates, and Legislators* (Praeger Press, 2018). Her work has appeared in the *Journal of Politics and Gender, Representation, Parliamentary Affairs,* among others.

Karen O'Connor is the Jonathan N. Helfat Distinguished Professor of Political Science at American University, where she previously served as chair of the Department of Government. She is an expert on American politics, the courts, women and politics, and interest group politics.

Heather L. Ondercin is assistant professor of political science at Appalachian State University. Her scholarly interests largely fall at the intersection of mass political behavior and gender and politics. Her research has been published in *Political Research Quarterly, Political Behavior, Electoral Studies, Politics and Gender,* and other peer-reviewed journals. She received a Ph.D. in political science and women's and gender studies from the Pennsylvania State University.

Tracy Osborn is associate professor of political science at the University of Iowa. She published a book on the representation of partisan women, *How Women Represent Women* (Oxford University Press, 2012). She has published many other peer-reviewed articles and book chapters on partisan women's representation.

Jennifer M. Piscopo is associate professor of politics at Occidental College. Her research on women's representation, gender quotas, legislative institutions, and gender equality policies has appeared in over 15 peer-reviewed journals, including *The American Journal* *of Political Science, Comparative Political Studies, The Latin American Research Review, Latin American Politics and Society,* and *Politics and Gender.* With Susan Franceschet and Mona Lena Krook, she is editor of *The Impact of Gender Quotas* (Oxford University Press, 2012).

Jessica Robinson Preece is associate professor of political science at Brigham Young University. Her research focuses on candidate ambition, recruitment, and selection. She has special interests in gender and experiments. Her research focuses on candidate ambition, recruitment, and selection. She has special interests in gender and experiments. Her publications include pieces in *The American Journal of Political Science, The Quarterly Journal of Political Science, Political Behavior, Legislative Studies Quarterly, Gender and Politics,* among others.

Kira Sanbonmatsu is professor of political science at Rutgers University–New Brunswick and senior scholar at the Center for American Women and Politics (CAWP) at the Eagleton Institute of Politics. Her research interests include gender, race/ethnicity, parties, public opinion, and state politics. She is the coauthor of the CAWP reports *Representation Matters: Women in the U.S. Congress* (2017) and *Poised to Run: Women's Pathways to the State Legislatures* (2009). Her most recent book (with Kelly Dittmar and Susan J. Carroll) is *A Seat at the Table: Congresswomen's Perspectives on Why Their Representation Matters* (Oxford University Press, 2018).

Monica C. Schneider is associate professor of political science at Miami University in Oxford, Ohio. She earned her Ph.D. in political science from the University of Minnesota, Twin Cities. She studies gender and racial stereotypes in American politics and gender gaps in political ambition. She is passionate about the advancement of women in the academy and improving outcomes for undergraduates. Her research has been published in many journals, including *Political Psychology, Political Research Quarterly,* and *Politics, Groups, and Identities.* She coedited *The Political Psychology of Women in U.S. Politics* (Routledge Press, 2017) with Angela L. Bos.

Jamil Scott is assistant professor of political science at Georgetown University. Her research is in the areas of political behavior, political representation, race and ethnicity politics, and gender politics. She seeks to explain individual's motivations to participate in political activities in conventional ways, particularly as candidates and officeholders, as well as in unconventional ways, like protest and political engagement via social media. Moreover, she examines the behaviors of officeholders within office as a means of understanding political representation and behaviors within institutions, such as legislatures.

Shauna L. Shames is associate professor of political science and Director of Gender Studies at Rutgers University–Camden. Her work focuses on women, gender, feminism, political ambition (especially of millennials), and dystopian government in speculative fiction. In addition to her monograph *Out of the Running: Why Millennials Reject Political Careers and Why It Matters* (NYU Press, 2017), she is coeditor of a volume on women in the Republican Party, *The Right Women* (Praeger, 2018), and coauthor of a textbook on dystopian government, *Survive and Resist* (Columbia University Press, 2019).

Beth Anne Shelton, a professor of sociology at the University of Texas at Arlington, has research interests in gender, work, and family and civic engagement. Her publications have appeared in journals such as *Journal of Family Issues* and *Sex Roles.* She has also published books on women's time use as well as contemporary families.

Rachel Silbermann is a senior consultant at Maxfield Strategic Communications Research. She received her Ph.D. in political science from Yale University in 2014 and served as a lecturer, policy fellow, and postdoctoral fellow there until 2016. She also served for three years as a researcher at the Analyst Institute. Her dissertation examined young women's attitudes toward running for political office.

Jennie Sweet-Cushman is assistant professor of political science at Chatham University in Pittsburgh, where she also served as the Assistant Director of the Pennsylvania Center for Women and Politics from 2013 to 2019. A former congressional campaign manager herself, Jennie's research focuses on women's political ambition and representation in the United States, as well as gender equity in academia. Her recent work has appeared in *PS: Political Science and Politics, Politics, Groups, and Identities,* and *Politics and the Life Sciences.*

Michele L. Swers is professor of American government in the Department of Government at Georgetown University. Dr. Swers's research and teaching interests encompass Congress, congressional elections, and women and politics. She has written two books on women and representation in Congress. Her book, *The Difference Women Make: The Policy Impact of Women in Congress* (University of Chicago Press, 2002) explores gender differences in policy-making activity on issues related to women, children, and families. *Women in the Club: Gender and Policy Making in the Senate* (University of Chicago Press, 2013) examines the impact of gender on senators' policy activities in the areas of women's issues, national security, and judicial nominations.

Dawn Langan Teele is the Janice and Julian Bers Assistant Professor of the Social Sciences at the University of Pennsylvania, and an executive board member for the program on Gender, Sexuality, and Women's Studies. She is cofounder of EGEN, the Empirical Study of Gender Research Network in political science. Teele is editor of *Field Experiments and Their Critics* (Yale University Press, 2014), and her book *Forging the Franchise: The Political Origins of the Women's Vote* was released by Princeton University Press in 2018.

Sue Thomas is senior research scientist at the Pacific Institute for Research and Education (PIRE) and director of PIRE-Santa Cruz, which specializes in the intersection of social science research, public health policy, and the law. In addition to her PIRE projects on substance abuse and pregnancy policy, alcohol policy, and cannabis policy, Dr. Thomas has published widely on analyses of women officeholders in U.S. politics.

Danielle M. Thomsen is assistant professor of political science at University of California, Irvine. Her research interests include American politics, political parties, U.S. Congress, and gender and politics. She is the author of *Opting Out of Congress: Partisan Polarization and the Decline of Moderate Candidates* (Cambridge University Press, 2017), which examines how the decline of moderate candidates has exacerbated partisan polarization in Congress.

Catherine Wineinger is assistant professor of political science at Western Washington University. Her research interests include women's representation, congressional politics, American party politics, and political ideology.

Alixandra B. Yanus is associate professor of political science at High Point University. Her primary research agenda focuses on the role of gender in American politics, particularly the representation of women in political institutions, interest groups, and social movements.

Index